FAIL BETTER

FAIL BETTER

Design Smart Mistakes and Succeed Sooner

Anjali Sastry
Kara Penn

HARVARD BUSINESS REVIEW PRESS
BOSTON, MASSACHUSETTS

Printed in the United States of America

10 9 8 7 6 5 4 3 2 1

Library of Congress Cataloging-in-Publication Data

Sastry, Anjali.
Fail better : design smart mistakes and succeed sooner / Anjali Sastry, Kara Penn.
pages cm
ISBN 978-1-4221-9344-0 (hardback)
1. Business planning. 2. Business failures. 3. Failure (Psychology) 4. Problem solving. 5. Management. 6. Success in business. I. Penn, Kara. II. Title.
HD30.28.S2724 2014
658.4'01–dc23

2014011869

ISBN: 9781422193440
eISBN: 9781422193457

The paper used in this publication meets the requirements of the American National Standard for Permanence of Paper for Publications and Documents in Libraries and Archives Z39.48-1992.

DEDICATION

To Mark, Kiran, and Harry,
who teach me every day.

—Anjali

To Adit, my partner in all things,
and to Ava and Kayla, my purpose.

—Kara

CONTENTS

INTRODUCTION

This book is about inspiration's overlooked but essential companion, the perspiration-soaked work needed to deliver on genius. No matter how great your ideas, in the end your impact will be measured by the effect you have on the world. Unless you're gambling on being incredibly lucky—a risky bet, we'd say—if you want your ideas to materialize, you need to be smart in your actions.

We're talking about bringing a new form of intelligence to your everyday efforts. You can't avoid missteps, of course. Yet there's scope for your mistakes to be *smarter*. With the right methods applied to their design, execution, and analysis, even the most unglamorous activities can yield new insights and fuel innovation. Workaday life may seem like an unlikely birthplace for brilliance, but it's where your ideas are hammered out, tested, and refined.

Join us, and you'll discover why we see great potential for you to remake your work practices so that you, your team, and your organization can do better. Your projects provide the sandbox for your actions. Using our method, you'll orchestrate your team's activities to enable smart mistakes and avoid uninstructive ones. You'll work your way toward impact, step-by-step. As you go, you'll be assembling the insight, knowledge, and evidence required for your ideas to succeed in practice. And as you learn to choose your path wisely and let go of false starts before they bog you down, you'll reach your goals sooner.

Don't get us wrong about the other stuff. We're all for inspiration—the cracking-the-puzzle, eureka-moment flash. Chances are, you've heard stories of brilliant discoveries that altered the course of history. But let's disentangle such tales from the realities on the ground. The truth is, that to make something excellent happen, there's work, more work, and then still more work. If you're fortunate, only *some* of it is inefficient.

We can't change the fact that innovation entails risk and that for anything novel or creative, you'll encounter failure en route to success. But because any movement from waste to value could pay off handsomely, we are looking to shift the balance of results toward the productive and away from the useless.

Our starting point is the idea that the right kind of failure—small-scale, reversible, informative, linked to broader goals, and designed to illuminate key issues—paves the way to success. The wrong kind entails waste, discouragement, rigid thinking, and reputational damage. For every potential good failure, the world presents us with many more ways to fail badly.

We know you can do better than simply accepting the hand you're dealt. You can benefit from failure by orchestrating the right kinds of actions, then figuring out what you have learned from every step, whether or not it is immediately seen as successful. To profit from both happenstance and planned failures, you need an effective method for extracting insights.

We mined our own experience to design and test the Fail Better approach.

About Us

Personal experience stands us in good stead as your guides: like you, we've encountered failure firsthand. As sometime change agents with an interest in social impact, we may have engaged in more failure-prone efforts than many. One of us even published papers on her own failures (which, we can tell you, is rare for a business-school academic).

Our interests extend beyond our own change efforts. We've worked closely, often over the stretch of years, with hundreds of students and managers. We've advised CEOs and leadership teams and stood outside organizations looking in as researchers and analysts. Along the way, we've seen teams blindly execute project plans, going along with the schedule and turning in assignments even as they come to realize that their work will never be implemented. We've seen people struggle to learn from their visible failures. Some dismiss them, others point fingers, and still others become mired in doubts or unproductive discussion. Yet we've also encountered individuals at all levels who relish failure's lessons. We've even seen people orchestrate effective mistakes to benefit their companies and organizations. To develop our ideas, we sought out these exemplars, interviewing them and watching them at work, to glean how they design projects, spend their time, and frame their work.

Our shared drive to understand how to create success when confronting the risk of failure has nurtured our own decade-long professional partnership. Together, we designed dozens of iterations of courses, trainings, and workshops that combine the classroom and the real world. By framing real-world, complex challenges, then supporting participants in tackling them, we've been able to link classroom and textbook learning with action inside organizations. We've used these innovative platforms to test ideas, gather data, and build our own evidence base.

For instance, since 2008, our framework has underpinned a unique effort that put hundreds of MIT students to work on real-world problems amid some of the most complex and challenging settings—on the front lines of health-care delivery in Africa and South Asia.

The MIT effort, dubbed GlobalHealth Lab, aims to help organizations delivering health care to the poor to tackle extreme need amid pressing resource challenges. Guided by the ideas you'll soon learn, advanced master's, PhD, and MBA students put their skills and toolkits to the test in Sierra Leone, Kenya, Malawi, Zambia, South Africa, Mozambique, Haiti, India, Botswana, Uganda, Tanzania, Ghana, Nepal, and Bangladesh, each time collaborating with workers and managers in the setting over the course of hundreds of hours. Each project takes on a pressing challenge identified by the partner. By 2014, it was clear that the first seventy collaborative action projects had provided two benefits. Not only did they enable remarkable learning and growth opportunities for students, but they also delivered positive impact on the ground.

When teams were expected not just to turn in great assignments but to generate enduring improvements for the organizations with which they were partnered, they began to think differently. For instance, they tended to be willing to challenge their own plans—which in turn helped them to identify and test core assumptions and hypotheses. We credit the built-for-learning design of the course that linked the students' action loops with their own research and an ongoing stream of collaborative inquiry enabled by peer and faculty interactions. This dual-track method leveraged classroom sessions and mentor meetings designed to refine and improve project plans and deliverables as well as deep partner engagement that included on-site work and field tests.

A follow-on study revealed some of GlobalHealth Lab's benefits. In close to seventy systematic semistructured retrospective interviews with project partners, the strongest result was that the staff, managers, and leaders sought more interaction with MIT, not just for the collaboration with student teams but for the methods, materials, and findings that underpinned each project. That the professionals who had worked with GlobalHealth Lab sought the same supports that the course provided to its students provided one of the sparks for this book.

Through this effort and others, we've built an in-depth understanding of the value of iterating via action steps before, during, and after collaborative improvement efforts. Our field experience reveals that extreme constraints provide fertile ground for innovations, and that seeking to improve management systems with the goal of enabling scale and sustainability helps to turn good ideas into positive impact.

To inform and extend our academic grounding, we both work directly with enterprises to identify where and how they can do better. Our professional experience also includes stints in corporate, government, philanthropic, and non-governmental sectors. We've worked at or with organizations as diverse as Bain & Company, the Bill & Melinda Gates Foundation, the Rocky Mountain Institute, Oxfam America, Lawrence Berkeley National Laboratory, a plumbers and pipefitters union, Management Sciences for Health, and the United Network for Organ Sharing, as well as political campaigns, local government institutions, airlines, software companies, and a range of technology-focused start-ups.

All told, our methods have been refined through our experience as professional consultants and collaborators with more than one hundred organizations. Over the years we've lined up others—from clients and collaborators to smart and willing students—to aid in the task of developing the methods for extracting the most learning from every project. In doing so, we discovered the power of recognizing that projects provide a crucible for development and innovation. Focusing on projects directs attention at the unit of work by which every organization innovates, solves problems, or changes.

The method you're about to discover is designed to not only make your current project more effective, but also to enable you to apply that learning in future projects while helping your team to develop.

The Questions We Aim to Answer

As we take you through the book, we'll be guided by a handful of questions at the crux of the fail-to-succeed dilemma. Our advice is designed to help anyone who wonders how to make progress on multiple fronts simultaneously. If you've ever asked the following questions, *Fail Better* is for you:

- How do I deliver on my work—get my "real job" done—and *at the same time* innovate and improve?
- How do I help my team develop the skills and capabilities that are most needed for the work at hand without squandering time and resources on training that misses the mark?
- How do I help my team to root out and test the most critical assumptions and explore the most important open questions while making progress on the project's deliverables?
- How can I learn from previous experience, within our organization or more broadly?
- How do I improve my own personal practices and habits to enable even better impact?
- How could I enable others across the organization to benefit from the lessons offered by our team's hard-earned experience?

Our Hopes for You

We have in mind an ambitiously broad audience because we think that such questions are common across sectors, organizations, and levels of hierarchy. We imagine that ideas about how to fail better will be valuable to all kinds of consultants, team members, entrepreneurs, executives, and managers. We'd be glad if our suggestions were to reach academic and policy-making colleagues, too. In short, we are hoping for readers who are interested in failure as a mechanism for higher-order success.

Through this book, we aim to empower you with the knowledge, tools, and inspiration to design your actions so that they yield success. But, as we've already mentioned, failure is an omnipresent possibility. If you must fail, we'd like to help you do so at the scale, scope, and visibility that in turn will enable better overall outcomes and deliverables, achieve the task at hand, build individual and team capacity, and assist others within the organization and beyond to learn from your experience.

As you'll see, although the overall method is integrated, it's not an all-or-nothing proposition. We hope you'll find that you can make progress right away, using our advice to shape your own practices. You may find a muse or two in our sample of real-world managers and organizations who have developed their own ways of enabling step-by-step improvement, and draw on their inspiration to guide your own practice. Real examples help to illustrate and teach, and can also inspire you to envision yourself as an expert Fail Better practitioner.

And, as you make your way through the book, we hope you will realize how much scope you have to lead positive change. We'd like you to appreciate that you have a great deal of influence within your current context, even if you have little formal power, because you can shape how you carry out your own work. To adopt our advice, you need not wait for a new organizational initiative, line up lots of extra resources, obtain special training, or even get permission to start implementing the approach. You can begin tomorrow within the laboratory of your own work, with the position you currently occupy. Begin where it's feasible, in imperfect fashion, and you can learn and revise as you go. The only requirement is that you must, in fact, begin.

Our book presents ideas that are practical and field-tested. Taken one by one, you may find that the elements of our approach are familiar. Our discovery of their usefulness in practice lies in drawing them together and connecting them in new ways, drawing on our grounding in systems thinking. At the end, we hope you will feel ready to take action and confident that you know what to try. Our vision is that you'll create better results, enjoy a richer work life, and maybe even acquire some new wisdom along the way.

And if our biggest hopes for you materialize, you'll take things further. You'll make the method your own, documenting and sharing what you do. You'll let us know what works and what you've tweaked. If you're willing to do this, we want to help to build a collective dialogue. Imagine a community of practitioners that shares advice, inspirations, and innovations, helping each other along the way. A more nuanced and wider discourse about planning for, designing, and learning from failure could help many to address the practical challenges of the fail-to-succeed dilemma. Along the way we could all discover more meaningful ways to work, develop, and collaborate.

Overview of the Book

Throughout the book, you'll discover plenty of practical advice for laying the project's groundwork at launch, then building and refining your products through action so that at the end you can deliver a great result, wrapping up by embedding and disseminating what you've learned so as to pave the way for even better future results.

Part I provides a foundation for your exploration of the Fail Better ideas. We start with a firm grounding in reality: you can't escape failure. A systems-based examination of failure's roots helps to establish why. Yet, as we'll argue, failure is not necessarily a bad thing. Accepting that smart mistakes could even be desirable moves us into more nuanced discussions about learning, failure, and success. Enabling productive failures calls for a systematic method, hence the Fail Better approach. We introduce it in chapter 2, previewing its three steps and providing real-world examples to illustrate the main ideas behind each component. Chapter 3, which concludes this section, offers you some very practical guidance on how to apply book's ideas to your work to start failing better right away.

Part II tells how to do it. Chapter 4 addresses the launch phase, explaining how to lay the groundwork for a new project in a way that enables effective learning. In chapter 5, we describe and illustrate the three essential elements of iteration—planning, taking action while capturing data, and examining results to decide on and plan the next action step. We show you how small steps can yield big results when action is designed carefully, explaining how to build in room for experimentation while still completing the work at hand. In chapter 6, we focus on how to embed this learning—for yourself, the team, the organization, and beyond.

In part III, we explore the practice of the Fail Better method. We begin by describing the Fail Better mind-set, a way of approaching challenges that you'll draw on as leader, manager, and change agent to refine your own personal principles and approaches. We then delve into the design-for-learning principles behind the Fail Better method to help you understand the foundation on which the approach is built, which in turn will set you up to improvise as you go. To ground all this advice in a detailed real-world example, we take an in-depth look at BRAC, an organization that over the course of four decades has achieved global change with limited resources. Building on our ideas about how the most ambitious of change efforts could benefit from the core aspects of our method, we take a look at how the Fail Better approach could help make the world a better place. We illustrate its potential with an example from the present and an inspiration from the past. We conclude with some parting advice for creating even bigger change in the world.

PART I

The Antidote to Failure

Part One equips you to embark on the Fail Better approach. We begin by looking at why you need a structured way to benefit from failure, exploring a few key ideas to make the case and introduce the method:

Everyone will fail, someway, somehow. A systems-based examination of failure's roots helps establish why.

Failure is not necessarily bad. Accepting that it's inevitable, and maybe even desirable, sets the stage for a more nuanced discussion of learning, failure, and success.

Not all failures are useful. The key is to enable the productive ones. You'll need to know what makes some failures worthwhile and others useless.

A systematic method helps you to benefit from productive failures. The three elements of the Fail Better approach work together. Real-world examples help show how, as you:

- Launch your project with the right groundwork.
- Build and refine your ideas and work products through iterative action.
- Identify and embed the learning.

You can start right away. Practical guidance on how to use the book equips you to apply it to your own work.

CHAPTER 1

Failures Are Inevitable

Failure is the new black. Blog posts and articles extol its virtues. Venerated CEOs, famous celebrities, and star athletes tell come-from-behind stories of horrible setbacks that led to happy endings. Accounts of success extracted from the jaws of failure are part of business lore: think of the marketing and product development legends about Post-it Notes, Apple products, Viagra, and New Coke. Today, a growing collection of books advises business leaders to adopt pro-failure philosophies. Entrepreneurs and would-be executives polish their "failure résumés," nonprofits issue failure reports, companies throw parties to celebrate their flops, and industry groups organize fail fairs. Every year scores of graduation speeches urge young people about to enter the workforce to embrace failure. "Failure," novelist J.K. Rowling told Harvard graduates in 2008, "gave me an inner security that I had never attained by passing examinations."

The idea allured us, too. Six words from Samuel Beckett—"Try again. Fail again. Fail better."—inspired our book's title, even though its source, *Worstward Ho*, reflects Beckett's fascination with futility. Cast as a mantra that turns failure into success, the phrase caught on with tennis players, tech entrepreneurs, and many more, infusing it with an optimism that no literary critic would credit to "the twentieth century's most depressing writer."[1]

If failure is all the rage, why does so much of the advice on failing seem to fall short?

Failures, Small and Good, Big and Bad

At one level, it's obvious that failing is bad. You wouldn't want your next project to be labeled "A Failure." Think of what it would do for your reputation, motivation, and sense of self, let alone your ability to attract customers, workers, resources, partners, and job offers.

Yet there can be value in falling short. Small failures enable discovery and learning. They help rule out options, unearth flaws in reasoning, and disconfirm incorrect hypotheses. Freedom to fail is linked to creativity and boldness. Stretch goals, by definition, run the risk of failure. Yet their very audacity encourages people to reach for radically new ideas and novel solutions. And we know that failure often proves less fatal than imagined. Over time, people recast their own failures and losses—even those that they would have at an earlier time predicted to be unbearable—to find meaning in them, in a sense eventually relabeling them as successes.

Such benefits, however, are far from guaranteed. Sometimes the right lessons are not gleaned: window-dressing a failure story with an after-the-fact gloss may make people feel better about the experience, but it obscures its lessons. Too often, potentially valuable failures go to waste because extracting their lessons is fiendishly difficult in practice. At the same time, truly wasteful failures are allowed to perpetuate, slowing progress, derailing projects, and fueling cynicism. Why? Managers lack methods for designing processes and leading teams through the right sequence of small failures that could pave the way to subsequent success. Amid the current pro-failure hype, you'll find plenty of enthusiastic exhortations to fail early and often, but little advice about how to do so when you're in the trenches. Retrospective accounts of how others created new products or turned around organizations may be fun to read, but it's difficult to glean, and much less to decipher how to apply, their lessons for your own work. No matter how compelling they are, these vivid stories do not provide reliable evidence that if you do the same things you will get similar results. There are few places to turn to for guidance on what to try, and even fewer sources of advice on how to appropriately adapt any given approach for your particular situation.

Our book aims to remedy this problem by offering practical ideas for you to make your own. Despite the lack of instruction manuals for good failure, there is much to inform our present effort. We draw on a rich base of knowledge of how adults learn at work, which is increasingly informed by neuroscience along with organizational and behavioral research on shaping and adaptation, as well as a growing body of documented professional improvement practices and academic research on innovation.

Project and Product Failures Are Common

There's plenty of evidence that most of us will encounter failure at some point, though it's hard to come by good data on how often projects, products, teams, and companies fail. Measurement methods are inconsistent and source data difficult to find. In 2013, the Project Management Institute reported that 17 percent of projects fail completely, part of an astounding two-thirds of projects that the institute said fall short of expectations.[2] A 2012 study of 5,400 projects found that half of all large IT projects came in well over budget, with one in six overrunning costs so badly that they threatened to put the firm out of business.[3] Change management programs are notorious for failing two-thirds of the time.[4] Across industries, the rate of failure of new products is thought to be around 40 percent.[5]

In some industries, failure risks are inherent. Pharmaceutical development companies, consumer products firms, and venture capital firms routinely invest resources and effort in new prospects, whether a novel drug, new supermarket item, or start-up. Each time, they are making a risky bet. They know that every year a good proportion will fail. That's simply the reality.

Yet despite the knowledge that failure is a possibility for projects aiming to accomplish something new in all kinds of industries, its acceptance is far from widespread. Even in pharmaceutical and venture capital firms, too often good failures go to waste and the right lessons are not learned. Perhaps our lack of understanding about the underlying causes of failure is to blame.

It's Not You, It's the System Complexity

You live and work in a social and economic system that is fundamentally complex. Think of how much information is available to you today, how many people you can learn about and even connect with, and how many ideas, products, and services are yours to explore. The sheer number of choices available to you as a decision maker is astounding.

Detail Complexity

Consider your choices when you buy a new car. In reality, there are literally millions of different options: brand, model, trim line, color, accessories and extras, used or new, price and financing options, bundled maintenance and roadside assistance services, and much more. Multiply the number of options across each dimension, and what experts would call the search costs—a measure of the difficulty of grappling with all of them—is daunting. No wonder so many drivers simply buy the same car again!

All of these options add up to what's called *combinatorial* or *detail complexity*, the product of the multiplicity of components and attributes, along with the relationships between them. But detail complexity, daunting though it is, can be managed through tools including decision trees, spreadsheets, search engines, and personal and professional recommendations. Of course, the actual version of any of these tools that you use may be flawed, leading to suboptimal decisions.

This provides us with one reason you may fail in a complex world—by investing too much or too little in searching across all the options. This widespread problem is likely already familiar, from your own experience as a consumer and manager, and it has been explored in recent studies of the downside of excessive choice.[6] Like others, you have worked out ways to address the plethora of options offered by the modern economy. As a car buyer, you may visit a trusted website to select a few options you explore in depth. Or you may base your choice on the brand you love and the model you can afford. In other words, most people are already aware of the challenge posed by combinatorial complexity and have settled on ways to tackle it, even if their methods aren't perfect.

Dynamic Complexity

There's another form of complexity that's harder to pinpoint and in many ways more difficult to handle: *dynamic complexity.* Systems that are dynamically complex are challenging to understand and manage because their behavior is shaped by hard-to-predict relationships that play out in different ways when conditions vary. As we'll see, when causes are separated from their effects in time (and in space), it's tough to draw a straight line from action to result. Nonlinear factors can dramatically change behavior with only small changes in their inputs, once a threshold or inflection point is reached. Simple heuristics, such as linear rules-of-thumb, don't apply in such cases. And more sophisticated statistical techniques are ineffective when the situation shifts into new regimes outside historical bounds, such as when a new technology dramatically changes costs or when environmental conditions result in previously unseen weather patterns.

Dynamic complexity is inescapable in today's organizations and markets. It's inevitable that you'll encounter lags and biases in noticing, measuring, and responding to the effects of this type of complexity. Let's take a closer look at why this matters.

Behavioral research is shedding light on human limitations in predicting and understanding complex systems—and their implications. For example, studies of decision making show that individuals, organizations, and markets consistently overlook the effects of delays and cumulative effects.[7] Scholars are not immune to these challenges; dynamic complexity may contribute the difficulty of inferring patterns of behavior from verbal theories.[8] Thanks to such factors, individuals and social systems encounter profound difficulties in learning from experience; persistent underperformance, unaddressed problems, and catastrophic failures result.[9] The tendency of social systems to resist attempts to improve performance has been traced to cognitive limitations in understanding dynamics.[10]

Mutual influence, or feedback, is a hallmark of dynamic complexity. Any system with feedback involves the temporal factors we mentioned: delays, adaptive updating of beliefs and expectations, accumulations, and other features that give rise to dynamics. To avoid getting blindsided by dynamic complexity, decision makers need to understand the interplay of these factors. This means paying attention to processes that unfold over time:

- **Cognitive processes** include noticing, altering perceptions, or elaborating mental models. Biases in these processes shape how beliefs are updated or adapt over time to new information coming in, in turn affecting the quality of decisions.

- **Affective and other emotional responses** shape how new information is processed; for example, when data that conflicts with a long-standing belief is ignored or downplayed.

- **Physical and social processes** account for the influence of quantities that build up or draw down over time. When materials, technical experience, market knowledge, or resources accumulate or deplete, they can change the equation of how efforts lead to results.

- **Delays** interrupt responsiveness. For example, when information is gathered on an ongoing basis but acted on only periodically, or when shipments or production occur in batches, the situation is set up for over or under responsiveness. The stage is set for secondary and side effects to proliferate. Responses are also subject to the timing of scheduled decision-making or strategy-setting cycles, as well as variable spacing of more sporadic opportunities for change, such as when new managers join the organization.

These aspects of dynamic complexity stymie learning from experience.

A quick example illustrates why. Today's decision to put off scheduled maintenance has an immediate consequence—the cost saved by avoiding the disruption—and a consequence at some point in the future, when your car, computer server, or factory machinery breaks down. But the manager who put off the maintenance may have moved on by the time this happens, perhaps even as a reward for saving on costs. Who learns the lesson about the need for holding the line when it comes to preventative maintenance if the negative effects are always in the future?

Let's look at another example.

A Start-Up Story

Imagine a successful start-up. "FlameTech" has come up with a brand new technology: a foldable device that collects and stores solar energy for sparking a campfire in the dark or on a cloudy day.

Outdoor enthusiasts love the product and its appealing design. Early on, FlameTech does well. Growth comes relatively easily as word of mouth builds, bloggers buzz, and magazines feature it. In this phase, it's all about managing the upswing. The limits of market size and the bounds of the new product's appeal to customers are simply not evident to the firm's decision makers, because everything is starting off a small base. At this stage, growing the company's market share consumes everyone's focus. Not only are managers, production staff, and salespeople busy handling the challenges of increasing their activities, but the forces that will slow the rise of FlameTech are not evident. By and large, the limiting factors that will eventually come into play are not easy-to-find, fixed properties that can be simply measured.

Nevertheless the seeds for an inevitable slowdown are being sown. The firm's prospects for future growth are shaped by the reverberating effects of its own past actions. Study after study reveals that initially successful new companies can be undone by the unfolding consequences of their early achievements.

In this example, several effects unfold. In part due to FlameTech's success, its rivals step up their attempts to compete, copycat firms enter the market, governments start to respond with new taxes and other restrictions, the press increases its scrutiny of the firm, its own consumers become more sophisticated and demand more, and needed inputs become scarcer.

The scene is set for a classic boom-and-bust experience. Just as things seem to be going better than ever, business collapses as the combined effects of these constraining forces come into play. By the time FlameTech's decision makers recognize that the company has encountered growth-limiting factors, it's too late. To those who led the growth phase, it really seems as if the downturn came out of nowhere.

For such a company, it's tempting—and typical—to blame the downfall on one specific development, even if the event is simply a proximate symptom of developments that have been unfolding over time. The analysis may purport to explain failure, but instead settles on a simplistic account. Something *outside* the organization is a convenient target: fickle consumers, interfering governments, unprincipled competitors, a recalcitrant supplier. Pinning the blame on things outside your control reflects an exogenous perspective—one in which you are at the mercy of forces beyond your reach.

A more sophisticated systems analysis would take the explanation further, looking at how the dynamics of growth, saturation, and slowdown arise from interacting forces within the industry, market, and society, including responses triggered by the firm's own actions. *Systems thinking* teaches us that it's more fruitful to take an endogenous view that seeks to explain how the results are a product of factors in which you play a part as well. You have much more power to shape outcomes if you can better understand how the problems and opportunities you face today are connected to your own past actions and are influenced by the structure of the industry, society, and ecosystem in which you play a role.

Dynamic Complexity and the Likelihood of Failure

When cause and effect are separated in time, drawing the right inferences is difficult. You need not be an entrepreneur navigating a boom-and-bust market to suffer its effects.

Not only is the separation in time a barrier to learning, so too is the separation in space. Actions in one part of the system play out elsewhere. Competition among Western mass retailers has consequences for factory workers in Vietnam, and demand for organic food in American supermarkets affects farming practices in Mexico.

We touched on yet another effect: nonlinearities that mean history cannot always guide. If humans, markets, and ecosystems respond in ways that vary, the future cannot be predicted by extrapolating from the past. For example, once a critical mass of consumers started choosing iPhones over BlackBerrys, the entire market shifted dramatically. BlackBerry's past experience was not a useful guide to its future once these defections reached a critical level.

Nonlinearities arising from multiple factors that interact and unfold over time are the hallmark of dynamic complexity. As in most of human life, developments in markets and society are the result of multiple factors operating together in ways that cannot be teased apart, analyzed separately, and then added up. The assumption of separability is an analytical convenience that makes study more tractable, even as it yields less insightful understanding. But let's not forget that in the real world, things are not neatly separable: actions cause effects; effects set the stage for actions and shape them. Mutual simultaneous influences are the rule, not the exception, even if your spreadsheet software complains about "circular references."

All of this means that when you are trying to accomplish anything novel, chances are that you will not get it right the first time. You may even find that your attempts to solve a problem actually worsen it, thanks to unanticipated consequences.

The Benefits of Accepting That You Will Fail

As we noted, failure's inevitability could be a good thing. Unpredictability makes life—and work—interesting by adding an element of suspense and raising the stakes, which in turn drives engagement and enables meaning. It allows discovery, surprises, and novel solutions to emerge. Under the right circumstances for learning (which we discuss in chapter 8), the experience of failure sparks new rounds of problem solving, unleashing innovation and creativity. People think more deeply when wrestling to explain failed results than when accounting for their successes. As we'll show in the chapters ahead, once you accept that failure is a given, you can design work to incorporate experimentation, variation, and iteration, creating small failures designed to prevent bigger ones.

In many industries and fields, we think that work would benefit from embracing the inevitability of failure. This line of thinking leads us to two important considerations. If you can connect systems thinking with actions, your activities can help to illuminate the relationships and processes that shape your project's outcomes. Acknowledging dynamic complexity is one thing, but to enable superior results you'll need to update your plans in keeping with what you discover along the way about your organization and market. Ongoing thinking and ongoing action are both needed.

But before we talk about how to link thinking and action in your project, we have a pressing dilemma to address.

Discerning the Acceptable from the Unacceptable

Even if you aim to tolerate failures, clearly not all failures are beneficial. You'll need to figure out which failures are warranted and which ones are blameworthy.

New efforts fail for many reasons. Some are smart failures that end up saving resources or delivering better solutions. These are the failures we seek to enable. Others are the product of random unpredictable forces. These failures need to be tolerated and managed. Unfortunately, some failures are just plain dumb. Such failures need to be avoided. If they do occur, you need to call them out, or run the risk of encouraging poor performance.

Researcher Amy Edmonson offered a taxonomy of failure drawn from her field studies.[11] At the blameworthy end of the spectrum are failures that result when people deviate from rules or practice. Safety violations are a prime example of such failures. Slightly more understandable are the failures that arise from lack of attention or ability, when people are not up to the task at hand. When failures are the consequence of poor process or overly challenging work goals, managers are more to blame than team members. It may make sense to shift the response from punishment and prevention to inquiry and understanding.

When the failures are due to uncertainty about the situation that is revealed only in the course of events, they can be instructive. Edmonson calls these "intelligent failures at the frontier" and notes that they can guide next steps and future choices.

In the most laudable cases, failures emerge from planned exploration of unknowns. Her advice is to avoid blame altogether in such cases, instead reward failures that result from a planned risk, such as hypothesis testing or a deliberate exploration of a promising but uncertain possibility.[12]

Harness Failure's Benefits: Link Action and Thinking

If you cultivate a clear-eyed understanding of the implications of dynamic complexity, you'll recognize that prediction and analysis may go wrong. Accounting for the limits of forethought in turn argues for a discovery-driven approach. Redesigning your projects to enable trial and error, thereby ensuring that failures are small and instructive, is part of the solution. Just as important is building the team skill of surfacing assumptions, making proposed linkages between cause and effect more explicit, and identifying the critical ideas to test, then discussing results when they come in.

As you do this, you will be choosing a new way forward.

Every time you and your colleagues face a new and challenging project that involves uncertainty and system complexity, you have a choice about how to proceed. You can stick to standard procedure and stay the course (even when people claim to be attempting change, this often ends up happening). You can choose safe, incremental tweaks to the norm—shifts that cannot alter the status quo, but that you can plausibly defend should things go wrong. Or the team could charge on, acting on whims, implementing the first idea it comes up with, or blindly copying others. Another apparently safe choice is to work back from the deliverables, executing a logical plan generated by deciding early on what the result should be, then simply developing the required components. Working to a plan without reflection can preclude potentially useful surprises, because your team is seeking only to support and not test its original ideas.

There is one more option. You could use our approach to design your team's work to reveal useful surprises and insights along the way. In doing so, you raise the chances you'll generate smart failures and avoid the uninstructive ones. And in the end, you could increase your successes, with fewer time-wasting false starts, better-designed end points, and more learning along the way.

The link to action offers a practical antidote to dynamic complexity that goes beyond just thinking about the system. Of course, it's still necessary to map and analyze interactions, feedback loops, and nonlinearities and to talk about and understand the important aspects of the systems in which we operate. But we've come to believe that the value of systems thinking is realized only when it informs and is informed by a series of iterative actions, allowing teams to make progress where success is not guaranteed for any given step. It's the *thinking combined with action* that provides an antidote to challenging situations—and projects are the domain where this all takes place.

Projects Are the Crucible

Any effort to make things better is a project of sorts. We think it's time to claim a more elevated spot for the humble project. Projects are the way we change the world.

If you are looking to do something specific that improves efficiency, solves a problem, innovates, or creates something new, you're working on a *project*, even if you don't give it that label. Our conception of projects expands on the more traditional, technical domain of project management by bringing in ideas related to learning, developing, and seeking epiphanies. Let's make sure that we agree on what kind of projects are right for the Fail Better approach.

By our definition, projects aim to create novel products, services, or results within constraints. These constraints include limited resources, specific timelines, scope boundaries, such as focusing on a given market, and the requirement to meet external standards for success. Projects also involve multiple people. When the goal is to do something that's urgent, ambitious, or complex, you need to work with others. Within organizations, new efforts are often built on projects that involve people who do not routinely work with each other. These sorts of projects—temporary collaborative work that entails deadlines, criteria for success, uncertainty about what course of action to select, and a set of inputs and constraints—provide ourfocus.

Thinking Broadly about Projects

In some fields, projects are widespread. New product development, information technology upgrades, building and infrastructure construction, manufacturing improvement, and software development all hinge on projects. Accumulated experience in these domains has given rise to professional project management expertise that includes formalized bodies of knowledge and communities of practice.

But even if the dialogue on projects is less visible in other domains, it's clear that projects are the unit of work and improvement for professionals in many fields. Today, a firm setting out to expand into a new market will use a project to make the strategic and operational move. A contractor may lead a project team to clean up a decommissioned chemical weapons site. A consumer products firm may harness a project to relaunch its line of shampoos. Management consulting engagements, new drug development, and retailer logistics improvement efforts—all entail projects.

Projects are the vehicle for innovation. Companies are trying out new approaches to innovation that are based on a strategy of harnessing projects. Google famously enables its employees to conduct their own projects on the side. Others from Lockheed to Procter & Gamble to Apple have used skunkworks, or separate innovation projects, to challenge their existing businesses with the hope of fueling innovation and avoiding becoming trapped by past success. Microsoft, 3M, and LinkedIn are just a few of the companies we found that offer internal venturing opportunities that support innovation projects, then select the best to develop. Even relatively small, young organizations are trying out employee-led projects. To encourage employees to develop new business ideas, Tough Mudder, which offers extreme obstacle course experiences, set up an internal business plan competition along with its own modest angel fund.[13]

Here's a more typical corporate example. In early 2010 the global financial firm Société Générale launched a challenging project. The original intent was to replace the company's cumbersome back-office software platform with state-of-the-art technology. Partway through its work, the project team was handed an additional task: enabling the start-up of the company's new US primary dealer business. With a staff of forty and $20 million dollars in investment, the project was done within eighteen months. Because they had successfully completed such a large-scale project with minimal business disruption, the team was much lauded and their project management approach documented so that it could be studied by others.[14]

Projects also abound in creative and social sectors. A team working to line up a new Broadway production or to make a movie; a disaster relief effort; a nonprofit agency developing a new program to support the region's elderly; and a parent-led effort to increase arts programs in local schools are all projects.

Our Mission to Make the World Better, One Project at a Time

What if every project enabled you, your team, and your organization to learn and at the same time to accomplish the work at hand? We see great potential for projects and learning to be linked. If you could embed systems thinking, skill building, and experimentation into the projects that you are on the hook for delivering, your own professional development would connect to your actual work instead of being seen as something separate. The promise of aligning the work that needs to be done with development of capabilities offers an antidote to the pervasive problem that learning, improvement, and development detract from the *real* work. As a result, products, services, and workplaces could all benefit.

Our aim is to deliver on this promise.

A Fail Better Declaration

The right kind of failure instructs, refines, and improves ideas, work products, skills, capacities, and teamwork. We aim to support your efforts to generate small, smart mistakes that enable your team to meet its work requirements (a first-order performance goal) while building capacity, habits, and insight (the second-order, deeper change). In other words, we want to help you harness the right kind of failure to get your day-to-day work done while you learn.

Now, we'll show you how to do this.

CHAPTER 2

Three Steps for Harnessing Failure

We've made the bold claim that your workaday projects could become crucibles for innovation, learning, and improvement. Yet too often, the reality couldn't be more different. Many projects fall short, instead plod along in the rut of status quo, good enough, what's always been done, safe, and no better needed.

Think back to *your* last project. Was it set up to maximize learning? Did you uncover valuable insights along the way? Did you deliver what you set out to? And once it was over, did your team reflect, or did you move straight to the next thing?

A systematic method for managing your projects can set up your team for useful epiphanies at every step. In the end, it can help you to create better deliverables with more lasting and further-reaching impact. At the heart of the Fail Better approach is a set of simple techniques to guide your work through three key phases: launching your project, iterating to build and refine, and embedding the learning. In this chapter, we preview these steps, showing how they relate to one another, and provide real-world examples to bring it alive. We start with an entrepreneur tackling his own very pressing need to fail better.

REAL-WORLD INSPIRATION

Ryan Tseng, WiPower, and the Need to Fail Better

It was a cold December day in 2007 in Cambridge, Massachusetts, when the young president and founder of WiPower, Inc., Ryan Tseng, found himself trying to pinpoint the causes of what he was dubbing his "8 million dollar mistake."[1]

A few years earlier, as a student at the University of Florida, Tseng had led the development of new hardware technology that could charge electronic devices wirelessly through magnetic pulses with an efficiency that rivaled that of a plug-in charger. Tseng knew he had a winning technology. The novel product solved many vexing problems: a slew of bulky cords and power strips cluttering work and home spaces, different charger types for every device, and the ability to charge only one device at a time. Tseng's charging pad did not require devices to be precisely aligned and could charge several simultaneously in a compact space.

Even at this early stage, the invention had attracted interest. WiPower was featured on television, appearing on CNBC's *Innovations* show, in the *Boston Globe*, and on the Engadget and DesignNews websites.[2] Now that he'd developed a working prototype, Tseng's next project was to get the technology to market. It was proving easier said than done.

As Tseng looked back on that summer and fall, he realized WiPower had been swept up in a tornado of progress. His team had braved technical, financial, and interpersonal obstacles to stay the course. In the previous month, they seemed to have turned a corner, and Tseng had begun to feel they were emerging above the clouds. Customers were in place, and the young company had lined up a strategic investor who seemed ready to make a significant financial commitment. But, as Tseng noted, "In a moment's notice, we lost our balance atop the turbulent vortex and crashed painfully back to earth."

Reflecting in the Midst of Action to Identify Mistakes

What had gone wrong? In the thick of things, Tseng offered his own take. "Initially, I took care to build a solid core with steadfast commitment to our vision and each other. Previously, when we were blindsided by obstacles, the team adapted and never splintered. [Our level of] commitment was built on thoughtful discussions and understandings of each other's passions, interests, and goals. We knew what we wanted, we knew what we were doing, and we knew how we could help each other," he reflected. But that fall, as the workload mounted, his core team doubled in size from four to eight people. Along with everyone else, Tseng was consumed with aggressively setting milestones and attacking an endless to-do list. As he looked back that December, he realized that the team had lost sight of the shared vision that enabled such remarkable initial progress.

The first blow had come when WiPower failed to meet a deadline for its first big customer, a large American smartphone manufacturer. As Tseng tells it: "We attacked [the task] with all of our emotional, technical, and financial resources. We pulled all-nighters and every team member worked 100-plus hours per week to meet the deadlines. The prototype was demonstrated in the lab . . . On the last day, [when the final demonstration was slated to take place] two of the key engineers were no longer on speaking terms and the ensuing miscommunication (or lack of communication) caused a disastrous component failure that ended our chance of making the deadline." Tseng had assumed his team's intensive approach to development would ensure on-time delivery, but it had left little room for component testing. The disappointed customer was forced to proceed without the charging system technology in place. Tseng had never before missed a production deadline, but there was no time to reflect. The team pushed forward.

Unfortunately, that was not to be their last setback. A few weeks later, a key strategic investor who had completed rigorous business, interpersonal, and technical due diligence was ready to partner with

WiPower and had indicated a willingness to invest in the start-up at a valuation in the region of $8 to 10 million. It all came down to a conference call. But with the investor on the line to finalize terms, the call went horribly awry. The now-out-of-sorts WiPower leadership team could not agree on technical and business issues during the investor conversation, and it was clear they were in trouble. After the call ended, the investor made the offer: $350,000 at a $2.1 million valuation, far short of the $8 to 10 million the team had expected.

Tseng saw the first mistake as a failure of communication, and the second as a failure of alignment among his team members. That December, as WiPower continued its start-up journey, Tseng analyzed his recent experience. "I failed to continue my commitment to building a solid core and as a result, when we were pushed, we splintered. We lost two team members, millions of dollars in valuation, and a large contract as a result."

Why was Tseng actively reflecting on and documenting where things had gone off track? He was in the process of applying an early version of the Fail Better method to his project as he worked—often at breakneck speed—on getting his product to market. As an MBA student at MIT Sloan School of Management, he was an initial experimenter with the method, and he was stopping to do something he'd made almost no time to do previously: assessing his actions and those of his team on an ongoing basis, documenting the learning as he went, and using his emerging insights to develop a course of action to move forward. The sting of his previous failures was motivation enough to do things differently, and the Fail Better framework supported his doing so.

The Fail Better Method

For many projects that aim to innovate, the goal is to learn by doing, but too often the doing doesn't lead to learning. In the rush to get things done and meet deadlines, workplace project teams take action without effective planning and assessment, and the potential value of taking action is lost. The Fail Better method (illustrated in figure 2-1) harnesses the power of iteration by linking three sets of activities: launching your project with the right logic, team, and resources; building and refining your deliverables through testing and iteration; and then embedding what you've learned to improve your own practice, the habits of your team, and the capabilities of your organization.

We've found that by engaging in a focused set of simple activities in each of these areas, managers can help their teams achieve greater success, identify and scale failure earlier, develop important personal and team habits, and help others within and outside their organizations learn from what worked and what didn't.

Launch Your Project

When you embark on a new team effort, you have a sense of the tasks, deadlines, and expected outputs that will occupy your team in the coming days, weeks, or months. As a manager, you likely have the basics of project management down. But can you go a step or two further by defining your project's scope for innovation and experimentation—the domain in which your team will work, explore, fail, and ultimately deliver? The goal of the Fail Better *launch* phase is

FIGURE 2-1

Overview of the Fail Better method

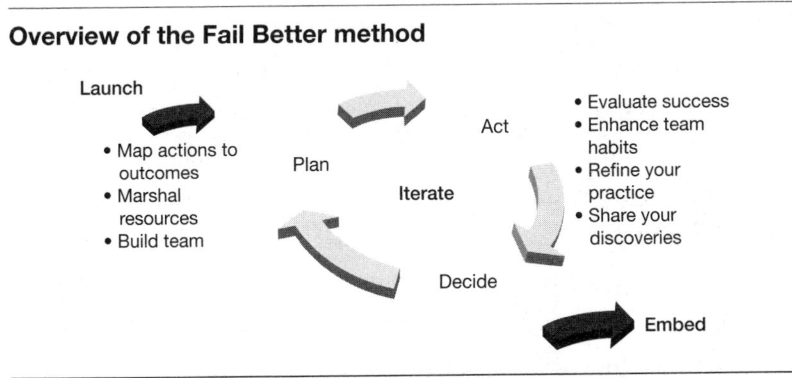

not to over plan and set things in stone, but to consider your project in its context, anticipate outcomes as tied to a series of logical assumptions, pull together your resources, and get the right people involved.

You'll begin by linking actions to outcomes by analyzing the project's goals and rationale to create a shared map of how your team's activities will create the results that lead to the outcomes you seek. Next, you'll marshal resources, accounting for the inputs and constraints that will shape the team's choices about what to do. Then, to build your team, you'll develop an understanding of skills, capabilities, and assets each person brings as you prepare team members to take action and work together effectively.

To demonstrate the importance of these activities, let's look at how a team in a health-care company laid out their logic for linking project actions to their desired outcomes, expanded the team with needed expertise, and leveraged the capabilities and resources of others to achieve a breakthrough growth solution.

REAL-WORLD INSPIRATION

Health-Care Managers Craft a Winning Launch Strategy

In the late 1990s, a team of Alaska-based managers at a US health-care company faced a growth challenge.[3] Seeking to develop new facilities to serve their region, they had submitted an unsuccessful funding request to corporate headquarters. Despite working hard to cut costs as requested by their higher-ups, months after the denial the Alaskan managers were still far from a capital business plan that would meet with home office approval. Realizing they lacked needed expertise to solve the problem on their own, the team turned to an expert in organizational knowledge sharing, Kent Greenes. His work in Alaska usually involved complex oil industry projects, but this time, Greenes's expertise would take him to a new domain.

Anxious for help, the team followed Greenes's advice and invited eight of the company's managers from Washington and Oregon who had accomplished what the Alaska team had not. Each invited manager had developed a successful capital plan. These individuals were asked to join an exercise called a *peer assist*. In the first of several sessions that Greenes led over the course of two days, the visiting peers shared their experiences. Advice quickly emerged: reduce the capital budget by shifting to a strategy based on remodeling or repairing existing facilities instead of building new ones. Such an approach had worked for these visitors. Their reasoning was supported by logical assumptions and evidence from past efforts. They had, in effect, linked planned actions to expected outcomes.

The Alaska team was skeptical of their colleagues' proposed solution. In their market, the team responded, remodels would not be sufficient to expand service offerings and draw in new customers. The group was at a stalemate of sorts, but they didn't let an impasse in their discussions prevent progress. Instead, they embarked on a joint field trip, visiting several facilities to observe patient care, operations, the settings, and more. Getting out of the conference room proved to be key to connecting the dots differently. Once they'd seen the facilities and met the people, the visitors agreed things were indeed different in Alaska. They changed their advice.

The group then set out to devise new ways to approach the budget request. They started by marshaling their resources—leveraging the expertise, insights, tools, and data possessed by those in the room. For example, one peer contributed materials from a recent market survey conducted in Oregon. Drawing on these, the group developed plans for a similar study in Alaska that would generate practical input for facility design. Working together, they customized the questions and survey approach for the Alaskan context.

Using data from the resulting survey, the Alaska team went on to improve its capital business plan and succeeded in obtaining the funds. The peer assist yielded other lasting benefits: increased understanding and knowledge sharing went both ways, and managers from all three states continued to collaborate.

What can we learn from this brief example? The Alaska team was innovative in borrowing the peer assist technique from the oil industry to solve a problem that had stymied their efforts to grow. A closer look at their activities reveals elements of the Fail Better launch phase. To advance their thinking, participants explicitly linked planned actions to anticipated outcomes, which allowed everyone in the room to examine and challenge assumptions. Because they made their logic explicit, team members could then revise their thinking to account for new evidence, which came in the form of their site visits. Another key step was to assemble the right people for the effort, supplementing local knowledge with different perspectives, skills, and expertise. Finally, they marshaled the varied resources that team members could provide, including data sources, market tools, and so on, to develop their growth expansion plan. Thanks to an early investment in testing their assumptions and challenging their thinking, the team—and their company—avoided a potentially flawed course of action, expanding or retrofitting existing facilities.

But beginning with a strong foundation is only one aspect. Completing the core work of your project, while refining as you go, comes next.

Build and Refine through Iteration

Now that you've built the groundwork for your project, you have a clearer sense of the project's goals, resources, and approach. As the project moves forward, it can be helpful to think of your project as a cauldron for experimentation and learning—in which you will plan, act, and assess to decide the next step.

Instead of thinking of your project as a monolithic effort toward the goal you've defined, approach your project in cycles or chunks.

Iterate to build and refine as we suggest by linking three activities via a repeated action loop: planning, taking action, and then assessing what has just occurred to make a decision about the next step. This process improves the chances that your failures will be small-scale and early rather than large and late. It also enables learning and refinement while allowing creative, or even seemingly outlandish, ideas to be explored. This loop is not designed to inhibit action by piling on additional work for the team—far from it. The goal is to harness the power of exploration while orienting your team toward action with a safety net in place. That safety net comes from intention, planning, and monitoring through data review and reflection.

You don't have to perfect your plans, consider every possible scenario or option, or calculate every detail in advance. Instead, you'll be iterating on your ideas by making repeated trips around the action loop. So rather than building your project around a one-shot effort, you can guide your team to an agile, responsive method of learning by doing. A team approach to tackling the key tasks and issues is crucial for this effort.

Consider an example from the experience of iconic American motorcycle producer Harley-Davidson. Changes in how the team designed its activities brought critical information to the forefront, where it could be acted upon swiftly and systematically.

REAL-WORLD INSPIRATION

Making Issues Visible to Prioritize Actions at Harley-Davidson

As General Manager of Powertrain Operations at Harley-Davidson Motor Company, Don Kieffer ran the motorcycle manufacturer's engine plants and oversaw the complex process of introducing new engines into production.[4] In 2003, as the organization hunted for new ways to increase quality and speed up its time to market,

Kieffer led an innovative new approach for making process, progress, and problems visible so that teams could prioritize their project activities. The idea was to bring into the open issues that otherwise could be revealed too late in a project's life and to avoid doing unnecessary work that didn't contribute to the end product. Eight months after adopting the technique, his engine plant was outperforming all others at Harley-Davidson, and Kieffer added the companywide role of Vice President for Operational Excellence to his responsibilities.

Kieffer's first step was to build the team's shared understanding of a set of simple but powerful principles borrowed from an approach called *oobeya* from the Toyota Production System.[5] According to Toyota veteran Takashi Tanaka, *oobeya*, which in Japanese means "big room," is just one of several linked elements of Toyota's process designed to bring the insights and practices of lean manufacturing to the domain of product development, where uncertainties often abound and progress can be unclear. As with improvement processes in manufacturing, the goal is to make problems and progress visible and to take on the most pressing issues as they are recognized and prioritized by team members. *Oobeya* also includes methods for clarifying a shared vision, specifying objectives, building realistic schedules, and aligning work streams. And as the name itself suggests, it all takes place in a room designated for the team's work. We'll focus here on one crucial approach that Kieffer and his team used, the issue board.

The team set up their room, taping big sheets of paper on the walls. Markers and sticky notes were the only other inputs. Once they kicked off their effort with an initial "spew" of all issues, the work team met weekly to add new items, note progress, and tackle critical issues, updating the board as they went. Each team member (or subteam) got a row, and there were just four columns: *potential*, *real*, *finished*, and *record*. In the corresponding cell went red sticky notes. Along with the name of the person raising the issue and the date, each red note listed two things: a clear, concise, and constructive definition of the issue and a brief analysis or recommendation. As the issue was tackled, its red note gained a yellow one recording the specific decision, committed action, or next step the team selected, identifying who would do what by when.

An issue began as *potential*, then moved into the *real* column when the team felt sufficient data had been gathered to indicate it was significant. Guidelines for taking on issues enabled the team to focus. Every week, two priority items could be escalated up the hierarchy if higher-level input or a decision was needed; and every week, each member or subteam selected a maximum of two issues to move from one column to the next. Teams would then take action to make progress on the focal issues.

Only when the issue was resolved could it be moved into *finished*. A subset of finished issues were tagged for *record* status if the team thought it was likely they or others would make use of the solution, providing a powerful conduit for learning.

In his 2010 book *The Lean Machine*, Kieffer's colleague Dantar Oosterwal tells what happened next.[6] Within months, Kieffer saw the normal daily flood of urgent emails and voicemails from his staff slow to a trickle. It was evident the process worked: things were going more smoothly, and there were fewer problems to handle.

In this example, we see the power the action loop at the heart of iterating to build and refine. The Harley-Davidson team had a winning approach for bringing critical issues and needed actions to the forefront, supported by evidence of why the issue was important and should be resolved. They were able to plan and prioritize their action steps, implementing just two a week.

With every action, team members collected data to ensure problems were solved. Only when the case had been made that the issue was resolved could the action item be moved into the completed category for reflection on what was learned and should be retained. The process would then continue, with new priority action items selected. This experimental and iterative approach, which demonstrates many aspects of the Fail Better iterate stage, led to major process and outcome improvements.

Embed the Learning

You've embarked on a project and led it to conclusion. What more is there to do? The final step is *embedding* what you've learned—from team processes to personal insights to larger project implications—so that you can share the lessons on a wider scale or apply them to future efforts.

From our work with everyone from students to CEOs, we know this is the most often overlooked aspect of effective action. Embedding the learning is really about what you do at the end of your project. The result of having developed plans and maps and then refined useful ideas via the action loop is a better set of deliverables. But all the effort you put into the launch and iterate steps does more than generate a better report, product, design, plan, study, recommendation, or decision. It also teaches you how to do things better the next time around. How do you embed the learning you've achieved for yourself, your team, and your organization—and even benefit others beyond your organization?

The first form of embedding takes place within your team when you agree to new habits you will preserve and old ones you will drop. The results and discoveries from your project are also potentially valuable to others, but managers often invest little in sharing and syndicating insights, data, tools, and techniques at the end of a project. And finally, the experience provides an invaluable spur to your personal reflection by illuminating your own values, revealing strengths and weaknesses, and alerting you to specific ways you can more effectively lead, manage, innovate, and create change.

REAL-WORLD INSPIRATION

Failure Reporting at Engineers Without Borders

In 2008, Canadian nonprofit Engineers Without Borders published its first annual failure report to document the subset of its development projects that had failed in some way during the past year.[7] The effort was orchestrated by EWB's Ashley Good, but the seeds were sown by another employee, Nick Jimenez, as he prepared to launch a potentially risky new project in Ghana in January 2008.[8] The organization espoused the values of striving for humility, dreaming big, working hard, and asking tough questions. Why, Jimenez asked the organization's leadership, did EWB share no stories of failure? Every account of the organization's programs and projects bragged about success. But it is common knowledge in the field of development that many efforts fail. EWB was no exception.

Thanks to Jimenez's probe, failure reporting caught on, starting with write-ups and presentations of in-the-field examples of failed efforts and then growing to include accounts of failures throughout the organization. The power of the approach became evident when EWB members not only reported on their failures but also found success in the next iteration of their projects. As Good tells it, the experience of another EWB staff member, Eli Angen, provides an illuminating example.

Enhance Personal, Team, and Organizational Practices

In the organization's 2010 Failure Report, Eli Angen described Bring EWB to Work, a program he designed to "mobilize volunteers across Canada to make presentations in their workplaces."[9] He was inspired by his organization's commitment to risk-taking and ambition that failure reporting exemplified. Angen explained: "I knew [it] was an ambitious initiative when I came up with the idea. That was the point. I wanted to push EWB to dream big and really shift how we engaged with corporations across Canada. It was way beyond anything I'd tried before but I also knew if I failed to achieve my goals I would still be recognized for the learning."

It didn't work, but Angen developed a presentation to share what he called his "dismal" failure. Why did he decide to tell his colleagues about his mistakes? Angen pointed to EWB's failure reports: "I'd seen authors of past stories get recognized and appreciated so I knew the painful act of sharing my failure openly would be respected and the learning would be used."

Interestingly, the benefit of this sharing materialized before the written report was even published. Soon after Angen put his presentation together, EWB began developing a new national campaign called "Solving Problems That Matter," and Angen's boss drew on the lessons of the earlier program's failure to refine the design of the new campaign. The result this time was a "wildly successful" program: within the year, the new outreach effort reached 85 percent of all Canadian first-year engineering students.[10]

What can we learn from this example? Failure reporting provided a substantive repository of insights and lessons via vivid first-person stories. This was a powerful way to embed the learning. As part of their failure reporting efforts, EWB staff examined their project results in depth. They could see where their own mistakes and personal shortcomings may have contributed, enabling professional development; they could also pinpoint vulnerabilities in their team's approach and methods, improving team processes. But the real payoffs came in sharing the learning with others. As the success of EWB's subsequent campaign revealed, helping others understand a project failure allows them to craft better courses of action in their next efforts. The move to failure reporting enabled a shift in EWB's culture that supported innovation and openness, a change that employees, beneficiaries, and donors lauded. Considering what can be distilled from every project you undertake—including the failures and setbacks revealed by your analysis—can help future efforts do better.

Failing Better Is Not Easy, but Its Rewards Are Clear

The Fail Better method of using projects as the crucible for learning provides both flexibility and guidance for the activities you'll do to launch, iterate on, and embed your project's contributions. The concepts underpinning our advice are not rocket science, but they are supported by research and best practice. And they are surprisingly rare in the hundreds of projects we have been able to study.

One reason is that nothing is free. Implementing Fail Better requires a commitment to the approach and an investment of your time, skill, and energy to begin experimenting. Think of all the work that went in to Engineers Without Borders' failure reporting, Harley-Davidson's issue board, or the health-care company's peer assist. But ultimately, which is harder: learning too late, after the fact, that you made avoidable and costly mistakes, or creating habits and practices that scale failure at a level you can afford and help you complete and refine your deliverables along the way? In addition, there's a bonus. All this commitment to learning, testing, and improving rubs off in the form of professional development of you as a manager and also benefits the skills and abilities of your team members.

Ryan Tseng and WiPower learned much about failure from the school of hard knocks, yet Tseng refused to let setbacks take him or his team off track. After his mid-course reflection, he did copious research on how to strengthen his team, developed an action plan that could help him learn from his missteps and move forward, and made time to reflect and learn—something he hadn't prioritized earlier while rushing forward with prototype development. Tseng also had a bold idea, a superior product, an orientation to risk, and a humble openness to learning from his experience. These qualities as a manager and inventor, coupled with his application of many of the Fail Better steps, meant he did not stumble in the pursuit of his goal. Even in the immediate aftermath of the difficult stretch that

WiPower endured in late 2007, he was optimistic: "We'll do better next time. It's all part of the fun."

Not surprisingly, with Tseng's tenacity and the skill of his team, WiPower landed on its feet and built an impressive track record in the years that followed. In 2010, Qualcomm acquired the fledgling company, ensuring its opportunity to scale and distribute its product and rewarding founders, investors, and employees handsomely. WiPower team members, including Tseng, went to Qualcomm to continue the development of the product. In 2012 Qualcomm partnered with Samsung to launch a new standards development organization (SDO) to standardize and commercialize the technology at massive scale for applications ranging from Bluetooth headsets to laptop computers.[11] By early 2014, the SDO had grown to approximately 90 members, including many world-leading device companies, and the technology had been incorporated into commercial products.[12] With Qualcomm on its way to success via a rapidly expanding consortium, a commercial product launch, integration into next generation chipsets, and a formidable patent portfolio, in 2013 Tseng left to embark on his next startup, confident that he'd learned and developed from all his experiences along the way.[13]

We invite you to take this journey, too—to learn and refine while implementing the work you do every day for better and more meaningful results, higher-quality deliverables, and the ability to grow as a manager and team in the process.

In chapter 3, we'll look at how to best experiment with the Fail Better method in your own context and to prepare for the journey ahead.

CHAPTER 3

Charting Your Fail Better Path

Your next big project might seem exciting at the outset, but there's no guarantee it will deliver big results at the end. If you're aiming to innovate, chances are there will be surprises along the way. Successful teams find and exploit these breakthroughs, from project launch to close, by using systematic practices tailored to their needs. This combination of exploration and discipline can shift outcomes from poor or just acceptable to surprising, groundbreaking, or even world-changing. Harnessing failure's benefits calls for a method to learn from failure and then do better.

It's this virtuous cycle that forms our focus. We designed this chapter to guide you in taking the ideas and inspirations from the pages of this book into your own projects.

Advice for Using This Book

We've introduced you to the Fail Better approach, illustrating how its concepts play out in four very different real-world examples. Chapters 4, 5, and 6 equip you with practical advice and essential details for implementing the Fail Better method through the steps needed to launch, iterate, and embed. Early in each chapter, you'll find a call-out box of key points summarizing its guidance, and the chapter itself explains every step, illustrating our advice with examples and diagrams. Each ends with a set of helpful tips for implementation: a list of guiding questions, an index of tangible products that we suggest you create, and a set of checklists to ensure you consider the options for each step.

This is a good place for us to mention some of our terms. We refer to you as team leader or manager, but you may not have that official title yet—or you may have a title that puts you higher up in the management hierarchy. We mean to include everyone who has a hand in shaping the projects they work on, regardless of title. Similarly, we'll often refer to your client, but we have in mind both internal and external clients. Your client may not be identified as such; it could simply be your boss. Please translate the terms into whatever's most relevant for you.

We recommend that you read through the entire book to get a picture of the method and its application. Jot notes in the margins, highlight ideas to try, call out the concepts that speak to you, and flag areas where you'd like to understand a little more. Everyone makes sense of content and its application a little differently. We've assembled a few suggestions that might work for you. Select one of these options as you read, remembering that a project example could draw from something at work, a community effort, or your personal life:

> **Consider a current or upcoming project.** Start with a recent project in mind as you think through the book's suggestions. Efforts that you are responsible for today or in the near future are likely to loom large in your thoughts, spurring you to ground the methodology in your own context.
>
> **Revisit a past project.** If you've ever experienced a failed project, you probably remember it vividly. Recall your experience with a past project that didn't turn out as you'd

hoped, reflecting on how the Fail Better ideas might apply. Not only will this thought experiment help you to understand the ideas and their application, but the analysis could help you pinpoint where things went wrong in the past and assess practices that went well and should be retained.

Look for inspiration and ideas. To get started, you need not apply every Fail Better idea to a current or past project. Instead you can simply follow up on what seems most interesting to you. As you read, look for what stands out to you because it complements your current practices and systems, or simply because it sparks your interest.

Once you've read through the book, we recommend that you review the end-of-chapter implementation guides. These walk-throughs equip you to experiment with the many ideas each chapter offers and put the entire method into practice, step-by-step. To make them easy to find, the pages have been edged in gray.

Fail Better Is Not One-Size-Fits-All

Adopting Fail Better could challenge you as a manager, not least because the steps must be tailored to your requirements. We don't provide a cookie-cutter recipe. On the other hand, even if they need to morph to work for your context, our ideas apply in varied project environments. We consider Fail Better to be a method that is prescriptive enough to offer practical guidance for its essential, interrelated steps while being flexible enough to allow you to adjust the effort, time, and focus devoted to each area.

Chances are, and perhaps reassuringly so, some aspects of Fail Better will look familiar. "Of course," you may think as you consider our recommendations: "Do some upfront predicting and planning, work toward deliverables through a certain amount of trial and error, and figure out and share what you've learned from your project."

Our experience, though, shows that many teams pay lip service to the value of such concepts but do little to apply the thinking, action, and discipline necessary to carry out these tasks in a structured way. Fail Better focuses your attention on the activities that can yield the most helpful results, linking your efforts to enable a more systems-based approach and avoiding the wasted efforts that slow success.

What does this mean for you? It's best to approach implementation with a commitment to applying *all three* stages of the method. All are essential for building new habits and garnering the results that we aim to help you achieve. This does not mean you must immediately take on a burdensome additional workload—in fact, we encourage you to make the ideas laid out in the book your own and apply them as lightly or as intensively as is feasible in your first attempt.

Starting at the scope you can afford means that you'll need to assess your project steps to uncover the best opportunities to implement the method. For example, you might already have a process for pulling your team together and outlining the problem that your project is designed to help solve, but you might never have developed a project map linking the actions your team will take to the desired outcomes. Allotting an hour to make these connections explicit and visible for the entire team may be the first addition to your typical launch process.

Taking Your First Steps to Implement the Method

We have some practical advice for making it easier to get going:

> **Jump in where you can.** Are you in the middle of a project right now? Knee-deep in creating your deliverables and already well past the launch phase? That's OK—begin where you are and experiment with some of the activities and thinking laid out here. As we've suggested, you can go back retrospectively to think through what you might have done

differently in getting your project off the ground, but in the meantime, keep going. How can you experiment in the context of project activities you are working on today?

Do a little bit in each area. You may feel better equipped to implement certain parts of the method than others. Don't skip everything that you're unsure about. If you see little leeway for experimentation in your current project or are concerned that you can't take a lot of risk, you can still try something out. Maybe you can test out new ideas for running your team meetings differently, compare it with the old way, and see which gets better results. Even a small change begins to orient your team toward innovation by testing the status quo to see if a better option exists. If you're jumping into the next project without much time to engage in the embed phase, you can carve out an hour or two to pull your team and key stakeholders together to identify what went well and what could have been done better. Document what you learn in a brief memo, highlighting three things you will do differently in the next project to improve outcomes and three things you will keep doing because they were successful.

Don't expect perfection. We believe it is more important to get started and do something in each area of the method than to create a perfect plan that is never executed. Get to it! Do what you can and find what works best. You can always add layers, implement new tools, or increase your level of investment in each phase down the line. The most important thing is to begin building a habit of critical thinking and action that allows you to view both the means and ends of your project, see the interconnections between activities and outcomes, and develop the mind-set and tools that can keep failure from setting you back as you drive development and innovation.

Involve others in your journey. Seek support from others and accountability for yourself by sharing your intent to implement a better approach to orchestrating and learning from failure in your next project. Perhaps you have a mentor or peer whom you trust or who supports your development. And, while you're at it, bring your team into the loop, explaining your intent to improve your outcomes and learn from experience by adopting a systematic project method. When others know what you intend to do, they can check in with you about how it is going, provide feedback and encouragement, and ask how they can help.

Pick a focal point. If it seems too overwhelming to apply Fail Better to all aspects of your project, consider picking a focal area, such as team process. You can think about ways you would like your team to work together, produce deliverables, and communicate better, focusing your launch, iterate, and embed efforts within this domain.

Try, try again. If you do fall off the wagon on a project while applying the method, consider what can be done retrospectively. Identify adjustments you'll make in your next project. To help support such course corrections, keep an implementation log—jot down what you try at each step of the way, noting how well it worked along with ideas to try next time around. Just keep at it, little by little, and let this book continue to be your guide.

The Road Ahead

Nobody ever said that it's easy to build new habits and adopt new tools. Planning to learn from failure is likely to require additional effort on your part, especially when you first start. Simply talking about failure can challenge the faint of heart! In the thick of projects it's all too easy to drift away from the discipline. And as a team effort wraps up, it's tempting to simply declare victory—even if you suspect it's not quite what you all wanted—and move on. It will require a conscious commitment to approach our method with an open mind and to pay attention to elements that may seem obvious at the outset but prove easy to overlook in practice.

But the rewards could be great if you master the tools and refine your own approach to maximize your learning from your next project. You'll soon learn how to create the right environment, enable testing and analysis, build shared capabilities to extract useful learning from every action, and more. Every effort that risks failure also offers the opportunity to make new discoveries. In building and supporting a method, you'll be developing skills essential for any manager leading a team or running a project in uncertain environments or complex markets. To make sure that your efforts yield the insights you seek, read on, keeping this chapter's guidance in mind.The promise of the Fail Better approach beckons.

Your Checklist for Making the Most of This Book

Our at-a-glance checklist summarizes our advice for taking advantage of this book.

- ❑ Read through the book to see how all the pieces fit together. To choose how to start, consider the following options:

  1. Identify a current or future project to which you can apply the Fail Better concepts and approaches.

  2. Think back to a finished (failed) project that offers a vivid example on which you can try out the ideas with your own thought experiments.

3. Look for inspiration and ideas as you read, pulling out the pieces that resonate with you and fit with your work context.

- ❑ Make the book into your own field guide. Take notes in the margins about how you might try things out in your own workplace, community project, or personal life. Highlight relevant passages and flag ideas for follow-up.
- ❑ Return to the implementation guides at the end of chapters 4, 5, and 6. Find them on the pages edged in gray. Use these to structure and guide your application.
- ❑ Commit to implementing some aspect of each phase of the method in your current project by keeping the following approaches in mind:
  - Jump in where you can.
  - Do a little bit in each area.
  - Don't expect perfection.
  - Pull others into the journey.
  - Pick a focal point.
  - If you fall off the wagon, try, try again.

PART II

Fail Better: Step-by-Step

Part Two puts together the steps of the Fail Better approach. Dive in for specific ideas on how to get your project off the ground, iterate to refine your ideas and deliverables, and retain what you learn from your efforts.

Launch your project. Explore how to lay the groundwork for a new project in a way that sets the stage for learning. To reach success sooner:

- Establish the rationale linking proposed actions to results
- Inventory and assemble necessary resources
- Build your team for successful interaction and learning

Iterate to build and refine. Uncover how small steps can yield big results when you design your work carefully, building in room for experimentation while meeting project goals. Harness the power of learning from action as you:

- Plan your action to allow you to test ideas
- Take action while capturing data
- Review results to determine the next action step

Embed the learning. Instead of losing hard-earned wisdom as you rush on to the next project, capture and share your findings. Make the most of your work when you:

- Examine the outcomes of your project
- Enhance project methods, along with personal and team habits
- Share your discoveries within your organization and beyond

CHAPTER PREVIEW

STEPS FOR A BETTER LAUNCH

You're embarking on a new project. Set it up to take effective action, learn as you go, and create success—without overplanning. This chapter shows you how.

- Link actions to outcomes:
  - Craft a crisp and vivid problem statement.
  - Define your products and develop a deliverables list.
  - Map your project's impact.
- Marshal your resources:
  - Inventory project inputs and pinpoint constraints.
  - Identify unmet project needs and extra resources.
- Build your team:
  - Assemble your team roster.
  - Obtain missing skills and capabilities.
  - Establish team practices and project culture.

Start your project on solid footing by clarifying your aims, mapping the context, and ensuring the right team, practices, and resources are in place. Establish a commitment to learning at the outset by showing how the actions you will take will lead to the outcomes you desire, so that you can update your ideas as the project unfolds.

CHAPTER 4

Launch Your Project

The day will come. Your project will hit a snag. Panic-inducing deadlines will telescope. Priorities will shift under your feet. Surprises will materialize. Unfortunately, no amount of preparation can prevent the unforeseen crisis. And in fact, too much advance planning is as foolish as too little, given changing environments and unknown factors.

But that's not to say that preparation is useless. Kicking off your project with the right kind of forethought enables your team to navigate unexpected complications more effectively and to make the most of happenstance discoveries along the way. What if your team could rise above obstacles, even benefit from them, by reaping the new information and ideas that each challenge reveals? Every new discovery could advance your work, improve your results, and help your team to develop. Hurdles could morph into springboards.

Yet all too often, team efforts fall short of this promise.

Launches Often Miss the Mark, but You Can Do Better

Why do so many failed projects trace the root of their problems to launch? Let's look at three common failure modes and our advice for avoiding them without overplanning.

Too Little, Too Late and Other Reasons Projects Fall Short

In the aftermath of challenging projects, people commonly wish they had invested more of their smarts at the outset. For example, one team we worked with realized that a better launch could have revealed an important lack of alignment between project goals and the rest of the organization early enough for it to have cultivated crucial sponsorship and collaboration. Another uncovered disastrous internal disagreement about project strategy so late in the process that the team had few options for refocusing the work. Had they discussed work plans, deliverables, and goals at kickoff, the team later realized, they would have surfaced the conflicts early enough to resolve them.

Again and again, we are surprised by how often it happens: in the cold light of hindsight, spurred by the pain of disappointing final results, teams look back with candor and openness at their experience and their analysis reveals new truths. In this moment, given the right opportunity, teams can be very skilled at detecting the seeds of their project's lackluster results. Yet far too frequently, the resulting hard-earned insights and resolutions recede into the background when the next project is launched.

Perhaps it's human nature. It's true that failure spurs deeper thinking than success, at least up to a point. The kicker is that such examination necessarily happens at the end of a project—when the bad news is in. At the start of the next effort, the mood is more optimistic and the conversations forward-looking, and few want to dwell on what went wrong last time (or speculate about what could go wrong this time). The team may not have the same members and the work may differ, complicating the task of applying lessons from the past to the future.

Then there's the constant tug-of-war between planning and thinking on the one hand and action on the other. In many projects we've studied, the combination of ambitious goals and constrained resources created pressure to get visible results quickly. There are many advantages to "just doing it." Examples of rapid-action approaches include scrum and other agile methods popular in the software industry today, and new versions of lean and quality-inspired approaches that are reshaping manufacturing and start-ups. You'll see their influence in our methods. But the buzz about these high-speed iteration techniques may heighten the pressure to get things done, making you feel as if it's better to act than to prepare. Unfortunately, there's no guarantee that the requirements for an effective project—activities and deliverables that are aligned with organizational priorities, access to the resources required to carry out the needed work, and more—will work themselves out in the rush to action if your efforts are not guided by some careful forethought.

There's one more reason it's all too easy to skimp on the critical work of laying the groundwork for your project. One of the biggest barriers to project impact is operational: most teams don't know how to launch their projects in a way that primes them for learning. A practical and customizable method to guide project launch is simply not available. This chapter is designed to fill the gap. Because time, attention, and resources are at a premium at the outset, our advice will help focus your project launch.

Keeping It Simple, Supple, and Scrappy

We send you off with some advice for this phase of the work: *keep it simple and supple.* This is especially important for high-pressure projects that call for a measure of scrappiness. Complicated grand plans could be a waste of time—or worse—for such projects. To innovate, explore, or problem-solve, scrappy projects need to be able to turn on a dime.

Investing too much in formal planning can squander valuable time and resources. The resulting documents may simply be irrelevant and do little to enable nimble action. Worse yet, they may limit innovation by over-specifying activities in advance, leaving little room for discovery and creativity. They can create a false sense of certainty that in turn makes it difficult to raise new issues and limits openness to new ideas and data. They may even engender cynicism.

Perhaps you've seen it: detailed color-coded charts, reports, or custom websites filled with deadlines, dependencies, and more are presented ritualistically to the boss and then fall by the wayside once the team gets to work. Of course, expertly constructed Gantt charts, status dashboards, and other components of the professional project management toolkit are essential for many projects, particularly when they involve technical complexity and logistical challenges. Such tools are invaluable for managing complexity and enabling performance for a wide range of projects. But let's not confuse the task management and planning expertise of project management professionals with what is needed for the team to kick off its work with the right understanding of the project and its context.

The truth is, you may well need both the Fail Better approach *and* project management tools. Our approach is not necessarily a substitute for the latter, but we know that many projects undertaken by professionals proceed with no formal planning or project management tools at all. And amid the full complement of traditional project management approaches, the domains we focus on here may get short shrift. Even if you select a project management method for your project, our launch advice will help you avoid the traps we've described.

Most crucially, as you work through our launch process, develop a set of materials to capture the most important things for your team to pay attention to throughout the project. Think creatively about how you can make the products of this early work both easy to use and easy to refine. Choose the format and design that meshes with your team, perhaps pushing a little outside the norms. Make it compelling enough to inspire engagement and interaction.

The materials you develop could be simple and informal in format. After following this chapter's advice, your team will have a set of meaningful materials. You may end up with three typed pages at the front of each team member's binder, or some handwritten lists on flipchart paper taped to the wall of your project room. You may create a set of inspiring hand-drawn diagrams that represent the team and its goals and principles, a Google Doc summary of your ideas, or a set of intranet resources that every team member interacts with weekly. What you produce at this stage needs to be simple enough for you to refer to often and to serve as a practical touchstone for every team member. Something rough is preferable: plans and other documents that are too polished can actually discourage participation, as team members and stakeholders are less likely to interact with and update something that looks like it is set in stone.

The simple-and-supple principle underpins our design of the three key activities that guide your project launch. Now, let's take the first step.

Link Actions to Outcomes

All projects entail uncertainty. In a sense, this is what defines a project. Projects aim to create an outcome within constraints of scope and resources. If your effort were entirely routine, you would not need a project; you'd just be doing regular, production-oriented work. The more innovative you aim to be, the less likely it is that your work will proceed in a straight line from project kickoff to activities to work products to desired impact. How will your team get its work done and ensure it ends up generating the impact you seek?

Inspired by effective practices in high-risk military settings, high-stakes projects across domains, and organizations undergoing successful transformational change, we've pinpointed a crucial first step: build an explicit understanding of what you are trying to do and how you *think* it will work. You and your team will then be equipped to revisit your initial ideas as you go, asking yourselves if your experiences, efforts, and emerging results are indeed playing out as anticipated. This exercise may sound abstract, but it isn't. What we have in mind is something very practical: build a map.

We'll guide you through three steps to do this:

1. Develop a problem statement to focus attention on the situation that your project addresses.

2. List everything your team plans to create in the course of the project.

3. Show how you think these products will address the problem that your team is taking on, connecting item 2 to item 1 to build your team's project impact map.

As you'll soon see, an impact map highlights the connections that underpin your project so you can check that you're on the right track and discover inconsistencies in your plans, assumptions, or understanding of key factors as your project proceeds. It doesn't have to be complicated. In fact, for the reasons we mention above, it *shouldn't* be complicated.

Craft a Problem Statement

Succinctly define the problem your project aims to solve (or prevent). A simple statement can anchor your team's focus. But to end up with something crisp and vivid, you may have to put more work into this than you think! Your starting point is the obvious question: *What is the problem?*

Make It Crisp

Boil down your answer to a specific, cogent statement that describes the issue or opportunity your project addresses from the point of view of the people your project aims to help. Try to do this in language that matters to *them*.

Our advice: define what a physician would call the *presenting problem* or *chief complaint*. Make sure to word it in a way that is meaningful to the imagined "patient"—the equivalent of the rash, stomachache, or sleeplessness that brought her to the doctor's office. In your case, consider the client's problem or opportunity that gave rise to this project. Can you sum it up in a sentence? If not, you already know this question warrants further attention.

If you're wondering what to aim for, it may be useful to know that a good problem statement is:

- **Concise.** Your statement should be short and to the point.
- **Specific.** Your statement should clarify who, what, and why.
- **Measurable.** Where possible, your statement should allow you to measure the degree of change.

The specific format will vary, so we do not want to be too prescriptive. But if you're stuck, try the following template:

> [*A focal group of people who matter to your client*] need [*product, service, or item together with its key distinctive attributes*] in order to [*accomplish or attain some specific measurable outcome or state that matters to them*].

The Lack of a Deliverable Is Not a Problem Statement

There's a common tendency to frame the problem statement as the need to create the end product.

Let's take a very simple example. Suppose your team has been asked to create a new brochure. Is this your problem statement: "We need to create a new brochure"? While this may technically be true, it's limited, and as a result is likely to be far from generative. Without knowing why a new brochure is needed—the challenge or opportunity in the world that it would address—the team would eventually face difficulties, either being forced to figure out on the fly why the brochure is needed or else going ahead with the task with little guidance on its requirements and a limited sense of how it fits in with other things. Either way, it's unlikely to be productive (or much fun) for the team to work on the brochure without knowing why or what it should accomplish.

As you define the problem, you'll need to think carefully about the situation your project seeks to address. As you analyze it, you'll probably find yourself thinking about the problem's origins and coming up with ideas about why this situation exists (or could exist). Jot any notes about origins in a separate open issues list, for later consideration. You're not trying to account for everything! Right now, you are trying to develop a simple problem statement.

Focus on the People Affected

Check that your description focuses on the people who are affected by the present (or future) situation you seek to address. They may not be your direct clients, but your statement needs to address them while resonating with the client.

Ask yourself: *Who has the problem?* This can be a subtle question.

Let's return to the brochure example. Suppose your company's salespeople have asked for the new brochure. In a sense, the sales personnel are the ones who have a problem—they do not like the current brochure—but a deeper examination may reveal that they have noticed few potential customers pick up the brochure at sales conventions, despite the known appeal of the product itself, or that sales agents often end up printing website pages to hand to prospects instead of the brochure.

If this is the case, it's *potential customers* who have the real problem. Customer prospects are not getting the information they need, or the appeal of the product is not evident from the brochure. In either case, your team will need to consider the needs of potential customers. But you will likely also have to get the sales department's participation in order to effectively design the brochure. Do the salespeople feature in your problem statement along with potential customers? Probably not, but you now have a new question for your issues list to include: how will you work with sales to make sure you address the problem statement in a way that works for them?

This line of thinking may prompt a new consideration: how will you incorporate these potential customers into your project planning, so that their needs are factored in? If you have the right resources, you may be able to interact with customers and learn from them directly to measure the level of appeal. If time and money were no object, you could run true experiments, testing different design options in real sales situations. If not, you need other options. One solution is to draw on sales agents as proxies for customers (for instance, by interviewing them). Alternatively, you may end up reviewing all your firm's brochures to identify those that work best. Perhaps you could use sales data to look for evidence of brochure effectiveness and then select specific attributes that correlate with a sales measure. Each method has its own strengths and weaknesses, of course. You will be planning tactics later, but notice how many useful ideas have been triggered by your work on the problem statement. Jot these down on that issues list, and keep going with the problem statement.

In the brochure example, your statement would target the two things we've been discussing: prospective customers and their need to appreciate the product when they are in certain situations (e.g., when they are not online or when they are interacting with stakeholders who play a role in the decision adopt the product). So, adding a few more invented details to make it more specific, your problem statement may look something like this:

> Potential customers need comprehensive, but not too detailed, information about pricing and service-level options

available in writing when they meet with their families to make a decision about signing up for our services.

To complete our analysis of the people affected by the problem, let's imagine a couple of alternative scenarios involving our brochure project. If the update is necessitated by a change in the company's graphic identity and there's no indication of customer dissatisfaction or request for changes from the sales force, the people who have the problem would be your firm's marketing and branding departments. In such a case, your problem statement would focus on the stakeholders your marketing and branding departments seek to serve. It may also aim to prevent future problems (confusion in the marketplace, reduced advertising impact, and so on) that would arise if your firm's materials were not well aligned and consistently branded. In this scenario, the statement might be:

> Potential customers need to be able to recognize our firm's brand instantly as a reflection of our quality and innovative services so they can quickly distinguish our company in a crowded marketplace of providers.

A third hypothetical case puts the sales force as your focus for the brochure redesign problem statement. What if the old brochure is ineffective because the salespeople dislike it and therefore won't use it—it's too heavy, it's the wrong size to carry conveniently, it includes no place for them to write their name or insert a business card, or it's too expensive to appeal to sales agents? In this case, your problem statement would focus on the features of the current brochure that sales personnel find unacceptable and seek to meet their criteria. An example statement in this case might be:

> Our sales people need a clear, concise, easily portable method of showcasing and communicating our services to potential customers to more effectively close sales.

You've probably had enough of that brochure by now, so let's move on. But as the example shows, even a half-hour spent thinking about the key problem statement can be invaluable. The process forces you to think very specifically about what your project aims to accomplish, why, and for whom, in terms that can be measured or tested.

Defining a problem can be a fun and creative activity. As you hone a sentence that presents the need your project seeks to address, think about how you can add some color to your statement.

Make It Vivid

To dramatize the situation, consider what the problem *looks* like. How is it visible? If it's something that hasn't yet happened, how would it be evident? Grab a photo, sketch some stick figures, imagine quotes from the people the project serves, or draw thought bubbles for a hypothetical customer to make it vivid. You could tell a story—in words or comic-book-style.

Alternatively, make the statement exciting by imagining an extreme case of the problem or opportunity. What will appeal to your team members and get them to put in the extra effort on this project? Define the problem in ways that are meaningful and vivid to them. This could be an add-on to the more straightforward problem statement and serve as a touchstone for the team. Invoking humor, tapping into shared values, or creating a tag line, slogan, or sketch of an extreme potential situation can remind your team what's important and align motivation when your project hits difficulties.

Future creativity is also enabled by the very precision we suggest you strive for in your problem statement. When you crisply define the problem or opportunity and make visible the people who experience, or could experience, the ill effects that would ensue if you fail to address the situation, the stage is set for your team to freely explore new ideas and approaches that could spur creative thinking.

FIGURE 4-1

Vivid representation of a problem

Source: http://groundwork.mit.edu/globalhealth-lab/hosts/.

Figure 4-1 shows an example of how a problem was made vivid for our global health projects class. A clinic was struggling with long waits for patients, resulting in untreated medical conditions that led to poor health outcomes. The image reminded the MIT team about this need, even when working from campus.

How You Will Use Your Problem Statement

As you wrap up this portion of your launch efforts, know your investment will pay off. An effective problem statement can prove invaluable. In the thick of your project, a vivid, crisp, and salient description of the problem can help your team sidestep the short-term, let's-just-get-it-done thinking trap. It can also spur creativity in thought and approach. When you remind yourselves of the real issue your project seeks to address, you may help your team to push beyond boundaries of narrow individual or team objectives to create a larger impact.

As you discuss the problem, you'll inevitably come to the question: What do we think the solution should be? This brings us to the specifics of your team's outputs.

Define Your Products and Develop a Deliverables List

Make a list of what the project will deliver. Include everything that comes to mind. Does your project output involve a decision, a prototype, a list of ideas, a set of narratives, a website, video content, data for others to use, a study, a design, a template, a rule, or policy? If you've been asked to create a plan, you may now realize you need to clarify what it should include. What are all the expected elements of a plan? Teams often start by asking these definitional questions, which makes a lot of sense.

Not all products of your work will be tangible. Does your project involve an event, experience, or interaction? What are the performance expectations?

Quality expectations for end products loom large in most teams' early planning and often lead to questions about their deliverables' attributes. If it's a report, what will it actually look like: what physical form or electronic format will it take? If persuasiveness is important, what sorts of evidence and data, pictures, stories, quotes, and charts should it include? Will the materials need to be polished and well-produced, or is rough and ready acceptable or even preferable? How detailed will it need to be? How formally written? Define what you imagine you will have in your hands at the end of it as specifically as you can.

Decide Where to Push the Envelope

And as you go, beware the tendency of new teams to model their report, plan, or other document after the previous one or to simply follow the organization's usual template for such items. While this can be efficient and even effective—and if your firm has perfected its report formats, using the standard one could end up being your best strategy—it's also a way to ensure your project won't innovate in this respect. That could be OK; not every project activity needs to be innovative. But you need to make that decision after careful thought. Where is innovation likely to yield the most value? If you are at all unsure, avoid rushing to either extreme of redesigning everything from scratch or simply copying earlier work. Plan instead to invest some effort in figuring out how much you would like to spend in exploring options for form and format. If you decide the formatting of your work is less crucial than other aspects, it may not be worth investing too much time in rethinking design.

Here's a big caveat. If you have already decided you are happy to simply produce what you've been asked to by the boss or client and don't seek to push the thinking about how or what you do, all you need to do at this stage is ask for clear direction and specifications. But if your project is aiming for excellence and impact, it's unlikely that the good-enough-and-no-better, checking-off-the-boxes approach will lead to true innovation. Instead you need to be willing to renegotiate your deliverables at some point in the process. Chances are, you will want to shape your team's deliverables to account for what you learn as you work on the project. You'll want some flexibility to be built into the deliverables specifications.

How You Will Use Your Deliverables List

Once you have a working list of project deliverables, you can use it as the basis for checking for agreement about your planned-for end products in conversations with your clients, project champions, and other stakeholders, as well as within the team. A wonderful feature of any list is that it helps you talk about priorities: what goes at the top of the list, and what would be nice to have but is not essential? You are now equipped to have this discussion with your project stakeholders at any moment you choose—when it is most valuable for your team. The wise project wrangler always has a plan and a goal but never treats every detail as set in stone. If you overplay your hand in negotiating for changes in your deliverables right at the start of your project, it may make it difficult to change the deal later on.

There are other crucial reasons to define your deliverables at this point. Knowing what you are on the hook for producing is a basic project planning requirement for obvious reasons: your activities need to be designed so as to enable the products to be developed, and you need to ensure you have the time and inputs needed to create them. So begins the work planning.

Lay the Groundwork for a Work Plan

As you list deliverables, you will naturally be thinking of the steps needed to produce them. We suggest you immediately start building a list of the steps and activities needed to create your team's work products and events without investing too much effort in specifying details at this stage. Simply jot down the tasks, inputs, and dependencies that come to mind that are associated with each major deliverable. You'll return to this list when you refine your work plan.

Anticipate Deliverables

There's a further benefit to imagining all your project will create. As you define what you will deliver to your clients and how they will use it, forming a concrete picture of what you aim to produce can inspire your team to keep going and maintain focus. Remember our clinic example above? Figure 4-2 presents an image that motivated the team to focus on desired outcomes.

A visual representation isn't the only way to achieve focus. Anticipating how you will feel on your deliverables handoff day can add inspiration. One team undertaking a complex and difficult project spent an early meeting anticipating the scene. Every team member wrote a paragraph describing the imagined final meeting with clients, which the team used to create a team statement, written just for themselves, that they could review whenever the project encountered difficulties. Their vivid picture of what the team and its stakeholders would be doing and talking about, and what they would literally have in their hands that day, helped to motivate everyone's effort.

FIGURE 4-2

Vivid representation of a desired outcome

Source: http://groundwork.mit.edu/globalhealth-lab/hosts/.

It also enabled deeper examination of the work in progress. Once team members had a foretaste, even if imagined, of their handoff day, they could handle moments of crux by asking themselves: *Would the choice we are making today enable us to walk away from the final meeting knowing we had achieved our vision of equipping our clients with the most valuable tools, plans, and approaches?* If the answer was no, they went back to the drawing board. Tapping into this vision not only inspired the team's hard work over the next six months but also helped it focus on deliverables that would be the most valuable for the clients.

Map Your Project's Impact

Defining your work products begets the next question. How will your team know if you're doing the right things to address your focal problem?

It may seem obvious that your project's work products will solve the core problem you have identified. After all, that is the rationale behind the entire project's existence. If your deliverables were guaranteed to address the situation at hand, your main challenge from now on would simply be execution—making sure your team delivers the specified output. Indeed, execution is a key challenge for projects. Poor task planning and weak management bring down their fair share of team efforts. Project management tools are designed to take on these very issues, which is why we recommend using every relevant tool at your disposal.

But surprisingly often, failures are not operational or managerial but broader in origin. Projects can underperform spectacularly when they are based on flawed hypotheses, off-the-mark thinking about the ideas and relationships that underpin the project's design and its reason for existence. Again and again, we see projects that fall short because their assumptions at launch turn out to be the wrong ones.

As a result, many a team has toiled away on projects that pass formal muster—that check all the boxes and generate the prespecified deliverables—but that in the end fall short of creating the anticipated change or improvement. A mismatch between the assumptions underlying the project's rationale and the realities of the organization or marketplace is often to blame.

Prepare for What You Don't Know

The truth is, you may not yet understand important aspects of how your project efforts will play out. In other words, if you're aiming to innovate in some way, you are likely to face *unknown unknowns*—complexities in the market, within your organization, or in the technical and material aspects of your planned activities that are invisible at this point but that could influence your results. These intervening forces could undermine or accentuate the effects of your efforts.

You cannot solve this problem today. No matter how smart you are, no amount of planning, thinking, discussion, and study can reduce all uncertainty, because the information is not yet available. Only when you take action on your project will some of that essential information be revealed. Other needed evidence will turn up by chance or as things evolve. At any rate, if your project aims to accomplish something novel, you are likely to learn more about the world as you go which could in turn prompt your team to revisit your thinking, then pivot in some way. Adjusting to surprises is a challenge for many teams, but we think you can do better than waiting for them to show up and their implications to sink in.

In this step of the launch process, we equip you to be ready to learn and respond as you go. The first requirement is to develop an awareness of the situation—and the wider system—against which to view your experiences. This baseline mapping of key relationships and assumptions will set the stage for you to make sense of interim findings and emerging insights to uncover new discoveries, rule out dead ends, and succeed sooner.

To crystallize your thinking, identify how you anticipate that your project's work products will address the need you defined. We recommend you take a first cut at laying out your logic now. You'll review and refine your thinking with team members at an early team meeting, then at several points during your project's action phase and again at its end.

Develop Your Project Impact Map

What we're calling the *project impact map* establishes the logic that connects your actions to the outcomes you desire. Your impact map may be most easily imagined as a diagram (Figure 4-3), as we'll soon see, but it could also take the form of an organized collection of notes or images, a set of linked lists, or even a step-by-step story about why the team is undertaking this effort. You may choose to put it into words if your team needs a narrative-style project charter.

Here's the focal question your map needs to address: *If your project does indeed work as planned and you generate the anticipated products, how exactly will your deliverables move the needle on the (real-world) problem or opportunity that spurred your team's project in the first place?*

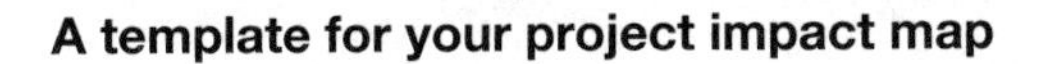

FIGURE 4-3

A template for your project impact map

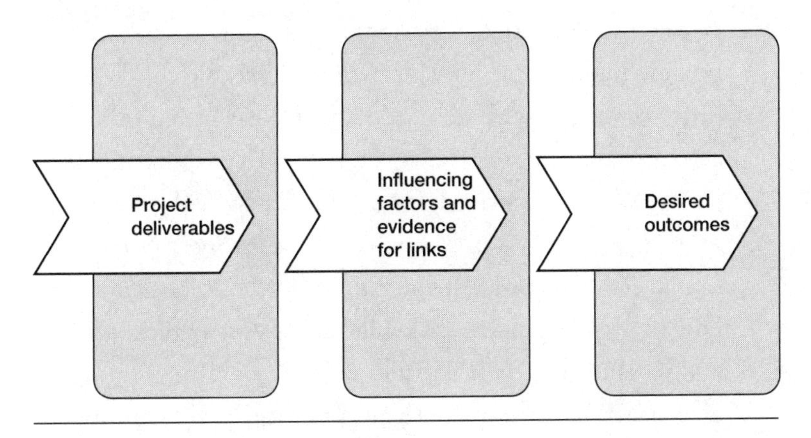

Now, let's look at how to map these ideas. To sketch out how you think the anticipated deliverables link to the problem statement, follow these steps to create a simple diagram using the template below. To do this:

1. Create your version of the template: divide a sheet of paper, whiteboard, or computer screen into three segments vertically.

2. On the right side, list the positive outcomes your problem statement seeks to enable; for instance, customers getting the information they need to select your company's product that best meets their requirements; patients getting critical services; or students who had previously been at risk of dropping out receiving diplomas instead.

3. On the left side, list your main deliverables. These may be a new brochure and other collateral materials, along with website blurbs and a set of internal messages and communications; a redesigned modular system of hospital beds and equipment; or an integrated set of

afterschool program offerings. This is what your project aims to produce.

4. In the middle section, describe your linking logic. You'll be showing how the left side is related to the right. What processes and inputs are needed for your team's products to actually generate the results you seek? To enable patients to get the care they need, for example, new equipment will need to be installed in hospitals, so it must meet purchasing managers' criteria. Hospital staff will need to be trained in how to use the equipment while supporting clinical care, and patients and their families will need to understand their options so they can make the most of the equipment's modularity. For the afterschool program to enable at-risk children to stay in school, it would need to address the reasons the students are dropping out; for instance, by strengthening skills, participation, or relationships that help them make the most of school opportunities.

In this part of the exercise, you may come up with many potential factors to consider. In the hospital equipment example, price, appeal, availability, and marketing could influence installation rates. Competitors could also affect adoption by offering rival products. Shifts in the health-care industry's payment structure as well as patient demographics are likely to influence how the new equipment will be used. If your team is responsible only for the product design, your project could not possibly take on all these factors! But it's likely that as you work on the design, you'll be learning about potential costs, materials, the marketplace, consumer attitudes, and other factors that could play a role in how effectively the new equipment helps hospital patients.

Your goal at this point is to identify *key* factors likely to intervene between project deliverables and your ultimate goal, keeping the list short by focusing on what you think is most important.

Place your top candidates for intervening elements in the middle of the page, drawing in arrows and steps to represent the routes by which the deliverables enable the results via the intervening factors you've identified.

How You Will Use Your Project Impact Map

Working on this map offers four benefits:

- First, it drives home why your work is important, a crucial requirement for motivation and focus. The act of linking actions to outcomes helps define meaning for the team by highlighting how your planned activities could address the problem.
- The exercise itself can help refine your thinking and focus, even at this early stage, by helping to prioritize the more influential attributes of your deliverables. Identifying the highest-leverage steps and activities in your plans will aid in your work planning.
- Refining your map of influential factors will be valuable when it comes to project handoff because it flags things you're learning that could be useful to others. For instance, if your design team will hand off plans to the manufacturing and marketing departments, imagine how useful it will be for your colleagues to get information about cost parameters, customer segments, competitors, or other relevant factors your team has discovered along the way, even if these things were not part of your formal deliverables.
- You will be uncovering new insights in the course of your work that could lead to shifts in your project, and the map will help you identify, locate, and analyze them.

The last point may spur some reflection right away. The million-dollar question to ask now: *Should we change our deliverables plan in any way to take these insights into account?* At this stage, a common insight is that you need to redefine your team's planned products. Some of the products you plan to create may not be needed; others may need to be changed or added. Take a hard look at your project plans, and make the changes needed to reach success sooner.

As you continue to explore linkages between deliverables and outcomes, your team can flag potential areas where, even if your team does all it is supposed to, other influences could undermine the effects of your efforts. Your map provides a method to explore and make sense of potential challenges to your project's intended impact. For example, you may come to realize your project is focused on the wrong thing, such as a factor whose influence is outweighed by other effects that lie outside your project scope. If you now suspect that your project is addressing relatively low-leverage determinants of the outcome you seek, you may need to redefine your work.

For instance, in the afterschool program example, if immediate economic pressures outweigh all factors in shaping kids' dropout decisions, then a program focused on exposing at-risk students to the arts may not be able to claim it is going to significantly reduce school dropouts. This is not to say that the program is not a good idea: exposure to the arts could build kids' motivation, inspire students to reach higher, uncover potentially marketable talents that in turn lead to more engagement in education, or in other ways help more students stay in school. Developing and revisiting the project map could help your team place the work in context, enabling you to marshal the most effective measures and evidence needed to permit the program to succeed. It could even help you think of new, creative approaches to the problem, like linking the arts program to a workplace jobs training program. And it can serve as a valuable tool for your team to manage its stakeholders' expectations.

To capture the insights from working with your impact map, flag ideas and considerations to keep an eye on, even if they cannot be settled right now. Key uncertainties regarding the results of project steps are good candidates for your issues list. Within your impact diagram, pinpoint specific means-ends linkages that are still up for question, along with any items beyond your scope that you agree are important to track.

You've now built the foundation for project launch by making explicit your hypotheses about the connections between the products you aim to create and the outcomes that matter—and you have an at-a-glance map that can be revisited and revised throughout the project.

Design Your Work Plan

You built your impact map with your project's deliverables as the starting point. But you have to create the deliverables themselves. A work plan shows the activities that your team plans to pursue, from launch to delivering your project's products.

Now is the time for you to refine work plans in keeping with the needs of your team and the dictates of your project, drawing on notes you made in earlier steps. Some teams develop detailed work plans, listing inputs, timing, interdependencies, and more; others treat priorities and activities in a more emergent way. A scrum software development team is a good example of the latter. A key tenet of scrum is to recognize that unpredicted challenges cannot be easily addressed in a traditional predictive manner, so scrum focuses instead on making the most of the team's ability to deliver quickly and respond to emerging requirements.

Now, do you have what you need to get the work done?

Marshal Your Resources

Our second set of launch activities establishes an inventory of your team's resources. To make the most of them, you'll also develop a sense of the boundaries within which your team must operate.

You'll use this information to identify where to shore up your team and gather needed resources to launch your project for maximum results.

Inventory Your Inputs and Constraints

First, make a quick list of the inputs your project will be able to draw on. Think creatively and broadly about all resources you may have access to: time, skills, physical space, money, relationships, partners, technology, personal capital, your team's reputation and goodwill, your organization's brand, team members' knowledge, your tools, and equipment. People and time are likely at the top of your list. We'll look at personnel shortly.

When it comes to time, know the official and unofficial aspects of your deadlines. When are you expected to deliver updates and products, and how negotiable or flexible are your milestones and deliverables handoff dates?

Know Your Sandbox

List constraints that could impinge on your team. These define the boundaries of your project activities and represent limitations on what you can do that come from your boss, your client, and your organization as a whole. To pinpoint them, ask: What can we *not* do? Is your ability to experiment bounded by something other than tangible resources? Some areas, issues, or stakeholders are sacrosanct. Are there any "no-fly zones"—domains that could impact your project that are simply not up for exploration?

Consider the social and political capital you can draw on and the organizational culture within which you operate. This accounting might include how people feel about risks, as well as the value placed on learning, reputation, and reflectiveness. If the organization values lessons learned, you may have more scope for experimentation than if the organization is risk-averse.

Find Problem Resonance within Your Organization

Pull up your problem statement, and consider the following question: *Does our project connect to themes and focus areas that are particularly meaningful in our organization?*

Identifying the potential for resonance will help you better understand how your project fits with organizational goals and needs. Consider how your project domain connects to trends and ideas that have meaning within the organization, including variations in this meaning for different parts of the organization. If you are successful in connecting your work to the bigger organizational picture, you have a strategic vantage point from which to view your actions and decisions.

Your project may address a domain that is near and dear to the organization—for instance, a historically important segment of the company's customers, the company's best-selling product, or an area of work that is tightly linked to the mission statement. These connections may benefit your project by raising its visibility and affording you priority in resources, but may also raise the stakes by making your project the object of increased scrutiny and high expectations.

Sometimes the connection is apparent: if your project seeks to develop a partnership model for your company's joint ventures in China and the CEO has just issued a major statement about the firm's ambitious goals for growth in China, it's likely your project will be seen as important. In other cases, the resonance between your project and the overall organization may be more difficult to assess. For example, what if your team is looking at one approach to online education, but a second team in the organization is investing in a different approach to the same thing? What might that mean for you? The answers may need to come later as you navigate the environment. So make a note of this issue and then come back to discuss it as you learn more. It's not always necessary for your project to be seen as important by everybody, but it's likely a bad thing if it's seen as important by nobody.

And to get to what's "important" requires some of the soft skills that are so essential for navigating organizational life. The formal mission and explicit organizational performance goals are one set of factors to consider as part of your project context: they provide an indication of what's officially important. But the trends, political shifts, and emerging power bases that shape the flow of resources and credit within organizations are important influences on projects, too. Don't panic if you have no idea of these yet: just note what you think today might be good to bear in mind and come back to this topic later.

Finding where your project resonates with the issues, opportunities, and needs that are important in your organization can help you align allies, uncover potential opportunities for sharing efforts and infrastructure, and build a broad audience for your project results. When you combine this activity with other Fail Better steps, you'll be better equipped to hold up under performance pressures because you have a structured process that can reveal potential failures (and successes) earlier in the work flow and help you to communicate them to others with the right framing.

Map Stakeholders and Shared Opportunities

List your project's stakeholders, making sure to include both allies and potential roadblocks. Consider people who hold informal power and outsiders along with higher-ups whose opinions and support explicitly matter. Identify the key stakeholders whose interests are most linked to your project, and, next to each name, note how that person could help (or harm) your project. You'll be factoring them into your key stakeholders.

As part of this inventory, also consider your potential to leverage the work others are already doing or committed to doing within the organization. Can you share any opportunities, scheduled events, or infrastructure to create efficiencies, build allies, or make your early work more effective? Some existing opportunities may not at first blush seem relevant to your effort, but they could offer a platform for connecting your work with others'. For example, if another team is already interviewing customers, can you add your questions to theirs? If there's a group responsible for newsletters, a speaker series, or other standing events, perhaps you can link your work to theirs by fitting one of your necessary project activities into their existing work responsibilities. Many teams fail to leverage these shared assets within organizations.

At this point review your notes to make sure you know how much you can spend overall. Tally financial and resource constraints and assets along with the social and political capital you can draw on, areas of resonance, and the organizational culture within which you operate.

Like the other documents you've been developing, your resource and constraints inventory will likely evolve as your project progresses. Use it to find feasible ways to refine plans as you go forward and take it into account when selecting your action steps, experiments, and tests.

Understanding available inputs, constraints, and resources could also be useful right away. You may uncover a constraint you realize must be addressed early on to ensure the success of the project, such as a needed stakeholder relationship that will require an investment of time to build.

Now, make sure to assess your deliverables list in light of this accounting.

Identify Your Unmet Needs and "Extra" Resources

Because you've been building your project map and work plan, you have a good sense of the products and events your team will create. You are now ready to review your list of deliverables and work plan activities with your resource inventory in mind to check if the team is equipped for success. List inputs required for project tasks and activities, noting how each resource supports your ultimate deliverables; identify which are essential and which are nice to have. Does it look like you will have access to what you most need to reach your goals?

You now need to figure out how to address any gaps you see. Knowing your sandbox and potential areas of resonance, you have a sense of how much scope you have to negotiate on project requirements. This is a good moment to advocate for what you need.

Approaching the fit between needs and resources from both sides can help you think about your options as creatively as possible. As you review the inputs you've been allocated or have access to, you may find a mismatch: for instance, you may have access to some resources that are not as critical as some essential ingredients that are missing. If simply asking for needed inputs won't work, a swap of sorts may be feasible. You may be able to barter your extra resources to get what you need from elsewhere in the organization.

If Your Team and Resources Are Already Set

What if your options are limited: the team is already selected, and the budget is already allocated, but you now realize you need more or different people for the project or to change inputs or scope in some way? Even if you face constraints with apparently little power to make early changes, you may have more influence than you think. Here are three options to consider:

- Set up an early discussion with your immediate clients about the project map, including the problem statement, deliverables, and project impact hypotheses. Ensure that key stakeholders—your client, your boss, others—are on the same page and refine plans if needed.

- Accept the current givens, but push now for an agreement that offers you scope to change things later. For instance, you could propose that if your project meets early milestones set by your boss or client, you would then get more freedom, resources, or client interaction for a later stage of the project.
- As your project proceeds, document exactly how your project is actively enabled or constrained by the givens that you have not been able to change, and use this to frame a dialogue with decision makers down the road, seeking more scope for you to shape project goals, expectations, and resources the next time around.

If you follow our advice for marshaling project resources, you'll be building an invaluable skill for many projects to come. And you now have a better understanding of the landscape in which your project will operate along with the resources you will be able to draw on to achieve your deliverables. You may have uncovered critical gaps as well as overlooked resources that could aid your project's success. You may even realize you are equipped to experiment more than you had originally imagined, setting the stage for more groundbreaking results.

The final part of your launch process is to build the team for success.

Build Your Team

So far, we've focused our project launch advice on activities you could do alone (but certainly need not do by yourself). Recall that we've insisted you treat your early work as provisional. Soon you will have your first chance to refine your ideas as you work with your team members to build a shared understanding of what your project will accomplish and how.

But before you get to this important discussion, you'll need to line up the right roster.

Assemble Your Roster

Who are your team members, and what do they bring to the project? Even if your team is already set, it's important to know its skills and capabilities at the outset. List everyone who will join the project in any capacity, and take the time to assess what each person brings to the table, including you. Include both strengths and weaknesses and go beyond résumé items to include personal capabilities, relationships and network membership, experience, and interests. As you gain more experience applying the Fail Better method, you'll improve your understanding of your own abilities and shortcomings and take steps to address them. And if you are in a position to influence the structure of your team, you'll be better equipped to select members who can balance out other team members' weaknesses. Equipped with knowledge of your team's capabilities, you'll be able to respond more wisely in the moment to new opportunities and challenges you encounter in the course of the project—you'll know if tasks that emerge along the way mesh with your team's abilities and interests, and you'll make smarter choices about whether to take them on.

It's tempting in the early stages of team formation to steer clear of difficult conversations. You'll need to plan and manage such conversations carefully, but they're worth having. To uncover potentially crucial gaps in team capabilities, can you encourage team members to identify their own strengths and weaknesses? Is it possible for you draw on other information within the organization to triangulate on your own assessments of the team's collective strengths and weaknesses? Gossip is not a good basis for this analysis, of course, but surprisingly often we find project leaders missing opportunities to learn from others about what their team members can contribute and where they will benefit from support and development.

The more you know, the better equipped you'll be to think creatively about how to leverage strengths while avoiding shying away from the weaknesses. One way to reframe your examination of weaknesses is to link it to each team member's professional development goals for the project. What does each team member want to gain from the project? What would others say is their biggest challenge in working on project teams? How would they like to address this challenge, in the context of the present project? Use their answers to ensure you are lining up the supports needed for your team to thrive.

Find Creative Ways to Shore Up the Team

Now that you know more about your team, you may need a strategy for addressing gaps that cannot be filled by the team itself as it stands.

You might return to the idea we've already mentioned—advocate and negotiate for what you most need. If a new team member is not feasible, it may still be possible to line up support from a technical team elsewhere in the organization, to get some funds for freelance help, or to acquire the time and budget allocation to enable a team member to get needed training on new software or project management techniques. And don't forget the creative routes: borrowing, bartering, or trading off an extra resource for something needed to fill a crucial gap.

If you succeed in getting extra personnel resources, don't overlook complementary inputs needed to make the most of them. For example, you may realize your team lacks data analysis capabilities essential to your project. You may make a formal request for consultation from a data analyst. Don't forget to also include what else is needed to make the most of such help: perhaps you need some new equipment or software to enable the data to be shared effectively. And if you are allocated expert consultation, it will also involve an investment of time on your part. Your work plan will also need to account for team members' activities related to managing your interactions with the expert.

Getting management time is an often-overlooked ingredient for project success. If you aim to help your organization to innovate, you may need to challenge established thinking. In our experiences, most bosses do not like surprises at the end of a project—even if your team thinks they are good surprises! Many teams underinvest in bringing along their key stakeholders. Now is the time to ask for regular interim meetings with the management team.

As you get to know the people on your team, consider other inputs that could help you to function better. It's surprising how much difference it can make for the team to have a dedicated project room where their ideas, artifacts, and inspirations can enable their work, as teams in creative, military, and manufacturing domains have already discovered.

Refine Your Project Map, Deliverables List, and Work Plan

However your team has formed, getting everyone on the same page is important early work. Engaging the team to refine your initial thinking and improve on it is critical to the success of the project.

Share your portfolio of working materials: the problem statement, deliverables list, open issues list, and work plan, along with what you have learned about organizational context—management goals, time frame, resources, and the boundaries of where you can experiment. Link these discussions to a careful exploration of the project impact mapping with all team members. Does it make sense? Do changes or updates now need to be made? With the full team engaged in examining the logic behind your project, everyone has a guiding project framework from which to make sense of his or her experiences and results.

Don't forget to discuss your expectations for how the team will use these working documents throughout the project, not just at launch. How will you make the entire package of materials meaningful to everyone? Reviewing the project impact map could provide an effective focal point for the team. Remind the team that it's all work in progress and that you will systematically revisit these materials to update them as you learn from your own experience.

Finally, this is an ideal time to explain that you plan to use the Fail Better approach for launching your project, iterating to build and refine, and embedding the learning. Make sure to discuss how the approach is shaping your project design and to make the case for why you think it's a good idea. Use your discussion of the initial materials to orient the team toward experimentation, data, acceptable risk, communication, and feedback.

Build Effective Team Habits and a Culture That Works

Whether by design or by chance, early meetings set the foundation for how your team works together. How will you your team create and support effective ground rules for collaboration? Crucial questions to address include: How will the team share data, run meetings, make decisions, and divide work? What are the key principles you all agree to maintain and defend throughout the project? Talking about how you aim to work together helps to build team-level norms and expectations. Early planning for teamwork allows norm violations to be called out later, allowing counterproductive habits that emerge to be addressed and effective new approaches to be preserved.

To round out our advice, we'll add one more idea to temper these early discussions about team process. It's one thing to discuss goals, work styles, and expectations in your early meetings, but the evidence shows that what you *say* does not matter as much as what actually *happens*. As teamwork expert Ed Schein reminds us, you can't simply mandate, or even collectively design, the enacted roles and relationships that play out in your team, no matter how well-intentioned the participants or how well-run the discussion.[1] Talk is important, but action matters more.

Individuals come into a project team wondering how they will act in the group, how much influence they'll have, whether their needs will be met within it, and what kinds of interpersonal relationships will develop within the team. Their questions are resolved only in situ—in the midst of team interactions. Is there a feeling of equity within the team, and has the group invested in building communication that serves its members? If not, members will not choose to contribute. If there's disparity in social status across the team, part of the work of the leader in the early stages is to create a special ethos within the team that sidesteps existing dysfunctional divisions or hierarchy within the organization in favor of more socially equal roles, at least within the context of the team itself.

How will you enable this feeling of equality within the team? Your actions could well speak louder than your words: bear this in mind when you run your first meetings. Design early interactions to enable team members to work through the questions identified above for themselves. In some situations, a light hand is far better than an overly explicit focus on process and norms. Choose the approach that works for you, your team, and your organization.

To Sum Up Our Launch Advice: Inspiration and Guidance

If you and your team work through the ideas we've described, you will have accomplished much by this point. Your team will have refined its understanding of why the project is important, specified what you aim to create, sketched out a work plan, and identified critical assumptions and open questions about how you will have impact. You also will have rounded up the right personnel and resources, developed a sense of what your team brings to the project, and know what may still be needed. Having scouted the landscape, you have discovered where you have leeway to experiment or change things and figured out the potential to connect with efforts already under way along with themes that are meaningful in the organization. You will have worked as a team to create the habits and approaches that will support a better project.

Our launch steps provide a foundation for your team's efforts throughout the process because they orient your team to what's most important for the entire journey. Establishing how your planned deliverables will help solve your client's problem sets the stage for your entire team to plan, take action, and learn from results while making progress.

Launching your team with the maximum capability for learning, discovering, and innovating could help avoid one of the most common—and wasteful—failure modes we've seen. Even the most diligent of teams that do everything they are supposed to, creating the specified products and events, staying within budget, and meeting milestones, can fail badly when, at the end of it all, their work fails to have any impact.

We want to help you to avoid building your project on faulty assumptions that never get challenged. *Don't let your team realize too late that you have worked hard to solve a problem that ultimately turns out to be the wrong problem.*

We also want to help you make the most of the team's discoveries about its own functioning as you work on your project. Setting off with a view of your strengths and weaknesses and a commitment to feedback and reflection can enable you to identify, in the moment, where the team needs to improve its capabilities in some way. The project could become a vehicle for professional development that is superbly aligned to the work at hand.

Investing in an effective launch will set the stage for your team to learn from experience and succeed sooner. The ideas we laid out are designed to equip you to lead your team to reach its potential for integrative, interactive, generative, and innovative collaboration. To help you do this, we've made our advice as practical as we can. Now, it's up to you to make each step your own. The guiding questions and action checklists that conclude this chapter provide a practical guide for every step of the way.

But first, let's look at a real-world story that could help inspire you to see how the ideas in practice enable a project to deliver breakthrough results. Our story highlights how an effective launch can guide iterative action at an iconic American company.

REAL-WORLD INSPIRATION

Herman Miller's Compass Project Invests in an Effective Launch

Furniture designer and manufacturer Herman Miller is admired for its innovation and value-driven philosophy. In 2008, a team from its Healthcare Division set out "to create a better patient experience" by redesigning the hospital patient room.[2] A charge that appeared straightforward at the outset quickly turned more complex as the team struggled to put their finger on the true problem to be solved. The more they learned about hospital rooms, the more evident it became that their initial ideas were off-base.

Redefining the Problem to Enable Lasting Impact

A breakthrough in the development of the Compass System, as the design came to be called, came only when members of the team realized that no matter how hard they tried, they could not design the ideal patient room. The problem, it turned out, was the ever-changing nature of health-care delivery. Adding to the challenge was the multiplicity of end-users. How could Herman Miller Healthcare embrace constant change in the requirements for patient rooms while meeting the needs of constituencies as diverse as patients, their families, nurses, doctors, and custodial staff? Lead researcher Doug Bazuin summed it up: "The perfect patient room today, if there even is one, will not be the perfect patient room of tomorrow."[3] This insight eventually led the team to focus on a design that could transform in response to emerging needs. Let's take a look at how their launch process enabled the team to make the most of their mistakes and succeed sooner. It started with the team.

Tapping Into the Power of the Organization and the Team

When Herman Miller Healthcare assembled the team that eventually designed Compass, its leaders were building on a successful model that had driven past projects like the design of the Aeron chair. Drawing on lessons they learned from their own experience, the company designed the team carefully, combining the knowledge and expertise of Herman Miller staff with external perspectives by partnering with outsiders. Lead designer Gianfranco Zaccai, then president and chief design officer of Continuum (a design consultancy that had produced innovations like the Swiffer mop and the Reebok Pump shoe) noted that team members also brought their personal experiences as patients and caregivers to the project.

Connecting to these experiences reinforced an aspect of the team's culture, an ethos that fostered a sense of empathy for everyone who would be affected by their product design. Shared values kept the human side of the equation visible and aligned the team's vision throughout the design process: "The collaboration was successful because all team members believe in great aesthetics, ergonomics, and in providing products that facilitate human interaction," explained Zaccai.[4]

Enabling Iteration with the Right Project Launch

The nascent team kicked off their effort by validating the need for the team's product, a requirement that called for evidence to demonstrate the rationale for the project. Such formal requirements may feel like a bureaucratic hurdle, but they can raise the visibility of new projects across the organization, helping open doors and secure resources, and can reinforce the commitment felt by team members and project sponsors.

At Herman Miller, once the need for it was established, Compass became a formal product development project. The team was equipped with resources, varied perspectives and skills, a well-defined goal, and a culture that embraced complexity, testing, and empathy.

Embracing Complexity to Find the Sweet Spot of Design

To tackle the complexity their early research revealed, the team switched to what they called a *systems-based approach*. It involved exploring how hospital dynamics, the health-care environment, and the unique actors within the system interfaced at the point of service delivery—where staff, equipment, materials, and other factors interacted directly with patient and family needs, ultimately shaping the patient experience.

To understand the larger context of hospitals and health-care delivery and to pinpoint the critical weaknesses in existing patient and exam rooms, the design team interviewed more than five hundred clinicians, hospital administrators, facility managers, designers, and architects. The team's engagement approach asked stakeholders to go beyond just listing their needs to prioritizing and explaining them. Four key issues came to the fore. Patient rooms needed to support changing technology, improve caregiver efficiency, improve the family experience, and be clinically appropriate (for example, prevent spread of infection).

A member of the design team noted that their systems perspective highlighted, rather than simplified, the complexity of the project's multiple interacting project requirements: "Hospitals employ many stakeholders, and the goals of these stakeholders on a moment-by-moment basis are not always aligned. This can create an unsettling environment for the patient and impede the patient's road to recovery."[5] To come up with designs that would help everyone achieve their shared goal—better patient care—the team built a nuanced understanding of the specific operational needs of each stakeholder in the hospital-care ecosystem. When their research illuminated potentially conflicting short-term needs, rather than splitting the difference or trading off attributes, the team dug deeper to understand the finer points of the apparent conflicts, then looked for solutions that could align key requirements to resolve the issue in novel ways.

When the project was complete, lead designer Gianfranco Zaccai reflected: "The opportunity for innovation was really finding the sweet spot of the areas of overlap between what's really important to the patient, what's really important to the caregiver, what's really important to the family members, [and] what's really important to the administrators."[6] Engaging deeply with stakeholders impacted by and contributing to the system allowed the Compass design team to pinpoint the things that were important to all. The final result was a system of modular components that could be reconstructed flexibly within a patient room to meet the demands of changing needs in health-care delivery and evolving technology.

How the Fail Better Approach Applies

Herman Miller's experience developing the Compass System demonstrates an organizational learning capacity that reflects core Fail Better principles. Learning from their early misstep, the project team tasked with developing the Compass System refined their problem statement to home in on a specific problem that accounted for the realities in the setting. By design, the team had the requisite skills and drew on varying perspectives, including outsiders to the firm. Team norms and processes were aligned with the needs of the project. And the team was well-equipped with appropriate tools and methods, including collaborative techniques and rapid prototyping. Testing was central to the team's approach, from early debates about the problem statement, careful observation of patients, hospital staff, and families, to validation tests of the prototype and final products developed by the team.

Let's look a little more closely at how the launch ideas we've been exploring play out in this story.

> **Linking actions to outcomes.** The team developed a problem statement—which they were not afraid to update, adding nuance as they learned more. The original goal was to perfect the design of hospital-room furniture and equipment. This goal shifted once the team realized that the changing nature of health-care delivery was not a separate marketing issue but a key design consideration from the start. In essence, they refined their project impact map in their early launch stages. The need for flexibility joined ergonomic requirements and other essential design criteria.
>
> In some respects, the team's deliverable was clearly specified from the outset: a design for furniture and equipment that would solve usability problems facing the different groups of people impacted by hospital rooms. But the eventual design concept—to make the furnishings modular—was not part of the original goal. The team was not afraid to change their plans once they learned about the need for flexibility. They also recognized that many actors were interfacing in patient rooms. Through systems-based research, the team identified pain points, focusing a large amount of their efforts on the specific areas in which

stakeholder needs conflicted, and did their best to ease those pain points with their design.

Marshaling resources. One critical resource the team used to great advantage were the many people who had a stake, in one way or another, in the attributes of the Compass design. Varied insights emerged from the five hundred stakeholders the team consulted, helping everyone on the team to understand the complex system in which the product would shape patient experience. Later on, when it came to testing the refined prototypes, supportive feedback from hundreds of potential users also helped move Compass ahead.

Building the team. Herman Miller Healthcare lined up a team that built on what the company learned from previous projects, combining an external design innovator to spur new thinking with internal members who understood the Herman Miller way. The team members brought relevant skill sets and connected through shared values, including an empathetic human-centric approach to the needs of patients and all those interfacing in patient rooms.

The Compass project example can take us further. It offers a preview of what's coming next: using iteration to create and polish the end product. The team employed rapid prototyping—designing inexpensive and quick mock-ups of the product to test for customer satisfaction—which proved to be central to the development of the end product. From small-scale modular components that could be configured in a miniature room to a full-scale foam mock-up that could be tested and used by a variety of stakeholders, Herman Miller Healthcare kept its failures small and inexpensive until the final system emerged. Only then did the Compass solution go into production. When it did, its innovations were much lauded.

At-a-Glance Guidance for Launching Your Project

We turn now to the practical, with a set of tools to aid your project launch. Guiding questions help you think through key issues that cut across domains. To help you manage things, we also provide a comprehensive list of the products you will create if you follow every launch step we've described. And a comprehensive trio of Fail Better checklists gathers the step-by-step details.

Guiding Thought Questions

This chapter focused on getting your project off on the right foot through problem definition, linking actions to outcomes, pulling together needed resources, and building the capabilities of the team. The following questions can help hone your Fail Better thinking to run your project in ways that sidestep common failure modes.

- ❑ **Getting the problem right**. What is the primary problem your project aims to address?
- ❑ **Planning for impact**. How can you link, through logic and evidence, the actions and outputs you will create to larger outcomes that your team aims to create?
- ❑ **Lining up what you need**. How do you fill resource gaps to set your project up for a better chance of success?
- ❑ **Supporting your team**. What skills, capabilities, processes, and culture will help your team tackle the work ahead?

Fail Better Process Products

Here is a list of Fail Better documents you may produce as you move through the steps. Not every team will create every document; in some cases, our advice may simply prompt a discussion or reflection. Choose the level of documentation that works for you.

- ❑ A crisp, vivid, end-user-focused statement of the real-world problem your project seeks to address
- ❑ An illustration of the problem situation that makes the problem tangible
- ❑ An ordered list of project deliverables
- ❑ A representation of anticipated end points that will motivate your team
- ❑ An open issues list to augment and examine as you go
- ❑ A draft work plan for completing deliverables
- ❑ A project impact map that connects your deliverables to the larger outcomes sought, indicating key intervening processes, factors, or interactions affecting these connections
- ❑ An inventory of project resources together with gaps in needed resources and an indication of potentially redundant resources
- ❑ A note listing constraints and no-fly zones for your team along with areas of resonance within your organization
- ❑ A stakeholder map and listing of potential shared opportunities within the organization
- ❑ A team roster that indicates unique skills and capabilities along with interests
- ❑ A listing of missing skill sets or capabilities and a plan for obtaining them
- ❑ Team ground rules and core practices

Implementation Checklists to Launch Your Project in Fail Better Mode

Use these checklists to guide launch activities, step-by-step.

Fail Better Checklist #1: Link Actions to Outcomes

This checklist will help you develop an understanding of what your project is trying to achieve and how the methods you will undertake and the deliverables you will produce lead to those achievements. Begin with the underlying problem your project is designed to solve.

1. Craft a crisp and vivid problem statement:

   - ❑ Define the core goal of your project—the specific outcome that would result if the focal problem were fixed or key opportunity were addressed.
   - ❑ Define who has the problem that is in need of a solution.
   - ❑ Identify the product, service, or other intervention that you think is needed.
   - ❑ Develop a one-sentence problem statement connecting these three elements, checking that it's meaningful to your core stakeholders. If you're stuck, try starting with this template: [*A particular focal group of people*] need [*product, service or other intervention*] to [*accomplish or attain some specific desirable outcome or state*].
   - ❑ Start your open issues list to track assumptions, excluded areas, impinging developments, and other things that lie outside this project team's boundaries of concern but that may affect your project or its impact.
   - ❑ Make the problem or opportunity vivid and memorable for your team. Consider drafting a user

case study, telling a story, or visually illustrating the critical situation.

2. Define your products and develop a deliverables list:

   - ❑ Develop a comprehensive list of everything your project will deliver to help solve the problem. Not all products of your work will be tangible, like a written report or new product. Consider a process implementation or one-off event. Note relevant quality expectations.

   - ❑ Start the work plan by listing corresponding activities, tasks, inputs, dependencies, and work efforts that will enable the project's work products to be developed.

   - ❑ Anticipate your deliverables by identifying what a successful output would look like or depicting the handoff moment. What will you have accomplished?

3. Map your project's impact:

   - ❑ Use the project impact map template. On the right, list the positive outcome your problem statement seeks to enable. On the left, list your planned deliverables. To connect the two, sketch out key factors and conditions likely to link project deliverables and your ultimate goal.

   - ❑ As you explore these in causal linkages, capture new insights and update your work plan accordingly.

Fail Better Checklist #2: Marshal Your Resources

Knowing what resources are needed and what is available to carry out your project is critical to success. Here are checklist items to help you identify your constraints, inventory your inputs, and address gaps.

1. Inventory your inputs and constraints:

   - ❑ List the person-hours, skills, capabilities, and other personnel-related assets available to your project. List other relevant inputs: budget, time, equipment, space, materials, stakeholder and team relationships, reputation, etc.

   - ❑ Identify areas of your project you have license to shape and influence, and what areas are not up for discussion or change. These define the boundaries of your project scope and activities.

   - ❑ Pinpoint how your project resonates within your organization: How do project efforts and goals connect to themes and trends that are meaningful to others?

   - ❑ List key stakeholders and their project-related interests. Include potential allies who could support your work and those more likely to be roadblocks. To find interests, consider how project activities and outcomes overlap line up with others' interests; in short, answer the question of what's in it for them?

2. Identify your unmet needs and extra resources:

   - ❑ Assess your work plan, deliverables list, and inventory of resources. Identify whether you have everything you need to complete your project. If not, pinpoint the gaps.

   - ❑ Consider whether you will be able to obtain more resources or personnel. If your givens are already set, devise a strategy for addressing unmet needs.

Fail Better Checklist #3: Build Your Team

Your project team needs to begin with a shared vision, clearly delineated processes, and the right skills to reach your project's goals. Use our checklist to work through team start-up activities.

1. Assemble your roster:
   - ❑ Identify who is on the team and what they bring to the project.
   - ❑ Engage team members in identifying their own strengths and weaknesses, including skills, capabilities, experience, contacts, relationships, and interests.
   - ❑ Help team members link their identified weaknesses to their goals for professional development. Find ways they can work on these goals as part of their project role and work.
2. Find creative ways to shore up the team:
   - ❑ You already identified gaps in resources. Now that you know more about your team, advocate for what you need. If you need to get creative, consider sharing a needed expert between two project teams or trading one resource for another. Check if your team would benefit from other inputs: training, software or equipment, a team room, or even management time. Begin implementing your gap strategy early on in the project process, so you're not stymied later in the project.
3. Refine your project map, deliverables list, and work plan as a team.
   - ❑ Review the problem statement, deliverables list, open issues list, work plan notes, project impact diagram,

resource inventory, and stakeholder map, updating to reflect new insights and information provided by the team.

- ❑ Set expectations about and jointly develop a process for how the above items will be made useful throughout the project, not just at launch.

4. Build effective team habits and culture.

- ❑ Design early interactions to enable team members to develop a functional level of equity, participation, and communication.
- ❑ Establish ground rules, team values, and team habits that all members support. Discussion is one way to do this. Bear in mind that it may be better to support the emergence of effective processes within the team by supporting interactions and modeling, or even giving team members space to navigate their relationships and roles.
- ❑ Orient the team toward the Fail Better project approach. Also preview what you will embark on in the next phase, including a commitment to experimentation, collecting and using data, taking acceptable risks, linking work streams, and gathering and using feedback on various aspects of the project.

CHAPTER PREVIEW

STEPS FOR MAKING THE MOST OF ITERATION

You've laid the groundwork for your project. Now it's time to get things done—in a way that enables you to test your ideas and iterate quickly for better results and smaller, more informative failures. In this chapter, we'll show you how.

- Plan your action:
  - Prioritize information-rich, critical-path activities that offer room to experiment.
  - Design some of these activities as tests.
  - Predict what you think will happen.
- Take action:
  - Put data collection systems in place.
  - Get out there and make it happen, documenting findings as you go.
- Make a decision:
  - Build a team habit of disciplined decision-making.
  - Check in on recent results, using all the data you can.
  - Decide what to do next.

The bulk of your project action and deliverables emerge here. Get to success sooner by making your work smarter. Track every surprise you encounter and proactively test your assumptions by designing experiments into your work, then use the information you collect to make better decisions.

CHAPTER 5

Iterate to Build and Refine

Join us for a moment to eavesdrop on the Firmwide Committee for the Future. Commissioned amid official fanfare, the committee is now meeting for the sixth time. But you soon realize it could easily be its first—or seventeenth!—session, because the conversation is indistinguishable from other discussions. Three of the eleven attendees have been analyzing a specific issue in detail. Then, with ten minutes to go, a previously silent participant interrupts: "Why are we talking about this? What is the goal of our committee anyway? Do we even have a problem with the future of the firm?" The meeting erupts. Each member has a different view; each advances a different set of ideas. The discussion feels like it's already been played through—though evidently, to no one's satisfaction. Watching the group, you realize this rehashed debate is undermining the raison d'être of the committee and casting potentially fatal doubts on its work plan.

Note that the interruption takes the form of what appear to be sensible questions. Yet when they are raised in this way, they are not productive. The session ends with no next steps defined—save, of course, the announcement of the next meeting—along with palpably deflated spirits and flagging motivation.

If you've been caught in similarly paralyzing debates or in their opposite—a headlong rush to deliverables—you've experienced firsthand a challenge facing every project: balancing analysis and action. This observation leads us to underscore the advice we've offered for launching your project. Invest in building an effective foundation, and early efforts will set up your team for constructive meetings. Laying out and agreeing on the initial rationale behind your efforts can prevent counterproductive, time-wasting debates, while at the same time enabling discussions to be fruitful when appropriate questions do arise. And developing ground rules for meetings will make your interactions more effective.

Yet by itself our launch advice will only take you so far. Not all problems can be prevented by wise preparation. Many of your best discoveries emerge only in the course of action.

What could have helped our committee avoid its paralysis? Had you asked its members at the outset about their tendencies to over- or underanalyze, most would probably claim to strike a happy medium. But as your team gets going, individual and collective behaviors will become more evident.

To avoid getting trapped by either extreme, be on the lookout for signs of either failure mode and address the issues as they arise. If you find your colleagues are prone to endless discussion, reinforce an orientation toward action. If you discover your team tends to avoid planning, reflection, and analysis, build effective shared practices to precede and follow each action step.

You'll be fine-tuning the balance of action and planning over the course of your project. The Fail Better approach is designed to help you do that. But it's also designed to help you uncover and make the most of new insights. In the course of your project, your team will intentionally or by happenstance unearth new information about itself, your customers, the market, your products, other parts of the organization, funders, and more. The Fail Better solution is to capitalize on these new realizations by interweaving action with thought as you go.

How you define and frame your activities is important. To scope team activities to maximize your learning, harness the power of iteration. Start by identifying the chunks of work your team can go through, not just once, but several times. Not only do you need to be able to test ideas early and then to try them again, but you also need to bracket each test with planning and reflection. Framing your activities this way sets the stage for the team to learn from each journey around the action loop. The right forethought in planning your actions can enable you to collect useful data as you go and to make sense of what you see. And because new discoveries often result from unexpected sources, an effective post-action process will help identify new learning from surprises as well.

In return, at every stage of your project, your team's actions do double duty: not only does every step enable progress toward deliverables, but it can also shed light on a key uncertainty, reveal or rule out important possibilities, or shore up essential knowledge and skills. Organizations and teams that experiment effectively are more innovative, productive, and successful than those that don't take such risks.

But simply knowing you *should* iterate through experimentation doesn't tell you *how* exactly to do it. For that, you need practical advice. In this chapter we'll show you how to use what you learn as you go to improve what you do next and ultimately, to deliver better results.

The payoff is exciting. When you make the most of the action phase, you free yourself from unrealistic expectations of perfect foresight. You don't have to hone every plan, consider every possible scenario or option, or calculate every detail in advance. Instead, if you're savvy and your work allows it, you can iterate by making repeated trips around the action loop. Rather than building your project around a one-shot effort, you can guide your team to an agile, responsive method of learning by doing. It all hinges on *iteration*—in which repetition of a series of activities or steps yields results successively closer to a desired outcome.

The Power of Iteration

Learning by doing involves extracting new insights, updating plans, and building skills from repeated actions. The idea that you should learn something useful from your work is deceptively simple. On the one hand, it seems self-evident that every activity should add something and lead to new knowledge or capability. On the other hand, without the right systems in place, even the most diligent team misses opportunities to mine useful guidance and learning from its work.

Luckily, there are appropriate methods that address this gap. Practitioners in a variety of fields have developed procedures that tap into the potential of action loops. Iteration underlies now-widespread process improvement techniques that have made industry more efficient than ever before. It is central to rapid prototyping, agile development, scrum, lean approaches, and other field-tested methods that enable new products to get to customers more rapidly than ever—and to meet customer needs in innovative ways.

Software, manufacturing, and product design teams draw on action loops to respond to problems, tackle critical challenges, and even to make ongoing improvement part of the regular work process. Let's look at one organization that has embedded continual testing into its everyday operations.

REAL-WORLD TESTING

Kayak Harnesses A/B Testing to Iterate

Paul English, cofounder and former chief technical officer of Kayak .com, credits iterative action for his web-based travel site's growth and evolution: "Demonstrate something small that people love . . . and then get more confidence . . . and scale up. I go against big grand plans. The original grand plans are usually wrong. Instead, I try to test ideas every day . . . and I remain open to variations of ideas every day."[1] Kayak has made this approach—what software companies call *A/B testing* or *split testing*—a way of life. Continual testing to compare options serves as the firm's engine for iteration. Here's how it works. Every week, two fully operational versions of the Kayak .com site, dubbed A and B, go live. Customers are randomly assigned to each, and by the end of the week, the company can analyze its data to figure out which performed better for users. The winner is then pitted against a new version the following week.

Like other innovators in software development, Kayak.com has made iteration part of the firm's culture and infused it into an integrated set of ongoing practices. In other domains, iterative action is enabled by the nature of the work itself. When the work at hand is inherently episodic, it offers natural opportunities to plan for and reflect on each round of effort. Because salient risks and rewards also tend to favor iteration, methods for harnessing action loops have emerged in organizations that face high costs of failure and have many opportunities to learn quickly what worked and what didn't.

After Action Reviews Systemize Learning

Opportunities to learn arise naturally in the course of ongoing execution in high-stakes environments where feedback is clear, outcomes are visible, and the benefits of reducing missteps are evident. Teams on the front lines of military battles, firefighting, and complex surgical procedures routinely use action loops to improve their performance and tap into new learning, and many have embedded end-of-shift and end-of-engagement habits for tapping into lessons learned and planning for the next day's work.

The US military offers an instructive example. In many of its branches, After Action Reviews (AAR) are used to systematize organizational learning. It may come as a surprise to learn that the value of an AAR arises not only in after-the-fact assessment but also *before* and *during* action. According to Harvard Business School professor David Garvin, AARs sprang up naturally in the field during the first Gulf War. Small groups of soldiers "gathered together, in foxholes or around vehicles in the middle of the desert, to review their most recent missions and identify possible improvements."[2] Such in-the-flow sessions of review and planning, Garvin argued, are also used by effective sports teams. Picture a quick informal postgame discussion with coaches and players analyzing what went right, what went wrong, and what the team should try next time. As one commander cited by Garvin explained, the approach creates "a state of mind where everybody is continuously assessing themselves, their units, and their organizations, and asking how they can improve."[3]

In the past decade, AARs have been used by teams in fire management and a variety of corporate settings.[4] Extensive military experience reveals that when they focus on the team's own use and value, when all participants are fully accountable, and when the process is built into a project from the very start, AARs enable organizational learning and success by creating "tight feedback circles between thinking and action."[5]

The military trains its members in the use of AARs and embeds its practices into standard procedures.[6] But for most of us, tapping into the power of action loops requires some new thinking, practices, and tools. The first step is to plan your action.

Plan the Action

Let's start with two important pieces of guidance. First, there's incredible power in designing your activities for iteration, yet we want to be clear that not every element of your project needs to be tested iteratively and reworked. Planning for iteration requires extra work, and only some activities warrant it. You'll be targeting just *a few* activities for the action loop, looking for steps that meet the criteria laid out below.

Second, not all discoveries are the result of planned tests. Some of your most valuable findings will emerge by chance. To extract these unplanned lessons, you'll draw on the later parts of the iteration loop, using the same process for debriefing and concluding from your experience. Missteps, lucky finds, and other happenstance events that arise in the course of your project could be grist for the after-action learning mill along with the deliberate actions profiled here, as we'll see later. At this point, we suggest you start by reviewing your work plan to identify your targets for iteration.

Identify Activities to Target for Iteration

To pinpoint the activities to prioritize for iteration via the action loop, begin with the list of your project's planned activities specified in your work plan. If you didn't do this at the end of your launch process, now might be a good time to further develop and refine the work plan. You need to do this anyway to carry out the work of your project. Typically, at this point, teams enumerate key tasks, responsibilities, lead times, input requirements, interdependencies, resource utilization, and other considerations to plan and manage their project work. Use the project management methods that work for your team, tasks, and organization to map out the steps in the detail you need.

But typical project planning, important though it is, is not our concern here. Alongside the work design, we are suggesting you add a *new* element. Working with your team, identify from this list a few target activities that you agree are critical for the following reasons.

The Proposed Actions Are the Most Informative–or Potentially Informative

Strangely enough, teams often fail to identify their most critical actions, only to discover that a crucial vulnerability (or opportunity) has been uncovered too late. Instead of prioritizing steps that seem convenient or low-risk, ask yourself: *What has the most riding on it, in terms of implications for our end results?* This helps ensure that you will learn something from it.

And how do you figure out what's most informative? Look for the following.

Priority in Activity Sequence. One indication of what's critical comes from path analysis and other sequencing methods that help determine the best sequence of steps for your project. Activities whose results determine subsequent steps, shape project direction, and influence final deliverables are natural candidates for prioritizing. Look for what you've already decided needs to happen early because it has the most riding on it.

You may need to reexamine your work plan sequence to check that you've slated the right activities early enough. It's a natural tendency to favor doing things that make you feel good—such as a relatively low-risk activity—and to put off difficult or riskier actions. And there could be logical reasons to do the easier things first: team members could advocate for early wins, momentum building, or learning more first. Such approaches may be warranted, but not if they come at the cost of avoiding more critical steps.

Disconfirmation Value. Another way to find what's most critical is to look for what could help disconfirm your ideas. Seeking disconfirmation doesn't always come easily, as we know from psychological and behavioral research. We humans are hardwired to favor evidence that confirms our existing ways of thinking. Your action loop may show that you—and possibly your boss, your client, and others—are wrong. But if scientists can learn how to test their thinking and seek disconfirmation, you can do so too. Finding out that something doesn't work, and finding that out *early*, is usually far more valuable than uncovering evidence in favor of your hunches and plans.

To assess where disconfirmation comes in, explore the underlying rationale for your project. If your plans rest on one or two critical assumptions that undergird the entire project, what activities would be most helpful in revealing early rather than late if you've made a mistaken assumption or left something out?

Your assumptions are indicated on your project impact map. How confident is your team about the logic that connects your tasks, planned deliverables, and eventual impact? Guide your selection of the most critical assumptions or arguments that your work rests on by asking: *How would we quickly and effectively show this is wrong?* In the Herman Miller example in chapter 4, the team built small-scale models of the modular furniture pieces, then tested their appeal by having different stakeholders use them to configure patient rooms to their liking. This method allowed the team to test their assumptions about how the room should be designed.

Consulting teams sometimes create a "dummy deck" early in the project. This is a draft representation of the team's best guess of the final day's report, with a placeholder for each element in the presentation deck laid out in a logical order. The team then gathers the information to complete each slide. If the team turns to blind execution in doing so, such a technique comes with a high price. There's little room for true surprises if every subsequent step involves simply filling in the blanks in a script that's already been written. Used this way, the dummy deck method represents the opposite of the scientific approach: instead of testing ideas by seeking disconfirmation, the team is seeking only confirmation—evidence that backs up and fleshes out their initial ideas. It's a dangerous approach to getting things done because the resulting document appears to be grounded in data and evidence, when in reality it's the team's assumptions that drive the data presentation. A shift in approach can make all the difference. Treating the dummy deck as a set of hypotheses to pressure-test rather than as blanks to be filled in enables the team to probe its own thinking.

If disconfirming something isn't quite the right way to think about it, you may choose instead to focus on the biggest area of uncertainty that your impact mapping highlighted. What are the most important open questions?

Actions that inform are natural targets for iteration, but there are some other considerations to take into account in prioritizing your action loops.

The Proposed Actions Offer Potential for Effective Feedback

Which steps offer you an opportunity to get data, information, or feedback? Push your team to think: Where do you have scope to develop something rough and ready that you can then use to elicit responses, collect use data, or gather information about performance or appeal? It's important to check that you will be able to get good enough feedback on which to act and to ask if what you learn will be sufficiently representative to inform your team's next steps, including potential shifts in project plans.

Consider the potential volume and quality of feedback as well as the domain it will address. What do you anticipate you will learn from the action? How good will the data be? What form will it take, and will that be relevant for your particular project?

The Proposed Actions Offer Leeway for Change

In considering potential activities, you'll exclude some simply because they offer insufficient scope for you to shape or change. Rule out the truly routine along with those repeated activities you have honed in past projects or that have already been optimized by your organization or profession. A good example of the former is a standard status update format you have developed by trial and error in your past projects. Firm policies may dictate some aspects of how you present your final report, collaborate with vendors, or interact with customers and give you little leeway for improvising new approaches.

The "no-fly" zones you identified at launch could rule out experimentation in areas that your organization considers sacrosanct. And you will need to exclude activities that are required to follow specific formats or procedures because of legal, contractual, or other requirements. A shop-floor team may be required to follow certain safety protocols whenever in the vicinity of active machinery, for example.

The Proposed Actions Are Drawn from a Wide Range of Options

Remember that actions take many different forms. The research, studies, interviews, discussions, and analyses needed to solve a problem, generate alternatives, or evaluate options are all actions. So are production activities like crafting needed text, writing and compiling required software code, building the physical prototypes, purchasing, and negotiating arrangements. Could any of these activities benefit from applying an action loop to their planning, execution, and examination?

Include less glamorous enabling activities in your consideration. For instance, your team likely holds meetings. If you decide it's important to you, can you and your colleagues use the iterative action loop to refine how you design and run your meetings? Is the team excited by the prospect of coming up with ways to make meetings more efficient, more fun, or more substantive, allowing your work to be more effective? Do you want to experiment with meeting design as you conduct this project?

By the end of this process, you should have a short list of varied activities from your work plan that your team thinks offer good potential for informativeness, feedback scope, and leeway for change.

Before moving on, allow us to take a quick detour to share a word of advice for handling the flip side of your investment in targeting. Let's examine the apparently noncritical activities that fall to the bottom of your list because they seem to offer little scope for change, feedback, or critical information. This offers us an opportunity to reconsider, not for inclusion in your action loop but for exclusion—or repurposing—in your work plan.

Assess Routine Activities to Eliminate or Repurpose What's Noncritical

What about all the *non*critical actions you are about to undertake? Teams tend not to put them in work plans, but consider all the things that fill your workday: the little things, the formal events, and all the routine activities you carry out. As you look at these tasks along with all the others in your plan, you may realize your team is about to spend much effort on activities that are not critical but that are on your daily schedules regardless.

If the activity doesn't offer an opportunity to learn or get feedback, why are you doing it? Consider eliminating it if it's not important. But you may not be able to eliminate everything you'd like to cut, and in fact there's often value in a more creative approach to these apparently noncritical activities. Any may offer valuable opportunities to advance your knowledge, understanding, and skills. Can you shift your mind-set by embracing the tenets of Fail Better and exploit, for the good of your project, the things you need to do anyway?

Examining your routine work in light of our ideas may push you to make small changes. If the activity doesn't offer an opportunity to learn or get feedback yet you cannot eliminate it, can you *change* it to serve your purposes? Asking yourself this question can help shift your thinking as you prepare for, say, a presentation of interim results. Your tendency might have been to consider such an event to be purely formal and symbolic, a useless but necessary evil. Don't let that assumption stand in the way of thinking creatively about how to repurpose the event to generate insight and knowledge.

The shift need not be dramatic. It may be as simple as editing your materials to highlight the open questions and elicit structured feedback from meeting participants, or ending the update segment of a conference call early enough to seek systematic input on a critical issue instead of a banal request for any questions or feedback.

Consider whether even the most mundane routine task could provide a ready-made test bed for quick experiments. A check-in phone call, a formal presentation, your organization's town hall discussion, the call for a newsletter article—such quotidian activities may not seem like the domain for substantive work, but if used shrewdly, they could turn into opportunities for you to inject a quick test of your hypotheses or to explore uncertainties and interdependencies.

Now that you have selected priorities for iteration, you are equipped to design your target activities.

Design the Right Tests

Design each of your selected target activities around the specific tests you anticipate will be most valuable. Begin asking your team: *What test can be worked into this activity that would provide useful information that could shape subsequent work?*

Consider a plan for combining different tests. A series of explorations may fit together—for example, by ruling out options or refocusing the plans, an early test can increase the value of more specific, complex, or expensive ones planned for later.

Encourage your team to think of tests that are quick enough to be repeated. Perhaps the most overlooked advice when it comes to testing is that quick-and-dirty trumps late-and-expensive more often than you realize. There's no reason not to do both! Start with the simplest options that are appropriate.

REAL-WORLD INSPIRATION

IDEO Bodystorms a Critical Insight in Under a Minute

Even the easiest of tests can prove informative. Tasked with designing interior configurations for a commercial airplane, a team in the European office of the design firm IDEO tested ideas with an approach they called "bodystorming"—a form of physically situated brainstorming. Before drafting complex designs, building scale mock-ups, conducting time-consuming ethnographies, and running expensive consumer interactions, the team tried out early ideas in their office. Team members simply grabbed conference room chairs to explore the physical and social experience of potential airplane seat configurations for a double-decker airplane bed. One person lay under the row of three chairs, the other on their seats. The team discovered it would not work: it was inescapably claustrophobic! A test that took just a minute to carry out helped the team rule out an idea on which they might otherwise have wasted much effort.[7]

Experience prototyping remains a key tool for IDEO, and the story of the chairs has entered its corporate lore as a reminder to teams to embrace rapid tests whenever possible. The company's designers advocate for creativity in the workplace to enable rapid exploration of ideas and experiences. Too often, they tell us, project teams sit in rooms, discuss things, and design surveys instead of interacting with the physical and social worlds directly to explore ideas generatively early on.

In this case, the approach worked because the IDEO team members were sufficiently representative of the airline passengers whose experience their test simulated, and the physical fidelity of the chairs to airline seats was good enough for the early exploration. Subsequent design decisions involved more faithful representations of airplane cabin arrangements and more carefully selected representative passengers.

We can't tell you if bodystorming will apply to your project. You'll need to figure out what works for you based on the time, money, personnel, leeway, and lead time you have. As you look at these potential costs, you'll also be weighing the information a test is likely to generate. How much data will the experiment yield, how relevant will it be, how specific, and how credible? Will it hold water with your key stakeholders?

And most importantly, will you be able to actually use test results to *change* the direction of your project? Will it allow you to choose between alternatives? A highly visible, time-consuming, and resource-intensive test can create its own unintended influence. If you invest in an expensive pilot program, for instance, unless you have appropriately set expectations for the team and its stakeholders, it may subsequently prove difficult to completely revamp the design and plan it is built on—even if results are not up to par. The test itself can create commitment to the course of action it is supposed to assess. This is why some proponents of rapid prototyping intentionally degrade the quality of the prototype to convey a work-in-progress feel that invites more critical feedback.

Options for Testing Ideas

There are more options than ever for testing your ideas as you go. Some are formal; others are downright fun. We'll mention a few alternatives and highlight some of the costs and benefits they entail.

We've mentioned product mock-ups as a way to look at basic physical or design feasibility. Teams tend to overlook the potential value of prototypes as tools for team members and project stakeholders to interact with. Seeing a mock-up of the final product can get people thinking and talking in far more ways than even the most detailed specifications document can. Prototypes also enable a very basic but critical test by making sure expectations for deliverables are aligned. You can use the prototype to check that everyone has the same general idea. In 2013, an MIT team exploring how mobile phones could be used to encourage health-seeking behavior change in the townships of South Africa had just a few hours to spend with a group of schoolchildren their product would serve. They turned a willing volunteer into a human prototype of the phone using sticky notes that indicated its keys, then had everyone in the room try out different scenarios by interacting with her. It was fun, and it also generated creativity that a more formal design specification exercise could never have allowed.

And of course, prototypes are invaluable for eliciting responses from representative customers, users, or beneficiaries. They provide the basis for all kinds of market research.

Prototyping options are many. For example, a team building new web software may start with a low-tech paper prototype, eventually moving to fully functional beta releases. An on-stage play starts with readings and then iterates through part and full rehearsals, the dress rehearsal, previews, and finally opening night—all are prototypes of the performance. A new product development team at a restaurant chain may try out recipes and menu concepts in its test kitchens to examine technical aspects of the new proposals and then bring in customers to try the new items. A teaching team developing a new curriculum may create a mock-up of a planned module to show to colleagues and administrators early on.

Virtual prototypes and computer simulations of new products are mainstays when physical prototypes are expensive to build. New car models are now tested in many different ways—from the most technical aspects of engineering systems to the subjective aspects of consumer appeal—via simulation. Stakeholders and potential customers interact with the virtual prototypes to provide the design team with vast amounts of feedback. Insurance and finance companies and governmental organizations test new plans and policies via computer simulation. It's often the only way to systematically explore the dynamics and ripple effects of proposed changes in policies, financial products, or service offerings.

Let's also include tests that play out in the world of ideas. Focus group discussions and stakeholder dialogues provide two common methods for getting feedback on plans, ideas, and designs. Computerized tools are used to elicit feedback from the crowd or from a targeted set of experts. In this case, the computers are not used to simulate the market or product but as ways of gathering and synthesizing customer or expert responses to the team's proposals.

There's also scope for testing your thinking within the team: consider thought experiments and scenario-based discussions that serve as what-if investigations to test the implications of potential decisions. Other structured approaches that shed light on and explore the implications of emerging project ideas include the systematic exploration of historical analogies and matched case study comparisons. Such methods can highlight issues with your planned deliverables that may otherwise escape attention. They enable a form of cognitive testing of ideas.

Field tests offer a further option. Consider pilot tests, proof-of-concept tests, and experimental tests that involve real people interacting with the product or service your team is developing.

One final consideration: many possible tests will explore some aspects of your ideas but not others. Along with tests of specific elements, make sure to include tests that are integrative. If all your tests involve decomposing the final deliverable in some way, you are missing opportunities to test an end-to-end integration of the final product. Can you design an early version of your entire product that incorporates all its proposed elements so you can explore its function or appeal? For instance, if you are writing a book, make sure to factor in an early integration of the entire draft as you seek feedback and otherwise test your content. Otherwise, you run the risk of polishing each chapter but failing to deliver a book that coheres. If you are building a complex computer model or software product, make sure to test how the parts work together well before the work is due.

Predict

Planning your activities is important, but in order to generate useful epiphanies, you need to also incorporate a basic discipline that involves thinking ahead. Learning—and insight—are favored by forethought. When people form expectations or predictions, even if they are not couched as formal hypotheses, they then have a basis against which to judge what does happen.

Without this form of thinking, even if things don't turn out as expected, it's easy to gloss over inconsistencies, unexpected results, or inklings that there are other factors or issues at work. Potentially instructive surprises are all too often explained away with vague justifications. In other cases, the *hindsight bias*—a type of after-the-fact sensemaking—comes into play, making people feel as if they sort of knew it all along. As a result, you may fail to identify and think carefully about the little surprises you discover.

The best antidote we know to this problem is: before you undertake the test, discuss and document what you are expecting to happen, then juxtapose what does happen against these expectations. This forethought need not be formal or extensive, but it does need to be explicit. In some teams, every task in the work plan is accompanied by a description of what the result will entail so that when the task is completed, the outcomes can be contrasted with the original description. This forces you to recognize that your team's expected outcomes did not align with actual results and triggers a more careful analysis of why.

Putting predictions into writing can enable review and learning. We studied an internet company that built a discipline around its key decisions. Coming into an investment or strategic choice, separate teams created presentations for and against the decision. The management team discussed both pros and cons in wrestling out its choice. Each set of arguments contained predictions about what would happen in the firm and the market. The learning was driven home by what happened next. Once the decision was made, both presentations were saved, and the entire management team returned to both decks after the results came in to discuss what they learned.

Adopt a form of this approach for every major decision your team makes, including action-loop tests that you plan where you are actively experimenting and any project activities that involve significant uncertainty, as deviations from expected results can be quickly revealed and discussed. A simple team habit of jotting down predictions before embarking on action and then reviewing them after action keeps this habit of mind alive.

Take Action

You've built your candidate list of action steps to mine for data, insights, and feedback. You've crossed off all the actions that would *not* help advance your project goals in any way. You've designed your tests and defined a method for making predictions about key activities. Now that you have identified what critical action to do next, your team needs to do it.

There is one important idea to bear in mind as you embark on every action step if you want to identify how predictions deviate from results, and it's a surprisingly subtle one. It's about gathering data as you go.

Plan for Data

Could catastrophic failures be avoided more often if smaller failures were better flagged as worthy of further examination? Our experience reveals that small failures can serve as warning signs and help avert poor outcomes further down the road. Yet they go unacknowledged for many reasons, social factors and organizational systems among them. But the critical barrier to identifying failure (or the potential for success) early is the unavailability of data that could trigger a different course of action.

Gathering useful data is as much about the discipline to collect and use that data as it is about the specific systems that enable its collection. Once you design an action step and predict a result, what will you be able to review *after* this action step that could tell you what works well and what doesn't? For some activities, a quick debrief discussion will suffice. But for others, the data may be dispersed and diverse. You'll need a plan.

In figuring out what data to collect, cast a wide net to make sure your team considers all forms of data at its disposal. If your team is exploring whether your users prefer one option over others, it goes without saying that your work plan would involve gathering relevant information from users' interactions. For instance, if you were conducting split testing for two website designs, your data plan might include agreeing with your team in advance what measures would indicate user preference: how long users stay on the site, how many links they click through, whether they make a purchase or enter a comment or complete a form, whether they come back to the site again. And of course, check that you are set up to collect the data and then to analyze and share it.

Some activities are likely to generate more varied data. What about the vast amount of information team members pick up in the course of all the activities involved in the project? Your team will encounter new ideas about the product, insights about customers or markets, and technical and resource issues. Your work involves interacting with others inside and outside the organization. Each of these interactions generates data. For instance, you glean information about others' assumptions from what they reveal in meetings, calls, or emails. You learn who supports your work and who seems to oppose it. In fact, the vast majority of the data at our disposal is *not* in spreadsheets, web stats, or formal reports, but instead embedded in experience. Effective teams develop specific ways of capturing this kind of information along with all the obvious, formal data. Meeting notes, end-of-day memos, "parking lot" lists of open issues that you uncover during the project, debriefing practices, and daily after action reviews are all ways to do this.

Organize the Data to Spur Learning

Knowing where your data are gathered and shared may seem like a trivial issue, but believe us, it's not. How do you offer the entire team access to the data, and encourage them to investigate it, rather than simply presenting the conclusion that a subset of the team has reached?

New tools make the task easier than ever: wikis, tracking in email, private blogs, and shared web work and storage spaces offer new modes of data sharing. You may need to experiment a little to find the tools and approaches that make sense for your team. A small investment in planning can yield huge benefits. A team of researchers, administrators, and students working on a complex study learned that adding simple instructions for file-naming protocols to their shared folders enabled a vast amount of disparate data to be quickly organized. Writing a memo on file-naming protocols and adopting the habit of checking that team members were both adding their new data to the shared folders and naming each item correctly was not exactly fun, but it took very little time to do and saved much wasted effort. Even more importantly, it meant that team members had a level of ease with the full set of data and regularly referred to it in their work, increasing the overall quality of their project. In the process of writing this book, we used online storage, strict filing systems to manage drafts and reference materials, and a web app that allowed us to curate and capture our information sources. Tools allowed us to effectively document, share, and archive our data despite being in geographically disparate locations.

Now you have considered how to gather and store data, and an orientation to using that data to inform your next steps and flag outcomes when results deviate from predictions. This forethought allows you to make the most of critical experimentation through action.

Just Do It

We repeat—just do it. Beyond this advice, when it comes to action, it might seem there's not much more to discuss: you just need to execute what you've designed. But, as we can't stress too strongly, document as you go. This is not a new step, just a reminder to check that you have gathered and are storing the data as planned using the approach you've identified and that your team has taken the time to record what you actually did (if different from what you planned to do). A quick check-in or friendly reminder can help reinforce the note-keeping and data collection habit, especially if it is one your team has not naturally been inclined toward in past projects.

Now comes the payoff for your hard work.

Make a Decision

What will your team do next? This is where the rubber meets the road! You have a plan that involves a logical sequence of steps. Are you still on track? Do you need to reconsider anything? Should your intended deliverable change in any way? As you assess results, this is the time to challenge your original project goals, reaffirm them, or simply shift emphasis and timing. You've gone through the disciplined effort of planning your action step, hypothesizing what that step will do to further your project, and collecting data that can confirm or challenge that hypothesis. Now it's time to use that data to inform your choice.

Define a Team Process That Works

All the data you've gathered is pointless unless it informs decisions that then lead to action. What will you do differently, now, as a result of this action step? Ground arguments for or against a particular next step in your data and do so as a matter of course.

Shockingly often, we see teams invest great effort in tests and activities that generate both quantitative and qualitative data—and then go on to make decisions about how to proceed without actually drawing on the data. The information appears to become irrelevant to the team almost as soon as it is gathered. As a leader, you can help set the team culture and reinforce the practice of ensuring collected data is actually used to inform the direction of the project. Every choice should be backed up with data of some sort, even if it's just a set of meeting notes or a team member's documented observations after spending a day with a customer.

A Simple Rule

To ensure that data drives your decisions, we'll share some advice that is deceptively simple: In making any major team decisions, follow these steps:

1. Gather varied data.
2. Avoid the divide-and-conquer method for key choices. Instead, analyze the data together.
3. If critical information is missing, find other sources that can fill in the gaps.
4. Make a decision that is supported by the data.
5. Do these steps in order.

It's really as simple as that. Think back to a particularly ineffective project you've experienced. We bet you can identify violations of these rules!

As you implement this process, figure out how your team will catch itself if you skip over any step. It's most likely to be looking at the data together.

We are not saying you need to follow these rules for everything. And they don't tell you all you need to do in order to make good decisions. (For example, you need first to decide what data to collect.) Also note that the steps require you to make the information visible and accessible to everyone. This adds a team responsibility that often gets short shrift: to share data at every step along the way. It also requires documenting decisions and the evidence behind them so that the linkage from data to decision is clear.

As you examine the data you've collected, you may discover that you'd like more information to make an informed decision. Identify ways the team can get that information or fill the gaps. A conversation with an expert, some desk research, or a follow-up test may be needed to equip the team for its after-action analysis.

Bring in the Experts

Using your data effectively means focusing on the information and evidence. Avoid privileging the most persuasively argued opinion or the most important person's idea. Commit to looking at all forms of data, including informal and nontraditional data. Make this a team habit and your work will benefit.

To examine and consider all the data at your disposal, use the methods that make the most sense for your team and project. Many teams design their own norms, habits, or meeting structure. Others borrow systematic techniques, such as the Toyota Production System. Still others bring in outside experts.

REAL-WORLD INSPIRATION

Eli Lilly's Rigorous Analysis Snatches Success from the Jaws of Failure

Rigorous techniques can help you to draw the right inferences from your results. You may need help with the statistical methods to do this appropriately. Mark Cannon and Amy Edmonson underscore this point with an example from the experience of pharmaceutical firm Eli Lilly and Company.[8] We tracked down the story they cited to learn more.[9] A once-promising chemotherapy drug, Almita, was deemed to cause unacceptable risk to human health when unexplained deaths occurred in clinical trials. The company was ready to give up. Suspecting this was the wrong decision, the physician conducting the trials decided to dig more deeply into the failure and was granted a limited time—two weeks—to do so. Luckily, a staff mathematician skilled in statistics and modeling could help identify and analyze the factors contributing to the bad outcomes. Working around the clock, the drug development team discovered that the patients who suffered negative effects from Almita typically had deficiencies in folic acid. Further investigation demonstrated that simply giving patients folic acid along with Almita solved the problem. Lilly was able to resume clinical trials with patients who were suffering from a specific type of cancer associated with asbestos exposure. Almita successfully shrank their tumors, and the FDA eventually approved the drug for these cancers. Further clinical trials cleared Almita to treat certain types of more widely occurring lung cancer, making the drug a commercial success and improving cancer outcomes in a large swath of patients. The physician's recognition that better data analysis was needed, the company's investment in the expertise for appropriate analysis, and the team's willingness to pull out all the stops to seek alternate explanations when confronted with an apparent failure enabled a promising drug to make it to market.

Refer to Your Predictions

The technical specifics of how you examine your predictions will depend on your needs, but there's one requirement, as we noted above: in some way or another, you need to juxtapose your predictions against the data gleaned from outcomes to highlight the surprises that you can then respond to. Identifying and describing these surprises is important for the team's own progress toward its deliverables. This is where you actually have the epiphanies. It's also important for presenting what you have learned to others: think of the stakeholders outside the project team whom you need to bring along, particularly if project plans change. Setting up the story with what was the original supposition and then contrasting it with what the facts reveal is an effective way to present an apparent failure or a change of course to others.

Checking against the data is the only way to add rigor to the inferences from action results, but just discussing it may not go far enough. Here some basic tools of systems thinking, logic, and research methods can come in handy. You may need sophisticated tools too, as the Eli Lilly example shows. Team process also plays a role. How will you use team meetings to check that you are drawing the right conclusions from the action? How will the team consult the data during meetings or decisions? How will the data be accessible to everyone?

Intersperse Deeper Project Check-In Points

Every now and then, revisit your entire project. The data you are amassing also allows you to reexamine the underlying project impact map developed in the launch phase. Have your mental models changed? How will you convey this shift in thinking about actions, deliverables, and outcomes to others? The process of engaging all stakeholders is crucial, but so is the data you invoke as evidence for your line of thinking.

Every few meetings, pause to check your resources, capabilities, and skills. Does your team have everything it needs? Are you working together well? Is there something that can be improved—in your process or within team member capabilities? Additional training may be needed, interpersonal or professional feedback may be required, or a coach, facilitator, or technical expert may need to be brought in.

Connect the feedback offered to team members to project needs, invoking evidence from a recent event if you need to drive home the point about a behavior or skill change, rather than making your feedback overly general. This way, people can understand how their professional development is connected to the work at hand, not an after-the-fact punishment.

It's also important to promote honesty at each check-in meeting so that problems surface before the deadlines are imminent. One study of engineering teams found that it was common for the existing organizational culture to discourage people from raising a problem unless they also had a solution, which dampened examination of complex problems until too late. In a firm in which multiple teams simultaneously developed interacting elements of a new product, each team delayed reporting problems to the collective group, hoping that another team was farther behind schedule and would "fess up" first, enabling them to catch up without taking the blame for the delay.[10]

But the delays in uncovering problems may stem from other causes. In many projects, for example, teams do not take the actions that could reveal major issues until late in the project. They may start with easier, simpler steps and put off the problematic, challenging tasks until later. Team members may argue for postponing more risky actions until they have gained more knowledge or sorted out other open questions—or they may simply be putting off until later the things that are least appealing to complete. Either way, the rationale may be a poor one. The risky or difficult step may be the most important because it sheds light on a key uncertainty or helps test a critical assumption. And, as we suggested earlier, this may make this step a priority for action and testing much earlier on in the project.

Finally, it is important to consider both planned and unplanned outcomes. Deeper project checks-ins present an ideal opportunity for the team to examine surprises. Consider unfolding events and insights from outside the project along with unexpected results from activities you had not targeted as tests. Try not to get so caught up in examining only the developments for which you formed predictions and for which you've carefully collected data that you miss insights and opportunities that unexpected developments can yield. For example, Teflon was discovered by accident when DuPont scientist Roy Plunkett realized that a sample of refrigerant gas he had been working on had accidentally polymerized, yielding a powder with low surface friction. The slippery material proved to be inert and had a high melting point, eventually finding use in a variety of products, including non-stick cookware. Had Plunkett not accidentally manipulated the gas he had been researching that day in 1938 and then been driven to explore the unexpected result just as he was cleaning up his workbench, he would not have made an unplanned discovery that spawned a commercially successful technology.[11]

Specify Your Next Steps

Making a decision about what to do next in your project is about more than following a hunch or shared assumptions about what's always been done. To make a conscious choice about next steps, focus on the implications of all the data you've collected as you've taken action, being sure to develop your team dialogue about how you are conducting the analysis itself and drawing conclusions. Make sure to retain both the data you've collected and the inferences you've drawn to inform future steps. Connect what you have learned from this round of work to what you will do next, and then do it all again.

To Sum Up Our Iteration Advice: Inspiration and Guidance

Our goal in this chapter has been to help you select, design for testing, and learn from your actions, while enabling you to meet the requirements of your project and complete your deliverables. We've guided you in choosing your first step and making explicit your predictions of what this action will achieve, and then thinking about how you can execute while gathering useful information that supports or disconfirms your prediction and guides the next steps. If you can test and refine your ideas at a level of affordable risk with time remaining for course corrections, you can replace extensive planning with more agile action, exit dead ends sooner, and discover new and better possibilities for your project.

The Fail Better approach to iteration equips your team to make decisions that are based on information and data, as opposed to driven by instinct or deadline pressure. We recognize that not every action is testable, predictable, or critical to results, so our goal has also been to help you identify the actions, both process- and production-oriented, that can deliver the most useful insights in a deadline-driven project made up of a swarm of simultaneously occurring activities by team members.

We hope this chapter has helped you to think of your project as a cauldron for experimentation. Approach your project in cycles or chunks in which you plan, act, and assess, then take the next step, and even big projects become more tractable while enabling your team to learn and refine its plans. Creative ideas become feasible to test when you develop the discipline that supports iteration, because failures will be incremental and early, and their lessons will not be lost.

Cultivating the skills and practices needed to refine the team's work through iteration calls on team members to move beyond their usual comfortable ways of working. We recommend trying the method described above by prioritizing a key activity where testing and data collection is possible and relatively straightforward. Then, see how the information and data you generate can inform your next decision. This helps team members see how building a habit in a project environment can get results, including insights that might otherwise have gone unnoticed until too late—either in the form of a costly mistake or a missed opportunity.

A key benefit of our approach to iterative action is that it will enable you to be more attuned to what you learned through the process. Taking these insights to the next level is what we explore in chapter 6—embedding new habits, practices, and lessons learned at a personal, team, and wider level to garner better results in the future.

But first, let's look at a real-world story that could help inspire you to see how the ideas in practice enabled an entrepreneur to pivot her software company.

REAL-WORLD INSPIRATION

Elizabeth Yin Iterates and Pivots Software Start-Up LaunchBit

"Stop coding!" Elizabeth Yin told fellow software entrepreneurs in 2011, shortly after launching her latest start-up. Like many of them, she was young and scrappy.[12] Now she and Jennifer Chin were on their way to initial success. Soon their new software company, LaunchBit, would raise close to a million dollars in seed round funding. The duo had generated positive publicity in the competitive world of tech start-ups and had landed paying customers after just a few days. LaunchBit aimed to enable advertisers to reach targeted audiences by serving ads within email newsletters instead of websites. Since users opt in to email newsletters, the idea was that ads placed there could efficiently reach potential customers with the right interests.

In 2013, LaunchBit was still in its early stages. Even if Yin couldn't yet tell how well it would succeed, she felt certain that its first years of success owed much to her learning from past experience. She'd already started several other software businesses, most recently investing over eighteen months to build a social shopping site that failed to gain customers despite much investment in developing the product. Yin had examined her failure from all angles to develop guiding principles that she now used relentlessly. And, strangely enough for a software entrepreneur, one mantra was to avoid writing code as much as possible.

Her reason: until you really know what customers want, developing elaborate software is not only a waste of effort, but a liability that could lock you into what may be a flawed approach. Working creatively, the LaunchBit team avoided this trap by offering prototype services to a small number of potential customers. The team could use early test versions of the product to see what customers liked, what worked, and what didn't. Even as they polished their landing page, the heart of LaunchBit's underlying software program—the ad server itself—was not fully functional. Those early test customers could not tell, and it didn't affect their service, because Yin and Chin carried out all the needed work manually. They hacked together a set of approaches that provided customers with the functions that LaunchBit aimed eventually to automate.

Testing the Product and *the Business Model*

In early start-up mode, LaunchBit's hybrid approach used spreadsheets, cut-and-paste methods, and other in-the-background shortcuts, stitched together with the minimal amount of coding needed to make it all work perfectly. The prototype would not work at large scale, but at this point, that was fine with Yin and Chin.

One such function they hacked together was an ad auction system. Other ad networks such as Google Adwords or Facebook Ads commonly allocated ads to ad slots through homegrown ad auction systems. Ad auctions determined how much a marketer paid for a shown ad along with what ads go into which ad slots. To make the auctions work, complex software typically factored in ad relevance, ad popularity, marketer bidding prices, and many other criteria. While Yin and Chin were experimenting with pricing models, they could not afford to spend a lot of time building out a complete ad auction system for each test, only to conclude that they would need to scrap it. So, to decide whether using an ad auction system was even a good idea, the duo faked it. They quickly developed an interface where their customers could enter in a bid price, but they did not develop the underlying code for the ad auction. Each time a customer would enter or change a bid, Chin would manually reconcile all the bidding customers to figure out where the ads should be allocated and then would manually deploy each ad accordingly. Even though this was tedious, LaunchBit could control how many customers to take on and not compromise on quality. And it could test different business ideas, such as varying the minimum purchase requirement.

Interestingly, LaunchBit itself was the result of iteration. For more than a year at its earliest stage, its founders ran a series of rapid tests to explore the most promising ideas for the company's focus, devoting one to four weeks of effort to each test. Evoking the idea of pivoting, Yin explained:

> We played our tests like poker; if we tested an idea and it looked good, we would invest more time and resources into. If it didn't test well, we would fold . . . [By the summer of

> 2011] we didn't know exactly which product we would build, but we did know which problem we wanted to solve. After testing many ideas that didn't work, we finally hit upon this e-mail ad platform idea and it looked promising . . . The first week of testing this idea, we received an ad from an advertiser and sent it to a publisher so that it could be manually placed in a newsletter. We measured the initial results and they looked good. So we kept pouring more resources into it until finally we were "all in."[13]

And though LaunchBit started as an ad network for email newsletters, Yin and Chin have evolved it even further. By early 2013, they realized they were hitting a wall with the business. Although marketers loved the product they had built and were able to run well-performing ads, the duo realized that it was very difficult to find email newsletters at scale. But they also learned something else: that their customers did not care as much about running ads in emails as they did about using their platform to get new customers. So LaunchBit pivoted again, this time to morph their product to accommodate distribution channels beyond email newsletters to help marketers get more customers.

In many ways, Yin reflected in 2014, the journey LaunchBit took in its early years followed the form of a snail shell, starting large and circling in on a specific need and solution. In the beginning Yin and Chin did not know what particular problem they wanted to address, so they made large pivots from idea to idea in different industries. Once they homed in on a problem they wanted to tackle—customer acquisition—they took their first stab at solving the problem: an ad network for email newsletters. Subsequent pivots were tighter and smaller, focusing on improving their platform continually to help it achieve what they saw as its highest value use, helping marketers acquire new customers at scale.

How the Fail Better Approach Applies

What can we learn from LaunchBit? Elizabeth Yin and her trial-and-error product development process provide an intriguing example of the tenets of the Fail Better method for iteration, including planning the step, taking action, and making a decision about where to invest next. Let's examine how:

Plan your action. Yin and her team selected activities that could generate useful information rapidly, with minimal cost. To avoid laborious code development, they hacked together a polished customer interface with an unsophisticated and low-cost back end to replicate the functions they aimed to eventually program in. By planning an information-rich and affordable first step, the team could continue to refine the functionality of LaunchBit. They also made predictions as part of their testing. For example, they predicted they would need to sell at a certain volume per customer to be profitable, adjusting that volume as sales data rolled in.

Take action. Central to Yin's efforts was structured, low-risk experimentation that generated useful information. She and her team were thoughtful and intentional about using their data to inform the next iteration of and investment in their product. Not only did they test different functions for LaunchBit, they also tested different business models (like the minimum purchase amount and the ad auction model). Yin's description of the development process as a poker game, where the team increasingly bet on the product eliciting favorable results, is a great way to think about how to keep failures small and manageable while moving toward an "all-in" success, as opposed to going all in on a seemingly good idea (Yin's earlier shopping website) only to lock into a failing course of action.

Running rapid experiments to test different versions of the product may seem wasteful or even unappealing to aspiring tech entrepreneurs—who, after all, are coders and builders at heart. Manual hacks like those behind the earliest prototypes of LaunchBit are inelegant and require hard work. But they're quick, and they're real. There's no substitute for learning from customers by interacting with them in connection with the product itself.

Make a decision. As a result of all their experience and information gathering, the LaunchBit team knew exactly how to shape their company's next steps as they narrowed in on their product design and business model. They truly were iterating to build and refine. They had data and experience to back up every key decision, which in turn allowed them to bring along investors who were also convinced by the data, until ultimately Yin could give the go-ahead to stop the behind-the-scenes hacks and code.

At-a-Glance Guidance for Iterating within Your Project

We turn now to the practical, with a set of tools to aid your project launch. Guiding questions help you think through key issues that cut across domains. To help you manage things, we also provide a comprehensive list of the products you will create if you follow every launch step we've described. And a comprehensive trio of Fail Better checklists gathers the step-by-step details.

Guiding Thought Questions

In this chapter, we helped you design and implement your actions to generate useful insights to inform your next step. Here are some big-picture questions that can help you harness the power of iteration:

- ❑ **Work design.** How can you help your team design core project work to test and iterate on ideas while meeting deadlines?
- ❑ **Information systems.** What systems and tools can you put in place to capture data gathered through experimentation?
- ❑ **Data-driven decisions.** How do you ensure you use collected data to draw critical insights that, in turn, inform your next steps?
- ❑ **Building buy-in.** How do you bring stakeholders along when a change from your original work plan is needed based on your data-driven discoveries?

Fail Better Process Products

Here is a list of Fail Better documents you may produce as you move through the iteration steps. Not every team will create every document; in some cases, our advice may simply prompt a discussion or reflection. Choose the level of documentation that works for you.

- ❑ Updates to your initial work plan, open issues list, and other launch documents prompted by this chapter's advice.
- ❑ A list of candidate action steps that lend themselves to experimentation.
- ❑ Brief documentation of the tests/experiments you've targeted for implementation. For each test, note how you will test and why, along with predictions of results and a practical plan to collect data on what happens.
- ❑ A feasible team approach to archiving and sharing data.

- ❑ Documentation of the data and findings generated by each test.
- ❑ An explicit team process for how to use the data to make a decision on what to do next.
- ❑ Documentation of the conclusions your team draws from your analysis of the data.
- ❑ Documentation of your selected next step and the rationale for it.
- ❑ Updated action plans and revisions to any other team documents.

Implementation Checklists to Build and Refine in Fail Better Mode

Use these checklists to guide launch activities, step-by-step.

Fail Better Checklist #4: Plan the Action

Your team is kicking into high gear to get the critical work of the project done. This at-a-glance checklist can help you prioritize and test the team's activities.

1. Prioritize activities to target for iteration:
    - ❑ Identify activities that meet the criteria: they are critical to your project's development; potentially informative; offer leeway for change; and are drawn from a wide range of options.
    - ❑ Flag the subset of these activities in which to incorporate tests and note why you chose them.
    - ❑ Eliminate or repurpose activities that score lowest against the above criteria.

2. Design your target activities as tests:

   - ❑ Design the prioritized actions around tests that could provide the most useful information. Consider the options laid out in the chapter (simulation, prototyping, etc.). In selecting a test, consider the utility, quality, and volume of information the test can generate along with its cost and speed of implementation.

   - ❑ Consider integrative tests that expose potential issues for the entire deliverable.

   - ❑ Once you decide which test to apply in each case, develop your action plan for carrying it out, identifying its tasks, inputs, timing, and responsibilities.

3. Predict what you think will happen:

   - ❑ For each activity where you've designed a test, jot down your prediction of what you think will happen and why, flagging specific assumptions that inform your prediction.

Fail Better Checklist #5: Take Action

Now that you've prioritized activities, designed tests, and documented your predictions, it's time to implement. Use the following checklist to guide your action.

1. Plan for data:

   - ❑ Identify what information will flow from the actions you take. Consider all relevant forms of data at your disposal, from meeting notes to interview summaries to available databases.

   - ❑ Organize the data you collect to make learning easier. Ensure all team members have access to the data.

Consider tools, such as shared organizational workspace systems and online options. Check that all team members are on board with the data approach and know their responsibilities.

2. Just do it! Implement your action:

- ❑ Implement your activities in the prioritized way you've identified, integrating the tests you've designed.
- ❑ Document as you go. Remind the team to remain disciplined in data collection. A little encouragement can go a long way.
- ❑ Continue to engage in overall project management as you move forward. Keep an eye on work flow, budget, and timeline. Keep in touch with team members and make sure they're communicating with one another as disparate parts of the project are implemented.

Fail Better Checklist #6: Make a Decision

You've done the hard work. Having carefully prioritized activities, designed tests, and implemented while managing your overall workflow, it's time for your payoff. Based on the information you've gathered, what will you do next? Make a decision.

1. Define a team process that works:

- ❑ Instead of reviewing data and making decisions in silos, pull the team together to review the information together.
- ❑ Share the collected data and discuss if any critical information is missing that's needed to make an informed decision, then fill the gaps to the extent that's feasible.

- ❑ If your team lacks skills to make the most of the information you've collected, bring in an expert to help.
- ❑ Once you have the best set of information you can gather, discuss how this information supports or disproves your prediction.
- ❑ Identify the ramifications of your findings for your project goals and deliverables.

2. Intersperse deeper project check-in points every now and then, as you take repeated trips around the action loop:
   - ❑ Identify the unplanned surprises and discoveries, both good and bad, that have emerged, along with your planned tests. Apply after-action analysis (looking at the data and making a decision) to the unplanned surprises to uncover any implications for your project.
   - ❑ Revisit your project's plans and rationale—your project impact map, deliverables list, work plan, stakeholder map, and anything else you think important to reconsider—to assess if your thinking and plans need to change in any way. Look at your experience and the data you've gathered with a critical eye.
   - ❑ Check on your project process. Consider whether your team has everything it needs, how team members are functioning together, and if communication processes are working as intended. Adjust as needed. Flag areas where you see the team as a whole or its members would benefit from professional development or other support.

3. Specify your next steps:

   - ❑ Choose your next step. Will you make adjustments to a product mock-up and gather feedback again? Will you change a core process your team has been using? Will you redefine the deliverable or pursue a different test or avenue all together?
   - ❑ Document the conclusions and inferences your team has drawn from the data. This provides a pathway back to your decision-making process.
   - ❑ Archive data that could be needed in the future.
   - ❑ If you're still in the process of creating your deliverables, testing ideas, or developing product concepts, begin again. Determine what's next in your journey around the action loop.
   - ❑ If you're done with deliverables and your project is wrapping up, it's time to move on to the next stage where you'll embed what you've learned through this project.

CHAPTER PREVIEW

STEPS FOR EMBEDDING THE LEARNING

While your project experience is still fresh, it's time to assess your results, make habits out of best team and personal practices, and share what you learned with others who might benefit. This chapter will show you how.

- Examine your results:
  - Assemble an archive of your project.
  - Build a timeline indicating developments.
  - Assess project outputs, team development, project impact, and underlying assumptions and logic.
- Enhance your practices:
  - Build better team habits for future projects.
  - Refine and improve project methods.
  - Update and create an action plan for your own management practice.
- Share your discoveries:
  - Hone your own story about what you've learned.
  - Prepare for wider impact so others can apply your results.
  - Reach a bigger audience to increase organizational knowledge.

Embedding the learning from your work is the most-often-overlooked stage of a project. Even if you're rushing onto the next thing or balking at the extra effort, set aside time to figure out how your experience could inform future work and your own development.

CHAPTER 6

Embed the Learning

Imagine how you feel on the day your team turns in its deliverables. Finally! This is a moment to savor.

Yet, as you send off those last emails, clean up your electronic files, and tidy up your desk—even as your attention is already turning to the project that's waiting in the wings, perhaps already under way—you can't help but think that you might be missing something important. Thanks to all you invested in the project, you now have a vivid, if somewhat inchoate, sense of what worked and what didn't this time around. This hints at the potential for improvement on many fronts, from project management to team process to the design of activities.

But, if you're like most people, these nascent insights will not be effectively documented. Even more important, they won't even be carefully examined. That's a problem—because without critically analyzing and then planning exactly how you will draw on these intimations of success and failure, they are likely to go unexploited, their full value underappreciated.

It's time for the embed step of the Fail Better approach.

Extracting the Lessons from Experience

Time and again, the failure to extract and use the lessons of experience comes up in our conversations with everyone from students to CEOs. This failure to learn isn't merely an academic problem. It has vast practical implications. Every time you miss an opportunity to learn from experience, your team risks wasting its future efforts, frittering away precious resources, or squandering new opportunities. And in the end, this widespread failure to learn engenders frustration as people realize that they are encountering the same problems in project after project.

You have a choice of how to respond to these missed opportunities.

You could choose a cynical or apathetic response: it's above your pay grade, nothing ever changes round here, our clients don't know what they want, there goes the manufacturing department messing up the work we handed to them, there's never enough time to think around here, and so on. While cynicism is unlikely to be a fruitful guiding philosophy, we'd like to point out that a realistic analysis of what went wrong is an invaluable ingredient for learning from experience. Without the ability to call it like it is, trying to figure out lessons learned is a waste of time.

How else could you respond to your organization's failure to learn? The alternative is to choose the wait-until-later option and look ahead to your imagined future: "Once I get a new qualification or job title," you say to yourself, "I will finally be able to change things. Until then, I just need to get by. But boy, once I get to my new role, then I'll be able to avoid these problems or make better use of the opportunities. I'll finally be allowed to call the shots and do it right!"

Of course, we're all for professional development! But if you look to formal qualifications as the sole means for you to change things, you're in for a long journey. And once you reach your goal and achieve more formal power, you still need to know how to wield it effectively.

We offer you a third option for avoiding the trap of failing to learn from hard-won experience. Working from the position you occupy today, you can choose to extract learning from your own experience. You can distill the most useful lessons it offers and use your insights to create a practical plan for embedding it into your own professional practice, your future teams' work, and perhaps even more widely.

If you don't run the organization, it may feel as if you have little power to change the culture, the rules, or the behavior of others. Even if you do not (yet!) occupy a position of great authority, you may have more scope than you realize to shape things for yourself, your team, and even for your organization and profession. This shaping takes some work, but, like any new discipline, it gets easier with practice. And as we hope you'll agree, it'll be worth it. It's easy to take the first steps. You can get going today, with a little review, reflection, and planning for next time designed to pay off down the road. It'll make your work more efficient, and it will also enable you to become savvier. And we think that the advice we offer will make work more interesting for you and your colleagues.

What we have in mind is not finger pointing or blaming. Our form of learning from experience involves figuring out what went right, along with what didn't work. We see widespread evidence that both failures and successes go unexploited because they are not systematically analyzed. In fact, there's evidence from research on social cognition, psychology, and organizational studies that medium-scale failures tend to trigger more careful thought than do successes, neutral results, or large-scale failure.[1] That's why the Fail Better approach seeks to enable failures that are scaled so as to be on your radar, but not overwhelmingly disruptive and damaging. Alas, real life is not always so easy to orchestrate.

Let's start with making sense of your project results.

Examine Your Results

Think of all you have to draw on as you wrap up your project. First, there are all the activities you've undertaken. Having carefully laid the groundwork, identified and iterated on key tests, and systematically gathered and analyzed data at each step of the way, you've planned your missteps to be small and instructive, and pivoted your team toward success. If it's gone as we hope, you've avoided making bigger mistakes. The Fail Better efforts you've already executed led your team to create a better product, design, plan, study, recommendation, or decision. That's the immediate payoff of our approach.

But we're also looking to tap into the second-order benefits of the approach: what you learned along the way. You'll be drawing on the trail of materials linked to all your efforts in the project. These materials are often distributed in different formats and different places, so you may need to invest some effort to make them accessible to all.

To set up your team to extract this learning, follow the steps laid out below. You'll find that the very same efforts that enabled your project so far provide an invaluable bank of evidence that can also teach you and others how to do things better the next time around.

Assemble a Project Archive

The first step is to build an archive of the materials your team created. You need not prepare an exhaustive collection of everything or implement a perfect filing system. The goal is to curate a sampling of what you did over the duration of the project, time-stamped as best you can. The more representative your repository of materials, the better you will be able to re-create your project path. This portfolio will ground your distillation of lessons learned.

Start by gathering materials. Along with the more formal content you've created, including your final and draft deliverables, pull together internal notes, such as meeting agendas, informal documentation captured in handwritten notes, mobile phone camera shots of whiteboards, cocktail napkin scribbles, emails, comments on drafts, and notes from phone calls. Get out a few different versions of your work plan from various stages of the project and make sure you have your calendar on hand. Your Fail Better launch materials are essential too.

The resulting archive will be a mix of content that reveals insights, data, tools, and techniques. Now you're ready to create a retrospective portfolio of your work.

Organizing your archive will help with all the steps to come. Can the materials be stored in a shareable format such as a shared drive? If you have hard copies of certain items, scanning these to file can make them easily accessible for many projects to come (shockingly often, work is lost simply because it cannot be found when needed for the next project). Possible ways to organize these materials may be by (1) project step; (2) date, week, or month; (3) key project area; or (4) products versus process.

Instead of renaming every item, you could design a file folder structure that makes it easy to find needed materials. Choose the organizing and labeling approach that will work best for your team. Make sure to create a quick one-page guide to your system—what's included, how files are labeled, and what approach underpins the organization of the materials. Save this guide in the main directory of your archive.

Once you develop your organizing approach, enlist teammates to help locate and upload items to build the archive. To make it all manageable, set aside a limited amount of time to do this. Investing even an hour or two is far better than nothing. Some teams create "archiving parties" and book a conference room for half a day when all team members help in the task, then treat themselves to a lunch or after-work drink to celebrate their hard work.

Develop Your Project Timeline History

Create a one-page timeline that depicts your project. Your most recent work plan can provide the starting point, but because projects often deviate from plans in the final stages, you may find that you need to update the plan to account for new streams of work that were added late in the process or planned efforts that were eventually set aside. Consult your archive to check that you've included all the major elements of your project. It's surprisingly easy to forget how much effort went into the project's various activities, particularly those that turned into dead ends or were abandoned for other reasons.

Working with your team, refine the timeline so that it shows the project work as a small number of key stages that represent the major focus of your team's efforts at each period. You may end up with overlapping stages if your team's size or the project's complexity necessitated simultaneous work streams. Give each key stage a name that captures team members' experience during that period. You're not going to be publishing this document and may not even end up sharing it beyond the team. It's designed for you and your team to use. So, as you label timeline stages, come up with terms that represent how you all *felt* and what you focused on—including what you wasted time on—at each stage of the project. Make the names brief and vivid to enable your team to draw on them in subsequent discussions. One team labeled their information-collection stage "Into the Weeds" and their push to create their final report "Rush to the Deadline." Informal labels that authentically represent the team's experience can enable everyone to frankly examine what happened during each phase of the process and provide the team with a common framework for referring to events and experiences as they analyze project lessons.

Under the label for each stage of project work, list the main accomplishments and discoveries that the stage entailed. What did you learn or deliver in that stage?

A word on timeline format: you can use special software or templates available online, create a hand-drawn diagram, use a spreadsheet, or simply make a bulleted list. Make your timeline simple and relevant to you and your team.

Your updated timeline depicting major work stages provides a useful basis for analyzing the triggers for transitions. Set the stage by first demarking significant milestones and changes in direction on the timeline. By and large, these transitions will mark the end of one stage of work and the beginning of the next. Transition events may be formal or informal. For instance, you may highlight key deadlines, official presentations, the addition of a new team member, and various disruptions to work flow (a government shutdown, a major weather event, or changes in the mandate coming from senior management or clients). Some transitions are planned, of course, such as moving from information collection to report writing in keeping with your established work plan. Others are the result of discoveries encountered during the project work itself. Jot down the important transitions your team identifies and locate each on the timeline.

Analyze Your Project's Trajectory

Your completed timeline now provides a retrospective overview of the project's evolution. Use it as the basis for a team discussion to analyze the trajectory of the work. Did you put too much—or too little—effort into any of the stages? Did you overreact or underreact to what you learned, external changes, or other triggers? Did your work follow the right sequence of steps?

Examine each shift in direction and note what triggered the modification in approach or plans. When your plans changed, what drove the change? Was it your own lack of foresight, the result of a deliberate test, changing an assumption disproved by data, or something unpredictable beyond the boundaries of your control?

Pay particular attention to the surprises you encountered during the project. Perhaps an action step test revealed new information that sent you down a different path. Or maybe a key stakeholder responded negatively to a mid-project briefing, forcing you to change course. Some surprises are pleasant: your team may have anticipated that it would have a more limited budget than the actual allocation. Identify a handful of your top surprises, and discuss whether they could have been anticipated better or managed more effectively. What would you do differently next time?

Finally, consider the timeline from the perspective of your project launch. By contrasting your initial project map with the timeline you've just developed, your team may be able to identify where your project went wrong or where a wrong turn was avoided due to your initial investment in listing hypotheses, testing ideas, and seeking disconfirmation. Sometimes failures are easier to spot than avoided failures or missteps. Make sure you keep an eye out for both—by uncovering a faulty assumption early, you may have saved yourself a ton of time, trouble, and cost later on. To do this, pinpoint deviations from the work plan in terms of what you expected to accomplish via various work steps. Looking at the stages, discuss with your team: where did you meet your plans and where did you deviate? Did you invest the effort and resources you had planned to, and did you get the results you sought by each stage?

In exploring the origins and effects of changes and developments in your timeline, you'll develop a sense of how well your team was able to create, exploit, or respond to shifts. This may point to capabilities you have—or need—as well as advice for future projects.

You'll draw on the timeline again in later steps to review progress and work flow and remind yourselves of surprises, discoveries, and evolving and emerging ideas and practices.

Assess Your Project's Results—Your Project Scorecard

Looking back in time also highlights how far you've come since the project's starting point. You began your project with a charge: an outcome to achieve. As you went to work, you clarified the purpose of the project, collaborated with others to refine the design and content of your deliverables, and likely had your share of twists and turns along the way. To assess what to keep and what to change, at this point in the process, you'll need to figure out how well you did in the end, in terms of what you produced. For this step, focus on the project's *results*—not the team, your personal role, or the politics.

Scoring your project's performance is essential for establishing how to frame the lessons learned. Does your project reveal things to avoid next time around? Does it offer an exemplar of effective practice? To figure out what you are learning, you need to look at what you did—hence the timeline—as well as at how well you did it.

It's important to assess what your project has delivered in four domains: the team's outputs; capacities developed by the team as a whole and its individual members; the real-world impact of your products; and the new knowledge you gained as a result of your work.

As you consider these domains, your team will be assessing what you've accomplished in each. Figure 6-1 shows a quick scorecard you can use to capture the headlines. For each of the four areas, you'll give yourselves an overall score—it can be as simple as low, medium, or high—and jot down the one or two best and worst aspects of your performance.

FIGURE 6-1

Template for your project scorecard

	Project outputs	Team development	Project impact	Assumptions and logic
Evidence and examples				
Score				

Column 1: Project Outputs

First, were your deliverables as good as you wanted them to be?

When you work in an organization with bosses and stakeholders, it's common to define success in terms of others' perceived satisfaction. Did the client, the boss, or your peers seem to think your work products were good? When others seem satisfied, it's tempting to whitewash things, even if the project didn't achieve what you initially intended. You may find yourselves saying, well, the bosses seemed to think it was fine, that's good enough. Is this enough if you truly want to learn from every experience? We think not.

Take an objective look at what you accomplished. Begin with what you delivered: the product, report, presentation, analysis, or service your project provided.

Review your team's final portfolio as critically as you can to establish your own assessment of its quality. See if you can triangulate with any other data. What do all the available sources of information—not just those that are most favorable or politically expedient—indicate about the quality of your team's project work? Include as much evidence as possible. If you think that the new guide, plan, or website your team created is good, in what ways is it good?

To put your assessment of the deliverables into some context, take a few minutes to review what it cost. Create a rough accounting of the inputs that you expended over the course of the project. What did your team spend, in terms of money, time, attention, social capital, and any other important inputs? In a sense, this accounting of overall costs provides a denominator for the overall assessment of project quality. If you have delivered an excellent result, but done so at a cost far beyond your budget, take that cost into account. If your work was simply good enough, but you managed to meet a crucial requirement of coming in on time and on budget, that's worth noting too.

As you do this, you're enabling your team to move beyond looking solely at the perceived quality of deliverables. While such perceptions weigh heavily in subjective assessments of success and failure, our more nuanced take on the results will enable a more sophisticated evaluation of the value you created. As we work though the rest of the embed process, we hope that you will see how useful it is to come up with your own take on your results.

Column 2: Team Development

This is a different kind of analysis that allows you to uncover the capacities that your experience generated, separate from the project deliverables themselves.

Look back on your team's experience. Take a moment to identify the capabilities, assets, skills, and knowledge your team developed as individuals and as a team in the course of carrying out this project. What are you now better at doing? One way to get at this is to ask: *What did you or members of your team gain that could be valuable in future projects?*

Some of these gains are team skills and capabilities—what you can do together. Team capabilities include the ability to make sense of ambiguous data together, such as debriefing a difficult client meeting, and the ability to carry out complex tasks, such as organizing and carrying out events or creating effective content and materials.

Some gains may represent individual professional development, such as a team member mastering a new software product or developing focus-group interview skills or quantitative research know-how. Consider improved technical, communication, leadership, and management skills that you can draw on again. Identify potentially useful domain knowledge and topical insights that your team members gained too.

Some gains may be shared assets, such as deeper relationships with different stakeholders, status within the company, or visibility within the industry.

Jot down the top few developments that come to mind.

Looking at your team this way, you may realize that you have also learned about gaps in capabilities, assets, knowledge, and skills. Do you now have some specific ideas of how your team needs to develop? Pinpoint anything you learned about needed skills or professional development of the team.

And as you inventory relationships and assets that your team created or strengthened, flag those that should be actively maintained, such as new skills that require investment to keep up or new connections within the company that would benefit from regular interaction.

Finally, consider the flip side: Is there any damage to stakeholder relationships or other interpersonal connections that now needs to be repaired or otherwise be handled?

Column 3: Project Impact

Team outcomes are not the only broader result that matters. You are likely to also want to know if your work was useful. The wise team looks for evidence of both output quality and its eventual impact on the world, because in the end the ultimate goal should be to understand how well the products of your work actually meet the real-world needs you set out to address. Only when you trace work to products to impact will you be able to assess the full value of what you have invested in. In getting this feedback, you may discover new things—features, strengths, and benefits of your work, along with its flaws and limitations—that spur further learning.

The problem is that translating deliverables into impact can be elusive. Your team may have developed a product design that your immediate clients think is great. Or perhaps you have mapped out a detailed market entry plan that everyone agrees is better than any in the company's history. Yet these indications of project quality are necessarily incomplete until your project's deliverables are tested on the factory floor or in the marketplace. Unfortunately, you often have to wait to learn. And in the waiting come challenges. For one, the project may now be out of your hands; its results have been handed off to the next team, who will be taking actions and making decisions that shape the application of your results. There are likely to be confounding factors en route to impact.

Some unlucky teams face an even bigger challenge if their work does not get tested in the real world. You may labor to produce deliverables that appear to be high quality, only to be deprived of this learning opportunity if your work is not used. For reasons beyond your control, the new product you designed may never see production or the new market entry you've designed not undertaken.

But in most cases, you will be able to find opportunities to glean feedback about your work that goes beyond the immediate responses from the client or boss. An investment in some creative thinking today could pay off down the road. How will you learn about the eventual impact of your deliverables?

For now, form a provisional assessment of impact and make a quick plan for updating your understanding as more feedback comes in. To start today, ask yourselves, what are the indications of the effect of your work? Even the simplest steps to gather more information can pay off. An informal chat with clients or other stakeholders in a low-pressure setting could reveal honest evaluations about how effective your work will prove, for example.

A quick visit to the production department could help you to learn more about the manufacturing aspects of your new product design—what worked well, what didn't. Think of creative ways to tap into your existing connections within the organization, in the marketplace, or in the community to glean any feedback about how your work is playing out for others. Even at the earliest stages of implementation, there is often more feedback to be had than you might realize.

But since you'll also need to invest in learning in the future, include this in your plan for assessment. Assessing value takes time. You may need to look at impact at multiple future points. Even if tracking actual impact over time is beyond the scope of your team's work, can you devise a shrewd way to learn more as consequences unfold? For example, are there others within your organization or with the client who will be able to assess near- and longer-term outcomes down the line? How can you stay informed? Consider setting calendar reminders at regularly scheduled intervals to check into the unfolding evidence of impact of your project and to uncover any emerging insights into the drivers of success or failure.

Column 4: Assumptions and Logic

In examining differences between what you expected and what actually happened, you learn where your assumptions were faulty. Examining the rationale for your work and its results can reveal where your prior mental models were correct and where they were flawed.

First, consider the big picture by reviewing your outputs and plans, including your launch-phase project map and the timeline history you've just assembled. What did your team plan to create, and what did you deliver? How do you account for any differences?

Check your understanding of how your team's outputs enable impact and then reflect on what this reveals about the world. This helps you to explore means-ends connections—the cause-and-effect linkages that relate the work you undertake to the outputs you create, which in turn lead to positive impact in the marketplace or community you serve.

To do this, revisit the project impact map and other materials you created in the launch phase. This map provided the rationale for your team's work. But is the rationale behind it correct? Considering the map in light of your quality assessment and timeline can provide key insights into the validity of your assumptions. How has your knowledge about the domain of your project become more sophisticated? Revisiting your project map can help you identify how, specifically, you have improved your understanding of the world. Flag the cause-and-effect relationships that your experience reveals to be important, and identify where your posited connections were spurious.

Look at the causal relationships that formed the basis of your original project plans. What can you pull out as new understanding that can be applied to future projects? Document what you see as critical to your reflections on the logic and assumptions that guided your process. This can help you diagnose where and how your project succeeded or went off track, and can inform future projects.

For example, one organization we worked with, a statewide nonprofit addressing hunger, carried out a public awareness campaign to promote a free summer foods program for children. They invested significant resources in the campaign, sharing information about the program in highly visible places via bus placards and billboards. They made a reasonable assumption that increased program awareness would increase program use. But the organization saw only a small bump in the number of summer meals served in targeted areas. It went back to the original approach to determine why. It checked in with those sites that had been anomalies, having successfully increased participation, and learned that localized efforts via word of mouth and trusted messengers were more effective. The organization was able to adjust future projects to increase program participation with this learning in mind.

Putting It All Together

Putting your assessment of these four domains together, you can look at the project as a whole to gain a sense of highlights and implications of your team's work and accomplishments. Knowing how well your project did is essential for you to responsibly assess what you will change and what you will retain from this project's experience. If your project scores poorly on all dimensions, your team's next steps in the embedding process will likely focus on things to avoid. If you log great success in some domains, you'll want to look at how to retain and share the knowledge, tools, and practices that enabled your performance. The next step focuses on how you turn this gained insight into changed or reinforced behavior through the development of team habits and individual practices.

Enhance Your Practices

Our daily experiences show us—often in dramatic, if small-scale, ways—techniques, habits, and practices that don't work. Think of the emails you routinely get that are unclear or overly complicated, poorly designed forms you're required to complete, or the waste-of-time meetings you've given up too many days of your life to already. These mundane aspects of work experience are more than trivial exasperations: they can belie a lack of attention to detail, convey a lack of caring about others, or engender feelings of disempowerment. They generate friction that slows the growth of new ideas and stymies innovation.

Even if you're not in a position to drive revolutionary change across the whole organization, your team can control many aspects of how you get your work done. Focusing on practices, we'll help you to work with your team to identify what you can change for yourselves next time around. Your team will be better equipped to avoid or fix such problems, whether they are seemingly small things like poorly designed meetings or ineffective report design, or larger issues like internal conflict or mismanagement of resources.

Sometimes, the contribution of reviewing team practices is to simply stop doing something that isn't working. If you've been preparing monthly newsletters that nobody reads, consider dropping the practice. Other times, you may need to label and then help each other to maintain a new habit, such as taking five minutes at the start of a weekly meeting for status updates. Effective teams consciously build in new ways of doing things—whether it is refining how emails are written, planning complex projects, or managing budgets—and discard unproductive practices.

So make the most of this opportunity to take into account *how* you did your work and pinpoint the ways in which your own practices contributed to your project's outcomes. Your goal is to figure out what to stop, change, or retain.

Build Better Team Habits

Draw on your entire team and tap into everyone's experience to uncover the potential to improve your team's habits. Insights into potential improvements come from people throughout the hierarchy, and those on the periphery often have as much to offer as insiders.

Plan an approach that will work for your team and time frame. You need not make this a long-drawn-out process. Many of the suggestions below can be completed quickly and informally.

A Proposed Plan for Identifying Team Improvements

Design a special team meeting to identify team processes that were successful and to determine what should be let go. Make this a different kind of session: hold it at an unusual time or in a new venue and use a novel design to convey that this meeting will be a break from the routine. You'll be looking back on the project in a critical but constructive way.

Signal your intent. Before, during, after your session, make clear that you'll keep all critical aspects of the discussion private. Creating a safe space for this conversation is key, since it's human nature to avoid examining the negative too closely. Set the stage to establish a shared commitment among participants to focus on the goals. Some teams use explicit terms to make this clear: "Leave your stripes at the door" is a common reminder for such review meetings in the military, for example. To underscore the importance of avoiding the blame game, you may want to set some ground rules that team members can refer to if the discussion gets off track.

Have your materials archive, project timeline, scorecard, and notes from the first stage of the embed process on hand.

To kick off the meeting, share the project scorecard and timeline. Prepare a handout, or sketch out the main points on a board at the start of the meeting, to direct attention to the aspects of team functioning that contributed or detracted from your collective work. If your team did exceptionally well in working with others and building stakeholder input and buy-in, what did you do to enable that? If the project's products and materials met a higher standard than usual, what aspects of team functioning do you credit? Similar thinking can be applied to areas where your team fell short of goals or expectations.

Elicit ideas from everyone: What should we remember to do next time? What should we never repeat? If your team is more formal, the meeting could begin with a review of the materials, like the project impact map you created in the launch phase, along with the timeline and your notes from the first step in the embedding process. You could then systematically review the project stage by stage.

If you have the freedom to do so, make this exercise creative and fun. You could create an anonymous list of best and worst moments. Or each person could complete colored sticky notes listing practices, habits, and activities that didn't or did help the project. Alternatively, before the meeting, each member could contribute a paragraph describing one thing he or she will never forget from the project.

Focus the next part of your discussion on things that will be useful in future projects. Review all ideas from the team to identify some candidate rules, practices, how-tos, or advice to remember. Then engage everyone in a joint decision-making process. A simple approach is to organize team practices into categories like *continue, add, drop*, and *change*.

Your candidate list should not be long. Focus your attention on a few key items that everyone can agree are important to remember. How will you make them stick? Once you've prioritized your list, spend some time as a team to identify how the proposed changes can be implemented. What will help your team cement a new habit? What will it take to drop an old process, and will you need to replace it with something else? Make sure you identify why the change is being proposed.

Finally, document and distribute to the team the changes you identify, in a format that works. Some teams make slogans and cartoons. One team we worked with selected a mascot—in the form of a stuffed toy—that symbolized their new commitment to learning. Some teams create checklists; others may create more formal memos or month-by-month guides for subsequent teams. An email with copies saved in your team's archive may suffice. The main idea is to document your shared thoughts about what changes will be most helpful to make in subsequent projects. This will provide a pathway back as you initiate the next project—you will know what the team wants to work toward and why.

If your team will continue to work together, embed the learning by agreeing to new habits that you'll preserve and old ones that you'll drop, along with team-generated ideas for how you'll remind each other of what's important. If your team will be changing for your next project, track a few lessons you want to take with you from one project experience to the next and share ideas about how to introduce, reinforce, and maintain needed changes in subsequent teams.

Enhance Project Methods

Along with the process changes that emerge from your examination of team habits you may also discover tools, methods, and approaches that contributed to the substance of your project work. Examine your action loop experiences to identify these. Did you figure out a new way to test early prototypes? Did you examine data using new tools? Did you try out a new technique for iterating on your initial ideas? Did you pinpoint areas of uncertainty within your project plans using a new method to prioritize where added knowledge would most benefit your team? Do you think your team decision-making method was innovative in some way? If so, make sure to capture these novel activities. Document what you did, what planning and inputs were necessary for each step, and how the results differed from standard practices used in the past. Your own team and others may benefit from the current review effort in the future.

As always, also be on the lookout for things you did that didn't help or that hurt your team results. You may identify specific areas of project implementation where your team went astray. Did you waste effort testing out ideas at too early a stage, or did you squander resources gathering more data than you needed?

You've now identified team lessons for action steps, managing the process, making decisions, testing ideas, generating new ones, and more, based on project activities that your team did well. By pinpointing those that are potentially reusable for future projects, you are equipping your team and yourself to learn from experience. You've also oriented yourself to look at your own professional practice by cultivating self-awareness and enabling action to strengthen your own management toolkit.

Update Your Own Management Practice

Even a quick review of your own experience can spur personal reflection, illuminating your values, revealing strengths and weaknesses, and alerting you to consider better ways of leading and managing in order to create the positive impact you desire to have in the world.

Set aside time to reflect about the experience of working with your team on the project, then line up some help to make sense of it.

Examine Your Own Experience

On the personal practice front, it's useful to ask the same questions of yourself that your team considered: What new habits should you keep, and what habits should be dropped? Your professional habits make up your personal management practice. They are the ways you manage and lead. Successful professionals build up and refine their own set of practices over time. As you change your habits, you are honing your personal practice of management.

Prepare by scanning meeting notes, your notebooks, and emails along with the timeline and project scorecard. Then gather feedback. Talk to team members, individually and together, to see what they make of the experience, and glean pointers from them about what works and what is not working for you as a manager and leader. Talk to higher-ups and external stakeholders too. The waning stages of a project can be an ideal time to get some honest feedback. This can be informal or done anonymously. Take care not to overlook this activity: not only could it provide critical professional development guidance, but it could also help you convey to others that you value improvement and even increase respect for you as a manager.

Don't assume that feedback will be only about areas for improvement. You will likely also learn of strengths you hadn't identified or valued before. Knowing what you are good at can help you line up assignments that leverage your strengths and compensate for your weaknesses. Too many managers we know are not ready with a professionally appropriate description of what they are excellent at doing along with a description of the supports and resources they require in order to leverage these abilities. If you are not ready with this accounting, you may miss a chance to line up the career-enabling job, assignment, or work arrangement you want and to negotiate for what you need.

Personal reflection and discussions with others about your strengths and weaknesses is often difficult to do in a work setting, where exploring emotional and social aspects of your experience can feel out of place. It may take some practice to calibrate these conversations so that you don't feel as if you're in a personal therapy session! Be easy on yourself if these conversations seem difficult. They will get easier. Remember that your aim is to become a more effective leader and manager, not to explain away your performance.

Setting aside some time to examine your personal practices has an interesting side effect: it helps you notice others. Soon you will find yourself observing the people around you, thinking about what works and what doesn't in their behavior in various settings. You have set the stage to learn from others by analyzing their management and leadership behaviors, picking and choosing what works for you, which is an invaluable skill.

We'd like to add one more piece of advice, based on the truth that you cannot be effective as a manager and leader without coming to an understanding of what it means to be helpful to others. Orienting your examination in this direction provides a fruitful approach to your discussions: ask others, and yourself, what you are doing that is truly helpful, and where your efforts fall short of helping. Later on, we will explore this helping orientation in more detail.

Develop a Personal Action Plan

Reflecting on and assessing your strengths, weaknesses, habits, and capabilities will be useful only if you act on what you learn. How do you translate the information you've worked so hard to gather into something actionable? Here are some specific tips:

1. First, make sure you've documented and summarized any feedback you've received and the self-reflection you've done. Categorize the things you've identified into three buckets: skills to develop; processes to establish; and habits to embrace.

2. Next, prioritize the areas you want to work on. Consider two levels: What most needs to change to give me the best chance of success in the future? And what am I poised to do and be successful at? Small wins matter!

3. Target what you want to embed in your personal management toolkit for your next project. Don't overwhelm yourself: consider a couple of things to make a top priority for future projects and at least one thing that you can immediately put into action. Develop and document one or two action steps for each area you identified that you can implement as part of your next project. For example, you may need to set aside ten minutes daily to do some personal planning. The vignette provided at the end of this chapter is a great example of how to cultivate a habit of reflection.

4. Let a trusted peer or mentor know what you intend to work on and how to increase your accountability to yourself and to enable feedback about your progress from this individual down the line.

5. Devise a method that will enable you to revisit your progress over time. Next time you consider your personal management practices, you'll see that you are on a path to ongoing improvement.

We've considered three different ways to draw practical lessons from your recent project experience. Whether it's by design or by chance, every project generates potentially valuable ideas for how to do things better. Yet too often, managers and teams fail to capitalize on these hard-earned insights. By identifying and planning for how to sustain improvements in how you work together, you can now enable subsequent projects to be more effective. Your effort will pay off handsomely as it helps to build a culture that supports high-functioning teams and avoid the process failures, ineffective activities, and counterproductive habits that contribute to subpar results in projects.

Many could benefit from these lessons. This leads us to the final step in the embed phase—how to take the learning from your project to a larger audience.

Share Your Discoveries

You now have a set of promising ideas that offer the potential for impact in your own future projects. But we think you could harness your learning for even broader benefit by putting in place a structure so that your learning can be of value to other teams, your organization, and even beyond. And only if you publish, disseminate, and share your results effectively will others be able to learn from it.

Hone Your Own Story

We'll begin by looking at how you develop your personal story of lessons learned.

For your next job interview or performance review, it's very possible you'll be asked what you learned from your latest project (particularly if it involved a failure!). Go beyond a pat explanation by drawing on your collected data, and make sure to include your own behavior and thinking as the focus of your inquiry. Are you now aware of a potential weakness or problem? Do you have inklings of a blind spot in your professional conduct? What will you be able to tell others that you now do as a result of this learning? Your answers could involve improving a skill or putting into practice a new personal habit to address your identified issue.

Telling a story about what you learned is also important for developing your ability to lead and manage others. Stories are the vehicle for persuading and enrolling others in your efforts and the way we explain why we do what we are doing.

Finally, as someone who manages and leads—or aspires to do so—within your organization, close the loop by thinking more globally about the organization. In the launch phase, you began by listing constraints and boundaries within which your project operated. You considered the attitudes and assumptions embedded in the organization's culture by asking such questions as: how is failure seen? How reflective are people? Is learning something that people value? The answers were initially your givens, but now that you are reflecting on your project, ask yourself what your responsibilities and options are for shifting the culture. Can any of these givens be changed in a way that would benefit the organization as a whole? How can you use your recent experience to support this change, and how do you line up your allies and the evidence to enable it?

One way to do this is to paint a picture for others of what the organization could look like as a result of the change. Come equipped with a plan for how to embed your recommended change across the organization. By making it easy for leadership to see the benefits of the change, while showing them how to accomplish it grounded in the evidence of your own experience, you're more likely to move the needle of your organization.

You can also encourage your team members to think in this way—to develop a story of their lessons learned, personal growth, and actions. And remember, it's important to give credit where credit is due, whether in your own story or the story of the project or the team.

But lessons learned go far beyond your own project story of what you have gained from a given experience. You have an opportunity for these lessons to be shared for wider influence.

Prepare for a Wider Impact

Your deliverables were designed for your project's clients—the people who asked for the results—along with the people you report to. There are also the ultimate beneficiaries of your work: customers, users, or other stakeholders that your client serves. You considered the value for them when assessing your project scorecard.

But your project offers much more than the formal products you deliver to your clients or bosses, and when these other learnings are included a far broader potential audience emerges.

Consider an even wider set of audiences to reach than those listed above. These are all the people who could benefit from learning of your work, both the content and the process.

Start by Identifying Who May Be Interested in Your Learning

Consider colleagues within your organization, collaborators in related projects, industry groups, social network communities, the profession.

Make a List of These Audiences

Your list of potential target groups may evolve as you consider your project though this lens. Allow for a little iteration and refinement in this process if you have the time do so.

Home In on the Most Relevant Audiences

Taking a quick look at your archive, timeline, project scorecard, and practice notes, ask: For the highest-scored areas of project output, impact, and practices, who else could most benefit from learning about what you did?

Identify the Information Most Likely to Be Useful to Others

You've already done the hard work of extracting the most valuable learning from all aspects of your work. Now the task is to mine a few of the best nuggets to share more widely. To pinpoint what to share, take a new look at the materials you have developed in the previous two steps in the embed process, but through the lens of the needs and interests of your target audiences.

Keep an Open Mind about What to Share

In considering candidate ideas and materials to share, look for what will appeal to many. For example, entrepreneur Elizabeth Yin, whose start-up experience you learned about in chapter 5, shared advice at industry meetings and conferences. Her talks could have addressed technical or market issues, but she reached a far wider audience by talking about her scrappy process for developing a successful product.

In general, the most useful products of your work include:

- What you have learned about the world (the market, for example), your organization, or the product
- New tools, methods, approaches, or practices that you used in your team to good effect

Review these products to prioritize what to share. Three considerations may help screen options:

1. Identify what products would be most helpful to others. Usually, this means looking at the potential for your work

to lead others to make different decisions or to change their behaviors. Given that goal, what information should you share to enable them to act differently? How much detail will they need, and how persuasive will the materials need to be? Reflecting on this question can help you to develop materials that are truly helpful to others and may lead you to reassess the top priority ideas to share. Your answer will also inform your design choices for how you will share your results. For each type of audience, note your ideas for the format and content that they would find most useful and determine how you will distribute these products.

2. As you select what's appropriate to share, think through the implications of making the information public. What are potential downsides? For instance, you may need to exclude proprietary client information where sharing could be restricted. It may be important to build appropriate buy-in from your boss, the client, and your team regarding your plan to share findings. Give credit where credit is due by crediting team members as appropriate, and respect privacy, reputation, and other aspects of disclosure as needed.

3. Make a realistic estimation of how much work you will need to invest in the existing materials to make them shareable. It's fine to scale back your ideas—the goal, after all, is for every step of the Fail Better process to be feasible. Sharing something small, but doing it well, is better than a grand but poorly planned approach.

Reaching a Wider Audience

Once you've targeted the most important things to share, there's just one more step: designing how to present your work and learning to others. Since you've already considered potential audiences for your project insights, you know that the results of your project likely have implications for the rest of your department and organization and perhaps for others—members of your profession, other communities in which you participate, and maybe even the general public.

Within your organization is an obvious place to start, but depending on your situation, you may target both internal and external audiences, select only one of these, or devise a two-part strategy to share internally first and then syndicate selected insights more widely.

Make sure to explore the internal supports at your disposal and to understand how your organization's culture and structure enable or hinder information sharing. Some organizations have internal sharing systems built into their structure; others are notoriously compartmentalized. How can you work within your current context?

If you have the opportunity to begin with just one step, we suggest you start small. Identify one other team for whom your work has relevancy and create a mechanism to share some specific and practical information. Consider hosting a team briefing or archiving your materials systematically and developing a quick materials guide for the other team.

When you can, go beyond your bottom-line conclusions. Aim to share a varied selection of the products of your work, including information on process, methods, and timeline. Consider how to make accessible the analysis behind the results, the content, and the tools, not just the conclusions, of your project. In every organization we've worked with, a vast amount of project work was not shared with others, and as a result many opportunities to benefit from past work were missed.

Make the most of any internal archiving and shared learning infrastructure your organization offers. But also know that knowledge management is most effective when it involves multiple channels. Contribute to specialized repositories and work with the staff, drawing on their collection of tools, but also take responsibility for thinking of how best to share specialized insights that you and the team developed. Of course, many organizations simply don't have the capacity to effectively document all learning. So, consider how to usefully share knowledge, insights, data, and work products. Luckily, today you have more options than ever to communicate creatively in tangible and digestible ways to make sure others benefit from your team's discoveries.

For many projects, combination approaches are most effective. Archive your materials, provide documentation, and complete all your reports and paperwork, but also plug into other methods of sharing, including via internal and external communication, so that people can find this material. Think of placing stories in newsletters, serving as an expert for press articles, or getting your blog posts syndicated on a site that many visit. Some other options include preparing a stand-alone memo that you can easily send out when someone asks for information; creating brief case studies detailing your project; making your expertise visible in internal and external networks, such as via a new tag line on your LinkedIn profile or email signature; or tweeting or otherwise sharing on social networks so that others can find your team's work.

Make sure team members' names and contact information are appended to the content you create, and develop your own plan for staying in touch with them as feedback or questions roll in. In many organizations, knowledge exchange takes place primarily through interpersonal contact, even when formal shared knowledge bases exist, so personal networks are crucially important. And remember to take into account what your client considers can be comfortably shared and to gain appropriate buy-in before distributing information related to your project.

In short, we're suggesting you think creatively about how to efficiently accomplish two things. For internal audiences, or more widely if your industry embraces open-source methods, provide access to a complete and organized set of your work products to others. For the highlights of your learning, share and syndicate selected results of your work by getting the story out in creative and compelling ways that encourage and enable behavior change. Recognizing that both aspects of sharing may be important can help you to choose the most impactful strategy.

And, finally, don't forget that broader audiences may benefit from your story. It turns out that stories are the way we learn from others, even in an age of databases of previously unimaginable breadth and depth. What is the story you will share to distill the results of the project?

To develop your project story, work with your team to analyze the experiences you had with the project. Perhaps the process itself is story-worthy? Or did you discover a new insight about the market, your product, or more broadly? Consider developing a case study that provides insight into the context, your desired outcomes, and the team's techniques, along with a sense of emerging insights and ultimate impact. An accompanying summary of lessons learned can help readers focus on actions or approaches they can implement in their own work.

Putting together a cogent and compelling story is not for self-serving publicity but for sharing something important you learned—perhaps via a failure along the way—with others. Know that having data and rigorous causal thinking behind your story helps to make it better. In fact, it's the only way to develop a story that is professionally valuable.

To Sum Up Our Embed Advice: Inspiration and Guidance

In the end, if you want to learn from every success and failure, you need to invest in a systematic process that can help overcome all-too-human predilections to explain things away with self-serving attributions, to brush things under the rug, to overreact to missteps, or to settle on simplistic accounts that fail to get at deeper truths. Equipping yourself with the right guidance can also help avoid the unproductive trap of ineffective rumination and pointless recrimination. In this chapter, we aimed to guide your review of experience with an eye to the future and a focus on the practical. To do this, we've focused on a simple question: *What are the key insights and discoveries you think will be most useful to improve behavior or thinking going forward?*

For a variety of reasons, without the right support, it's challenging to examine your experience in situations where you perceive a level of failure to have occurred. Social barriers, both organizational and psychological, along with our own cognitive hardwiring, discourage reporting and analyzing failure, just as technical barriers such as system complexity and causal ambiguity inhibit recognizing failure and accounting for it effectively.

Preparation is part of the solution. In the launch and action phases of your project, we equipped you for this culminating moment when you have the opportunity to learn from your experience. Your project map, iterative action testing, and documentation provide a powerful set of tools for improving the quality of your insights from each project. You've also invested in enabling a team culture that values learning and testing to support the team's identification of where things may be going wrong before catastrophic failure occurs.

Now you've worked through a carefully designed process to extract the lessons of your experience, making sure you're critically analyzing your project and then planning exactly how to turn the insights into practice.

Sharing the resulting discoveries could help advance your practice as a professional and manager, help your team members to develop, and enable improvement for your organization, your profession, or even more widely. It encourages a learning culture and builds a reputation for you and your team members as potential collaborators, experts, and visionaries. You are looking beyond yourselves to the strategic ways that information can improve others' work while opening yourself for increased opportunity. Helping others learn from and build on what you've discovered strengthens your chances of achieving a higher level of impact. The value of these contributions is multiplied in resource-constrained environments where meaningful professional development is hard to come by for many managers. By focusing not just on results but also on how your processes, skills, capabilities, and habits got you there, you can guide your own development and strengthen the development of your team.

All the leaders we've met tell us they value learning from experience. But few people are able to develop on their own the open-minded orientation, disciplined practices, and comprehensive approach needed to make the most of the learning that arises in the course of their everyday work on projects. We've argued that whether your project is an unequivocal failure, an unabashed success, or occupies a more complicated place in between, the knowledge and experience it yields can enrich your organization's learning and shore up your own skills and wisdom, once you adopt the approach we've laid out in chapters 4, 5, and 6.

From here, we'll look at considerations that can take your application of Fail Better to the next level and further hone your orientation to and ability to help others learn through their experiences. In the end, what we aim to enable is nothing short of a transformation in how we learn at work, one project at a time.

REAL-WORLD INSPIRATION

Venture Investor Eric Hjerpe Reflects on His Decisions and Results

A venture investor must make decisions with scant information. To many, it seems that sheer luck, at least early on, determines a VC's ratio of wins to losses. Eventually, the veterans will tell you, instinct honed by experience and accumulated wisdom comes into play. Few would agree that there's a set formula for how to approach opportunities. And all would agree that even on a good day, every venture portfolio includes quite a few items in the "draw" column with plenty more in the "loss" column.

Failure is inevitable. And it's visible—the companies a VC invests in are rarely a secret. Their subsequent performance in the market is evident to observers. Yet ability to shape performance is limited: no matter how deep a VC's pockets may be and how wise her advice, results are influenced by forces beyond her direct control. Shifting economic conditions, leaps in technology, and fickle markets all come in to play. Add in the norm of long, meeting-filled days, together with an individualistic sink-or-swim approach to decision making and constant pressure to make the right call (or at least, to do so more often than your competitors)—VCs must survive in contexts that offer little prospect for the rapid and unambiguous feedback and supportive environment that optimize learning.

Yet, given the lack of formal rules and universal methods for making investment decisions, learning is vital for survival and success.

Disciplined Approach to Learning from Experience

In 2007, Eric Hjerpe was a seasoned investor.[2] As a partner at Atlas Venture, he'd seen high-tech start-ups burst onto the scene, then progress—or fail—though developments that played out over the course of months or years. The most visible type of decisions he made were which companies to invest in and which to pass on. But these choices represented only a small fraction of his day-to-day choices.

Like other VC investors, he also shaped the trajectories of his investee companies by weighing in on key decisions. Hjerpe could determine the hiring (and letting go) of key personnel, including

CEOs. He could influence a nascent firm's direction by selecting markets, design options, pricing, and more. His role offered vast scope for him to get involved with the leadership, management, and operations of new companies. And nowhere in his job description did it say exactly how involved he should be in the companies he worked with.

Every day, he participated in key entry, exit, and strategy choices. Often, he turned down opportunities. Sometimes he wrestled with choosing whether to change or retain top management. He found himself drawing on his early career experience in managing IT projects, not just for the technical orientation essential to his current work, but also in his personal professional practices. These included gathering data assiduously and managing his time carefully. And amid the hectic rush of back-to-back meetings, conference calls, and industry events, he did one thing that none of his colleagues did: at regular intervals, weekly or monthly, he devoted an hour to writing and reflecting. It was an hour he could have spent squeezing in more meetings, yet he was vigilant in protecting this time.

An Hour Well-Spent

Hjerpe used his hour carefully. First, he wrote a memo to himself, systematically documenting the choices he had been making, including decisions to do nothing or hold course. Each time, he jotted down his rationale and listed the evidence backing up his analysis. He noted areas of uncertainty and conflicting arguments and data. He added a quick summary of his doubts. And then he'd save the document. For the remainder of his hour, he would open up an old file to review his notes for a past decision. Was he right in his overall approach back then? Did he make the right call, given what he knew? Sometimes the reflections centered on personnel decisions; other times, he examined a choice to turn down or delay taking an investment opportunity. In reviewing this past choice, he didn't rely only on his own thoughts but also drew on information he'd gathered since that decision was made. He used the time to iterate on his own decision-making methods, to ferret out weaknesses in this thinking, and to derive new rules of thumb to test out the next time he came to a comparable situation.

As part of this personal discipline, Hjerpe would also schedule appointments for himself to revisit his notes from the day, ensuring that he was selecting times to reflect on his recent decisions that were be far enough in the future to reveal something of the outcome, yet close enough to enable him to explore potential connections in how today's decisions could be linked to the outcomes he hoped to observe. He'd schedule multiple review sessions at different points in time, if he felt that would help.

His own practices, Hjerpe felt, enabled him to learn from his own experience in a way that would not have otherwise been possible. He didn't always have an entire team to collaborate with on all aspects of his decisions. In its place, he embedded a personal habit for revealing, investigating, and generating improvements in how he did his work.

How the Fail Better Approach Applies

Few managers, VCs or not, invest in such disciplined self-reflection and analysis of key decisions and results. It's easy to chip away at protected personal time by squeezing in one more thing, whether a conference call or an end-of-day errand. Hjerpe's experience illustrates the payoffs of defending such personal practices. He could trace improvements in his professional decision-making to his reflection habit, and he felt he was more stimulated by his job than he would otherwise have been. Years later, he was still continuing his practice of writing and examining his memos to himself, and attributed his success on the job, in part, to this personal habit. It also made daily work more engaging to him, fueling his intellectual curiosity and allowing him to connect disparate types of data from his professional experience in new ways.

In 2008 Hjerpe joined Kepha Partners, where he and two partners raised $185 million, thanks in part to his track record along with his contributions to the partnership's distinctive framework for understanding and guiding software firms. We can learn from his discipline and connect his efforts to the Fail Better approach for embedding what you learn from your project.

Examine your results. Hjerpe viewed his documentation and review efforts as an investment in systematically learning from his work in a complex and constantly changing domain. He was meticulous in maintaining his habit, which in turn allowed him to iteratively hone his decision-making skills, which he regarded as the most important ingredient for successful venture investing.

Enhance your practices. Hjerpe didn't just review his notes. He actively applied the insights he gleaned from reflecting on their implications to become more skilled and perceptive. In essence, he built new personal habits that enabled him to better replicate successes and avoid failed courses of action. He also learned more about how and when he should involve himself in the management decisions of a new venture and formulated and tested new ideas for identifying and supporting nascent software companies. In short, he drove his own professional development through one simple habit.

Share your discoveries. Like his colleagues, Hjerpe often worked as a lone wolf, yet over the years he realized that the results of his disciplined practice had implications for others within and outside of his field. He created opportunities to share his learning with others as a Techstars mentor and in the 12 × 12 initiative, a collaboration for identifying, enabling, and mentoring next-generation technology entrepreneurs.[3] The father of four, he applied the same methods to reflect on his own parenting and to serve as an example for his children.

Hjerpe developed a personal practice for gleaning actionable insights from his experience by reflecting on his own decisions and results. This, in turn, enabled him to improve his investment approach and grow in both professional and personal domains. That a fast-moving venture investor found value in practices designed to identify and embed learning demonstrates some of the benefits our approach can offer.

At-a-Glance Guidance for Embedding the Learning from Your Project

We turn now to the practical, with a set of tools to aid your project launch. Guiding questions help you think through key issues that cut across domains. To help you manage things, we also provide a comprehensive list of the products you will create if you follow every launch step we've described. And a comprehensive trio of Fail Better checklists gathers the step-by-step details.

Guiding Thought Questions

Find and preserve your new insights, cement new practices, and develop the story about what you've learned from your project to make the most of your efforts, now and in the future. To inspire your thinking, here are some overarching questions:

- ❑ **Protected time.** How will you build in time at the end of your project to examine your experience and pull out key lessons?
- ❑ **Tracking outcomes.** How will you figure out if your project has the eventual benefits you sought at the outset?
- ❑ **New practices.** What team practices and personal habits will you retain and cultivate?

- ❑ **Discovery sharing.** What are two to three ways you can share the findings of your project to benefit others in your organization and beyond?

Fail Better Process Products

Here is a list of Fail Better documents you may produce as you move through the steps. Not every team will create every document; in some cases, our advice may simply prompt a discussion or reflection. Choose the level of documentation that works for you.

- ❑ An archive of the materials your team created throughout the project
- ❑ A one-page timeline of project stages, inflection points, major efforts, and discoveries
- ❑ A one-page project scorecard, assessing project outputs, team development, project impact, and underlying assumptions and logic
- ❑ A brief plan for monitoring the end result of your project's impact over time
- ❑ A short list of team habits and practices to retain (if applicable, also those to change or drop)
- ❑ Documentation of novel project methods, such as testing approaches
- ❑ A personal action plan to build on the strengths and tackle the weaknesses you discovered in the project
- ❑ Your personal project story, capturing lessons you learned, skills you developed, ways that you grew as a manager, and how you shaped the project

- ❑ A prioritized list of audiences with which you can share some of the work and learning from your project
- ❑ Materials you choose to syndicate to benefit others

Implementation Checklists to Embed the Learning in Fail Better Mode

The following checklists are designed to help you implement step-by-step.

Fail Better Checklist #7: Examine Your Results

Your project offers second-order benefits beyond the deliverables you've produced. To identify what you learned along the way, begin with what you delivered: the product, report, presentation, analysis, and/or service your project provided, along with notes, materials, project plans, and drafts.

1. Assemble the project archive:
   - ❑ Gather a representative selection of your team's work materials.
   - ❑ Time-stamp each item so you can recreate how the project progressed.
   - ❑ Create and organize an archive of the selected materials.
   - ❑ Document what's in the archive and how it's organized so others can navigate and access materials at a later date.
2. Develop a project history timeline:
   - ❑ Create a project timeline that maps steps, events, and project stages, giving the latter names that are meaningful for your team.

- [ ] Analyze the timeline to locate moments when surprises emerged, along with transitions and shifts. Analyze deviations from plans.

3. Assess project results to create a project scorecard that systematically assesses your accomplishments. Document the following four items on a one-page summary that lists key examples and scores each area:

   - [ ] Assess the quality of team's work products and other project deliverables in relation to the cost of producing them, using your own take along with other perspectives. Assign a rough score to the outputs.
   - [ ] Examine developments in skills, capabilities, professional development, relationships, as well as team capacities and assets. Include improvements along with drawbacks, and give yourselves an overall grade.
   - [ ] Form a provisional assessment of your impact on the problem or opportunity that your project aimed to address, keeping in mind the situation or people in your problem statement.
   - [ ] Identify one or two ways you can assess impact of the work over time.
   - [ ] Critique your logic and assumptions underlying the project's rationale, referring to your initial project impact map and where you ended up. Give a score that reflects the accuracy of your logic along with the benefits of lessons learned from inaccuracies.
   - [ ] Once the scorecard is complete, review the four domains together to guide your next step.

Fail Better Checklist #8: Enhance Your Practices

Taking into account the quality of your project's four performance dimensions, this checklist will help you identify the practices that contributed to your outcomes. Your goal is to figure out what to change, what to add, and what to retain.

1. Build better team habits:

   - ❑ Design a special team meeting to assess team processes.
   - ❑ Review your timeline and scorecard with the team to set the stage.
   - ❑ Working as a team, list the habits or practices to retain and to discard. Identify other practices that could be helpful to try in the future to remedy a negative experience in the current project.
   - ❑ Document the list of retain/add/drop/change items and share it with the team. Determine an action plan for how the team can be accountable to the list.

2. Enhance project methods:

   - ❑ Identify specific tools or methods that helped or hindered project results. This may be a test that was particularly illuminating or a way of sharing data.
   - ❑ Determine and document which methods you would like to try again or expand in future projects and which you want to avoid due to their poor outcomes.

3. Update your own management practice:

   - ❑ Examine your own experience and personal performance by asking the same questions—what habits and practices did you engage in as manager that should be retained or dropped? Supplement your own reflection with feedback from others.

- ❑ Select your top priorities by considering what's most needed along with what's most feasible.
- ❑ Create your own action plan that includes specific steps and a plan for assessing if you've improved in a specific area. Share your action plan with a mentor or trusted peer who can help keep you accountable to your goals.

Fail Better Checklist #9: Share Your Discoveries

Identify project discoveries to share that will benefit your career, your team, your organization, and a wider audience.

1. Hone your story:
   - ❑ Review your role in the project outcomes and craft a story about what you brought to the project, what you accomplished, and what you've gained and learned in completing the work.
   - ❑ Whether you see your project as a success, a failure, or something in between, you're in the driver's seat when it comes to telling your story. Take ownership of it.
2. Prepare for wider impact:
   - ❑ Identify audiences that you may want to reach.
   - ❑ Prioritize the list based on who is likely to find your results relevant and useful.
   - ❑ Determine what is most appropriate to share. Consider process improvements, data collection methods, team

habits, key findings, among others. Screen based on three considerations: potential helpfulness, appropriateness for sharing, and ease of sharing.

3. Reach a wider audience by sharing your work:

- ❑ Make the most of internal archiving and information sharing networks within your organization.
- ❑ Develop a varied selection of products that capture process and results, not just bottom-line conclusions but how you did your work.
- ❑ Share results in a way that captures the attention and imagination of the intended audience (storytelling is often one of the most effective ways).
- ❑ Consider other methods of disseminating: newsletters, blogs, panels, conferences, white papers, staff meetings, and memos, among others. Vary your approach for different learning styles and needs.

PART III

Moving from Ideas to Practice

Part Three equips you to foster a mind-set for implementation, understand the method's underpinnings so you can customize it, and become inspired by innovators who have taken on some of the world's toughest problems.

Cultivate your mind-set to overcome challenges. To help you manage your own implementation journey, draw on our ideas to:

- Adopt practices and an orientation that are truly helpful
- Talk honestly—and with nuance—about failures
- Manage time frames wisely, keeping potential time-related traps in mind
- Build resilience for the ups and downs to come

Understand the foundations. Learn about the design-for-learning principles behind the method to:

- Design calibrated challenges
- Provide freedom and safety to explore and fail
- Enable meaningful feedback throughout the project

Learn from a frugal innovator. An in-depth look at Bangladesh-based BRAC shows that clear goals and a disciplined and responsive approach enables people starting from even the most modest beginnings in resource-constrained settings to create global change.

Help make the world a better place. To discover how the Fail Better approach could help you take on even the most complex challenges, take a look at an inspiring example from the present and an inspiration from the past.

Get started today. Ready yourself for the work—and rewards—that lie ahead with our parting advice.

CHAPTER 7

Developing Your Mind-Set for Implementation

So far, you've seen lots of advice about steps to take. This is an ideal moment to consider how you'll implement them. If you're ready to swing into action, you face some decisions. Now that you've seen the entire set of Fail Better activities, you are equipped with suggestions, examples, guiding questions, and checklists. You'll be choosing what to try first. But there's something else you need to do: cultivate your own Fail Better mind-set.

Your workplace interactions, activities, and decisions are shaped by your mind-set—how you approach difficult conversations, select which battles to fight, and make tough trade-offs. Every action you take reveals what you think is important and what you are willing to let slide, among other things. Your mind-set guides how you make sense of your experiences.

In your implementation journey, you'll encounter both success and difficulty. Some steps will be easy to carry out; others will reveal unexpected challenges. To guide how you handle these, it's helpful to cultivate a conscious approach to implementation. The idea of a mind-set may seem like an abstraction, but we'll be taking a practical view here, driven by our work with successful implementers. By identifying how you will handle potential challenges ahead of time, you can be ready to effectively address any that you encounter.

This isn't an area where we can tell you exactly what do to. Nor would we want to. You've accumulated experience and developed your own unique wisdom from the challenges you've already weathered. You have much to tap into! But there are some specific aspects of a mind-set for failing better that are worth considering as you set out to implement the method.

This chapter gathers ideas to inform your thinking in several domains:

- Helpfulness, compassion, and supportive management
- The ability to talk about failures with courage, honesty, and nuance
- Managing time frames and shifts in projects, with an eye to potential traps
- Resilience for the journey

To help you cultivate the perspective that will aid your efforts to come, we link ideas in these domains to specific aspects of the Fail Better mind-set that we think will be most helpful to you.

By drawing on findings from recent studies to support our discussion, we explain how the ideas are related to what we know about human behavior and organizational life. For each idea, we offer useful advice, either our own suggestions for how to incorporate supportive practices or links to practical guides you can find online or in books.

With this aim in mind, our advice is designed to help you identify and develop your own mind-set for success in implementing the Fail Better method. We're not going to be talking about what might go wrong. Nor will we provide you with a step-by-step recipe for cultivating the right perspective. Instead, we'll be sharing ideas to support your doing things the right way in the journey to come—ideas that we hope you find inspiring. Use the advice to refine your own personal principles and approaches, and you'll be equipped to make these ideas a reality.

As you consider the concepts, use what's helpful and set aside for later anything that seems less relevant now. If you'd like to learn more about the research and practice related to an idea you find interesting, look for additional information in the Notes section at the end of the book. Dip into any of this chapter's sections, and feel free to move on if the ideas don't resonate at the moment.

At the end, we hope to help you build on your personal strengths. As a leader, manager, or change agent aiming to create improvement and innovation within your organization, you'll do better if you can clarify for yourself the ideas you will build on and defend throughout the implementation journey.

Helpfulness

How do you help others? The answer may seem obvious, but if you examine what it takes to be truly helpful, you may discover that it's more nuanced than you realize.

Consider the definition of *helping*: enabling others to better accomplish something. Working as a team means helping each other. In fact, by many definitions, that is the quality that defines a true team. If team members' efforts were not interrelated and mutually supportive, there would be no reason to operate as a team—work could simply be broken up into separate parts. Teamwork is essential for tackling *simultaneous interdependency* (when team members are working at the same time on things that affect each other's work) and *sequential interdependency* (when earlier work affects subsequent work).

In a successful team, interdependence isn't merely task-related; it's also psychic. And, as we'll see, the consequences go beyond the purely psychological.

For a team to gel, everyone has to both give and receive assistance on an ongoing basis. This give-and-take is the stuff of relationships. Helping is part of the social glue that connects team members. In every successful team, depending on the task at hand, team members shift roles from helper to recipient and back.

Unfortunately, in many teams, members quickly settle into fixed roles that reinforce a set hierarchy, and roles of provider and recipient of help rarely shift. There are two downsides to this trap: lost opportunities for both individuals and the team as a whole to develop, and lackluster project results.

To explain how this happens, Ed Schein, an expert on process consultation, places the act of helping at the center of work life.[1] Because asking for or getting help triggers a feeling of vulnerability for the person being helped, individuals giving the help need to select their approach carefully to enable the person they're helping—whom Schein labels the *client*—to actually benefit from the interaction. Effective help, Schein tells us, requires a sense of equity in the helping relationship. Too much of a one-up, one-down feeling blocks open interaction. Flawed helping relationships result in poor information flow, sub-par teamwork, and lower satisfaction.

Here's the mind-set question: *How will you approach the act of giving and getting help?*

Modes of Helping

Schein offers a typology to guide your thinking. You could be an *expert* who provides information or advice to others. Most people assume this is what helping is about: sharing knowledge or skills that the other person needs. A *doctor* role adds diagnosis to the interaction: identify what's wrong and then offer the solution or cure. If you've worked in a business consulting relationship, this may sound familiar: the doctor-style consultant analyzes data, identifies and classifies the problems and then presents specific recommendations to the client. A third option is to act as *process consultant*: at the beginning of the interaction, focus first on building your understanding by investing in what Schein calls *humble inquiry*. This form of helping goes deeper than delivering an expert response to an overt question. In humble inquiry mode, you ask what kind of help would be useful, why it is sought, and how it could be most effective. As a result, you can avoid some common traps. For example, instead of reinforcing social status differentials, this process evens out the score. Both sides of the interaction learn more, including highly useful insight into what help is needed.

How to Use Humble Inquiry

In an interdependent team, members—and especially leaders—need to draw on humble inquiry approaches. Team members need to cultivate both helping and client roles in order for the team as a whole to develop in the course of their project. An excellent point at which to shift away from more familiar expert and doctor roles is when your team first comes together or is joined by a new member or group. Avoid the tendency to jump into planning, tell people what to do, or move into problem-solving mode, and you'll cut the chances that you are focusing on the wrong problem or delivering help that misses expectations or fails to be taken up. Instead, to understand the other party's interests and situation, take time to *inquire*.

To equip yourself for the task, develop your own repertoire of inquiry skills. The methods you use will depend on the situation. At some points, ask simple, direct questions to learn the other's view of the situation. For example, you could ask the other person to describe the problem. To truly listen at this early stage, you may have to override your tendency to assume you already know what is needed and resist the urge to offer suggestions. Later in the helping process, as you learn more, shift your inquiry style to a more focused exploration of underlying causes and effects; for instance, by probing the other's attitudes and beliefs and seeking to understand how and why things are the way they are. Later, it may be appropriate at times for your inquiry to take a confrontational turn and push for the other to think about alternative courses of action—including what they did not consider.

Compassion

To be willing to accept smart failures—your own or others'—you need to identify, explore, and make sense of failures in ways that are compassionate: empathetic, nonshaming, and kind. It's difficult to imagine an effective dialogue about a failure taking place without compassion. Compassion is also critical in both giving and seeking constructive, helpful, but honest feedback. It shores up your ability to have difficult conversations.

Compassion has an important role to play in the workplace. Researchers are amassing evidence showing that compassion and other qualities that support dignity, psychological safety, and positive work experiences need not be at odds with the pursuit of excellence. To explain the role of compassion, let's take a quick look at emerging findings relating compassion, positive work environments, and team performance.

Strong work relationships that involve mutual positive regard and the capacity to handle forceful emotions, both negative and positive, can help your team to face challenges and constraints. We're learning that teams built on high-quality connections are better at drawing on varied resources and at enabling their members' professional growth.

Our specific advice for shoring up team relationships includes infusing positive interactions into team meetings, making everyone on the team aware of each member's strengths, and facilitating downward and lateral communication. Clear and frequent communication that incorporates problem solving in nonjudgmental and mutually beneficial ways also enhances team performance. There's evidence that showing compassion by visibly putting others in front of yourself can enhance work interactions.[2]

Cultivate Your Own Compassion

Watch others around you: how do they identify mistakes, missteps, and oversights without sapping morale or undermining themselves or others? Select practices to borrow, pinpoint the traps you will avoid, and cultivate skills that foster compassion. Doing so will help you lead more effectively with the Fail Better method.

You can also work on its foundations on your own. Increasing your mindfulness could drive awareness and acceptance of your own and others' emotions, including in the moment. *Loving-kindness*, a special type of meditation that builds warmth and caring for yourself and others, may increase compassion and help you better understand others' emotions.[3]

Supportive Management Practices

The right kind of managerial help makes work meaningful for team members. The study of successful work teams reveals some practical insights, including in the psychosocial domain. In the midst of a challenging project, the best team managers provide or facilitate interpersonal support, encouragement, and emotional comfort, inputs that are truly helpful to the team. These supports help to build members' sense of belonging, fulfilling a basic human need for affiliation, a key ingredient for a positive experience at work. In turn, productivity and project results benefit. Teresa Amabile and Steven Kramer found in a longitudinal study of dozens of teams in varied organizations that successful managers get more out of their staff by enabling their team members to create good inner work lives.[4]

Amabile and Kramer offer excellent advice for managers to help teams carry out their project work: visibly, and repeatedly, remove obstacles that stand in the way of team members' work; keep in constant touch with every aspect of the work being carried out, making sure to check in with team members and sharing with everyone what you learn; and every day, deduce or ask what kind of help is needed and do what would be most valuable for the team.[5]

These suggestions require managers and leaders to be plugged in to the team and stay connected both informally and formally with all the work streams involved in the project. For you to be informed on what's happening with the team, you need to understand the details of their work at a level that allows you to figure out what would be most helpful at each step. Of course it does not mean interfering or micromanaging. As Amabile and Kramer put it, focus on checking *in*, not checking *up*.[6]

Then, to figure out how to help, diagnose what's most needed and customize your intervention. You'll need a repertoire of interventions for removing obstacles, bolstering the team, and in other ways directly enabling effective work. Cultivate these capacities by observing others, trying out your own approaches, and asking your team for feedback on what's most helpful.

Talking about Failures as They Happen

Perhaps the most revolutionary aspect of Fail Better involves presenting and analyzing failures in a professionally appropriate way. Looking at missteps and mistakes analytically, as they happen, can feel unnatural and go against the grain of your organization's culture.

Talking about what went wrong in the thick of a project is an essential requirement for learning from smart failures while preventing ineffective ones. Even as the change agents we studied aimed to do this, we saw how difficult it was to present and defend failures as they happened within the organization—especially in cases when there was not just one failure but several. Despite the lip service offered to the notion that failure is instructive and necessary, we live in a culture that does not look kindly on failure—at any scale, with any adjective in front of it. The norms and culture of your organization may layer on negative implications of apparent failures, making them difficult to own up to, share, and analyze effectively. This underscores the need for you to develop your own principled stance regarding smart failures and to reiterate and reinforce your principles in varied ways, both formally and informally. You'll need to do this in interactions with your peers, your subordinates, and your bosses, maybe even with external partners, customers, and stakeholders. Consistency in your approach matters. You'll also need a measure of courage to do this.

To defend the process, you'll need to frame and present instructive failures so that others understand the value of outcomes that may appear to be undesirable. Because you will need to lead by example for this culture change, along with courage, you're likely to need your advocacy, sense-giving, and persuasion skills to make the case for the better ultimate result while guarding against the perception that your efforts are self-serving attempts at *impression management*—that is, controlling how information is presented to influence how others perceive you or your behavior.

The steps in our method are designed help you avoid the appearance of impression management by guiding you to set up each risky activity with a clear prediction of what could happen and a discussion of the value of disconfirmation, both of which establish the backdrop against which a failure can be presented. Chapters 4 and 5 provide you with a framework for showing why and how a given failure is justified in terms of the overall project aims and the specific course of action undertaken in the action step. Documenting your work as you go and keeping key stakeholders in the loop, along the way, can also help avoid the appearance of after-the-fact self-justification. Yet this won't mean it's easy.

Owning Up to Failures That Fall Short

Another crucial requirement is the courage to identify the "bad failures." You'll need to call it when a failure falls short of the Fail Better criteria and should *not* be explained away as a necessary, smart failure. If it's the result of poor planning, execution, or analysis, you need to own up to that or else risk cynicism. Not every failure is worthwhile, and many—perhaps most of those that currently happen—should not be lauded. Even if Fail Better reduces the number of undesirable failures, you're likely to still create some. You will need to be prepared to handle these failures while defending the instructive ones.

Living with Ambiguity in Labeling Successes and Failures

We're reminded of a Shakespearean quote at this point. Reflecting on his experience, Hamlet tells us that "There is nothing either good or bad, but thinking makes it so." These musings prompt a few words of big-picture advice: *What seems like a failure in one frame of reference can look like success when viewed through a different lens, and vice versa.*

One issue to contend with is the labeling itself. A given action step involving a test, experiment, or innovation may be called a failure if its results don't support your initial hypothesis. But an apparently negative result can expose important limitations in your thinking. We'd call it a success if it advances your knowledge and improves the impact of your overall project.

And at the end of a project, your results may reveal that the value of the idea driving your entire project is not borne out by your results. You may conclude that the new product, process, or material you aimed to develop will not work in practice and the work should go no further. As a result, your organization will abandon this course of action. That can feel a lot like failure, even if for the organization as a whole, the exit decision delivers real value.

A related challenge is the human tendency to assess the quality of a decision by its outcome. Yet when uncertainty is involved, you cannot look at the result alone to establish if the decision was the right one. Instead, you need to look at whether the choice was warranted when it was undertaken and to weigh the full set of costs and benefits, including insights and learning, that flow from the action you decided to take. Here, too, the term *failure* is a misnomer, but that may be how the result comes to be known.

So, adding some nuance to the notion of failure, along with a commitment to actively communicating, is part of the work to be done. Taking on our approach may require you to analyze and present the experience of an apparent failure with your team, with stakeholders both in your organization and outside it, and even in how you talk to yourself about your experience. This act of framing and giving interpretation to results is something you'll be called on to do in a variety of situations.

Managing Time Frames

Here's an idea you may have overlooked in your previous thinking about harnessing failure: the importance of managing time frames. Cultivating an awareness of time scales, temporal factors, and trade-offs between the short term and the long term can help your project in many ways.

We discovered that project teams tend to treat time lines as given until they can't avoid admitting that they will be late. Often, teams fail to add the critical activities to their work plans that will reveal earlier in the process if they are on the wrong track—in part, we suspect, because they are not equipped to renegotiate time frames if they uncover midcourse feedback that necessitates changes in plans. Let's look at the dangers of approaching your project with the wrong time horizon.

If your project aims to innovate or improve, you will encounter trade-offs between the short run and the longer term. Here's an example. Improvement projects are notorious for delivering lower-quality results in the short run, even if they lead to eventual performance improvement.[7] The worse-before-better phenomenon is an unavoidable consequence of the extra work that improvement entails: people are gathering data, solving problems, and running experiments while the regular work of the organization goes on. During this period, performance often falls. If you are guided only by performance indications, you may end up pulling the plug too soon, before you reach the payoff of all your hard work.

A similar danger plagues new product development. Innovations may fail in early market tests because adoption plays out more slowly than imagined—and they get written off too soon. What if Apple Computer had stuck with the Newton, an early version of a portable tablet that it discontinued in the 1990s? The same phenomenon holds for the diffusion of new ideas and practices. It took decades upon decades for simple insights, such as the discovery that Vitamin C prevents scurvy or that a sugar-saline solution can prevent children from dying of diarrhea, to spread widely. If you were to assess either of these ideas by their early uptake, you might conclude that they were not effective, but you'd be wrong.

In such cases, projects are doomed because they are given insufficient time to generate useful results. The innovations they could have yielded are abandoned prematurely.

In other cases, projects go on far too long and should have been canceled weeks—or even years—before they finally end. For example, negative aspects of the promising new idea you're developing may surface only later in time, and you could be making the wrong call if you assess project results too soon. New products and technology innovations often fall into this trap. Many an organization has invested enormous effort in new portals, sites, and databases that initially appear to work well, only to discover that the intended audiences find the new sites too cumbersome to use routinely. In other cases, the team developing a new product becomes so invested in it that they fend off pressures to pull the plug, in effect pushing for an overly long time frame for their project. This phenomenon is so common that it has been given a name: the *escalating commitment trap.* We'll discuss it in more detail a bit later.

First, a word about why it's difficult to account for temporal factors.

Why It's Difficult to Choose the Right Time Horizon

Some projects end too soon and others go on too long. The nature of these two extremes means that we can more easily find examples of the projects that went on too long. After all, these projects tend to be more noticeable since they've been around longer. It's harder to discern, after the fact, if you pulled the plug on a promising project too soon. Because those projects ended quickly, they are not visible. And an opportunity missed is difficult to see. If people are more concerned about projects being too long instead of too short, they may systematically allocate too little time to novel projects.

In many ways, the tension between these failure modes provides the motivation for Fail Better: we need a systematic method for managing our innovation projects because what looks like a failure at one time scale could actually be a success at another, if you manage things well. Or, it could go the other way: you may scrape together some quick apparent wins and declare an early victory, yet later discover that things are actually worse, when negative side effects subsequently emerge. It all hinges on the time horizon you select for your assessment.

Other Challenges in Thinking about Time

Why do we get timing wrong so often? There are some consistent explanations for why it is difficult to appropriately factor temporal effects into thinking and planning. As we showed in chapter 1, people tend to underestimate the effects of nonlinear rates of change. Consequently, they are blindsided by effects that appear to come out of nowhere but are actually the result of compounding processes playing out within the system. A similar tendency is at work when people assume that the future will be similar to the recent past: the normal human tendency is to guess that the future will continue current trends. If you imagine trajectories of change over time on a graph, the equivalent of this mental shortcut is to simply draw a straight line that projects ahead based only on the last few points in time. For anything that's cyclical or exponentially growing or declining, this heuristic ensures that you will at some point be wrong—and that you will be dead wrong at those crux moments when rates of change are greatest (peaks and troughs in cyclical markets, for example).

Knowing that your prediction of rates of change could be wrong is the first step. If you suspect that there are potentially complex temporal issues shaping your project's tests and forecasts, factor an investigation of patterns of behavior and trends into your project plans. If your early tests show low uptake by consumers, pay attention not only to the number of adopters but also to the trends underlying their growth, looking for evidence of nonlinear effects. A snowball effect could accelerate uptake down the road, for example. If you suspect that there are interacting and compounding factors that shape an aspect of your project results, consider gathering more data, running longer tests, or bringing in experts to help untangle interactions and form better predictions.

In other words, length of project is not the only temporal factor to manage. Three important time frame considerations come in to play for many projects.

- First, there's the pacing of the project itself. Is it moving at the right speed—one that matches the needs of the market or the community you are serving: fast enough to capitalize on developments, yet with sufficient time and resources allocated to enable the right quality of results?
- Is your project's time frame linked to timing that's important within the organization, such as budgeting, model release, or other cycles that shape decision making? If your project timing is off-kilter with your organization's pacing, you may miss valuable opportunities simply because your milestones don't line up with cycles of attention or resource allocation. Awareness of organizational rhythms can help you line up your project's resource requests, discussions of midpoint results, and final deliverables with opportunities when others in the organization are ready to engage. Experts call this idea *entrainment*.
- Third, as we've already seen, there's the time horizon you select for assessment, both within your project for individual tests carried out, and for the project as a whole. The time frame for assessing results can affect whether your effort appears to be a failure or a success. *When* you decide to assess results—what we call your *temporal horizon*—can shape the results of your assessment and even the lessons you take away from a given effort. If you call a halt to the project too early, you may miss insights that are just around the corner. Such insights may be slow to emerge for several reasons. If a failure

along the way creates negative feelings, individuals may need time to make sense of them. In other cases, the results may take a while to cumulate and reach you. And elsewhere, you may not even realize what you have learned *until* you see it playing out in another experience.

In every come-from-behind story of initial failure giving way to eventual success, it's clear that the time frame makes all the difference: a battle may be lost, but the war won. But let's not go overboard here: even if many projects fail because they are planned with too short a time horizon, others limp on when they should have been canceled or redirected. In such cases, as we'll soon see, persistence is not a virtue—it's simply stubbornness.

Mind-Set Tips about Time Frames

How will your team keep in mind that they may have the wrong assumptions about time frames, rates of change, and payoff times? There's no single antidote to the temporal complexity of the modern world, but we have four suggestions.

- First and foremost, be aware of common flaws in thinking about timing, for instance, the tendency to assume that trends are linear.
- Second, bring in the experts to help think through timing issues if needed. For risky or large projects, more formal methods of dynamic modeling ensure that temporal factors are more systematically considered.
- Third, discuss the time horizons you, your team, and your stakeholders consider appropriate for assessing failure and success. If you are like the people we studied, you may discover within your organization—and even within your team—very different assumptions about how long it will take before you can assess success or failure. Experts tell us that a

useful rule of thumb to keep in mind is that most people err on the side of selecting too short a time horizon. For example, even in high-stakes IT and construction projects, professionals consistently underestimate how long big projects will take.

- Finally, along with defending instructive failures, you may need to advocate within your organization for longer time horizons for assessing innovation and change projects.

By better understanding the dynamics at play within projects and across them, you can form better plans for how long to persist and how often to revisit the project's overall rationale vis-á-vis its results to date in order to consider whether you should end the project or change course drastically. Foreknowledge of the downside of persistence could also help.

Avoiding Escalating Commitment

The trap of escalating commitment plagues high-risk projects, particularly when they are visible and long-term. People tend to become identified with the course of action they are taking, and can be loath to give it up, even if it is not paying off. Within organizations, social factors can worsen this tendency when people are identified by others with the project, and their reputation and social identity becomes entangled with the project's existence. Another contributing factor comes from behavioral economics: the *sunk cost trap* is created when someone invests so much in a course of action that the past investment itself becomes a reason to continue the investment, illogical as it seems.

Imagine you work in a pharmaceutical firm, charged with developing a new drug. Your team has been working on it for months, maybe years. What if your action-loop tests show that the drug is a bust—that it will never work as planned? The fact that you have the budget, the team, the time frame, and the job title that line up with the drug can tend to make you continue with its development, even when it is not in the organization's best interest to do so.

How will you avoid the trap of escalating commitment?

One antidote is to develop a set of critical questions about the project's timing to revisit at key points. Follow the advice in chapters 4 and 5 to plan and schedule project check-in meetings where you examine these issues. Referring to the project impact map and problem statement can help to highlight clues that your work is not heading in the direction you seek.

Simply being aware of the trap is also going to help. To tackle the implications of these negative clues, you'll also need the mind-set to enable open discussion and a receptivity to negative results, other aspects of your Fail Better mind-set that we've already described.

Adapting Work Modes and Focus

In projects, as in most of life, the secret to success lies in balancing countervailing tendencies. Instead of engaging in a constant tug-of-war or a simplistic splitting of the difference between two seemingly opposing needs, the wise manager shifts focus according to the needs at hand. A concentration on details is important at the close of the launch phase, in the thick of the iterate phase, and in the mid-stages of the embed efforts. But to shape the overall project and share the insights it generates, you will need to look at the big picture, too. You'll consider broader perspectives early in launch, then during project check-in points during your action phases, and again at the start and end of your embedding activities.

As your project evolves, be attuned to its shifting needs and adapt your work style to them. Let where you are in your project's cycle guide your focus as well as your responsiveness to feedback. In the mid- to later parts of a project, if the tendency is to continue with a course of action, you may want to impose stricter discipline to weed out bad ideas or stop an ineffective work stream. Knowing how to respond to your team's investment and experience with the project and to adjust decision making criteria is another aspect of time frame management.

All of this advice is useless if you are not open to an even bigger shift in approach—to cancel or pivot the project if all the signs tell you to do so. It may be counterintuitive, but pulling the plug on a foundering project could be the best thing for your company—and even enable the aims behind the project to be reached sooner. To succeed, every leader calibrates personal persistence with adaptiveness and willingness to learn and change course as needed. Even if politicians are sometimes criticized when they change course, we know that excellent battlefield leaders and CEOs change plans when the facts on the ground shift. You'll need to do the same with your team.

Resilience

Few would advocate blinkered perseverance that ignores emerging results and feedback. Yet when we talk to people about learning from failure, one of the first things they mention is perseverance. What they are talking about is not a blind commitment to a given project that ignores the data at hand but an ability to stay the course in service of their goals and vision, to find new ways to achieve what's important. Indeed, most stories about failure resulting in success involve the hero staying the course despite disappointments along the way. One specific trait—resilience—turns out to be key.

Resilience helps people deal with adversity and actually enables learning from experience. In countless accounts of their lives, successful leaders and managers say the capacity to handle setbacks is essential for surviving failures to reach success. Simply knowing that projects have their ups and downs could help your team to navigate upheavals, but you can go further, by building up a stock of resilience that enables you to learn from and handle the difficulties you encounter.

Why is this important? Remember, we set out with a focus on projects that meet our criteria—collaborative efforts that aim to accomplish something novel within the constraints of limited resources, scope, and time. The projects that stand to gain the most from Fail Better methods aim to address a pressing problem or to take on a new opportunity or emerging need, amid time pressures and other limitations. The combination of novelty and constraints ensures that most Fail Better projects will encounter challenges and difficulties at some point. Resilience can help you to handle the experience.

Personal resilience, some experts feel, involves realistic optimism. You can develop this outlook by acknowledging your challenges in the moment while also maintaining your aspirations for overcoming difficulties and reaching success. One idea to try out: balance an evidence-based, realistic view of the present situation with more forgiving views of the past and future. So, take a clear-eyed look at the deadlines, tasks, and requirements facing your team today, acknowledging what you do not know, while being a little more self-serving in identifying past experiences that ended well and in painting a hopeful picture of the future you are working toward. Sandra Schneider calls this "fuzzy meaning" and advocates "being lenient in our evaluation of past events, actively appreciating the positive aspects of our current situation, and routinely emphasizing possible opportunities for the future."[8]

Research on learned optimism offers more advice for cultivating this capability. Some of the ideas we've already mentioned also build resilience, such as the practice of mindfulness, along with many aspects of positive workplaces.

Organizations benefit when employees build capabilities related to resilience, and there's evidence that investing in team members' development in this domain pays off. Increasing team members' flexibility and adaptability by providing supportive resources and autonomy in decision making in turn enables them to improvise when confronted by uncertainty and contributes to resilience.[9] A central idea emerging from the study of resilience is the importance of a learning orientation that enables people to extract and internalize useful lessons from a setback experience.

A Learning Orientation Enables Resilience

How you view the events in your life shapes how you handle them—and what you achieve as a result. Another component of resilience involves looking at your experiences with the right mind-set. Like optimism, it's something you can cultivate in yourself—and even in others around you. Carol Dweck and her colleagues have developed a body of knowledge on how to cultivate an orientation that helps you enjoy challenges. Their advice: replace limiting attitudes that stem from a fixed mind-set with a more expansive growth mind-set.[10]

The origins lie in the study of how learning is influenced by internal thoughts. People who are overly focused on performance, believe that capability is fixed, and think that the only driver of success is innate talent tend not to handle failure well. To them, every misstep is just a visible demonstration of their limitations. In their ongoing efforts to display their capabilities instead of developing them, they tend to avoid challenges, and as a result lag behind their peers in developing knowledge and skills. They may organize their lives so that they do not fail often, but as a result they avoid opportunities to learn. They do not fare as well in life as their growth-oriented peers.

Others think that hard work and perseverance matter just as much as, if not more than, inborn talents and intelligence. They tend to view failures along the way as sources of valuable information about what did not work—information that will be useful in their next steps. People who think that you can always learn to do better and who see challenges not as tests of ability but as opportunities to increase ability have a growth mind-set. They relish challenges and are more resilient.

From the work with children, sports teams, and companies, we know that mind-sets can be changed. Carol Dweck's suggestions for cultivating learning mind-sets can help to shift fixed-capability perspectives toward growth.[11] The payoff can be vast. When children are praised for effort, rather than intelligence, they become more engaged in their learning, for example. And too much focus on grading and evaluating can weaken growth mind-sets and limit the learning that schools are supposed to deliver. Many see the same tendencies playing out within organizations. The effects could chill any Fail Better effort.

Managers with growth mind-sets create innovation, enable better work environments for coworkers, and seize opportunities to build their own capabilities and skills. By creating a culture that supports growth, they enable everyone to develop. And teams with growth mind-sets outperform others: they aim high, drive ongoing improvement, and collaborate more effectively.[12] By supporting experimentation with specific steps that lead to learning and development, the Fail Better method can reinforce your team members' growth mind-set. Cultivate your own awareness of the growth orientation to further a culture of growth and development for your team.

Resilience Lies in Action

To cultivate resilience, start by shifting your thinking. But to make it real, you need to take action. Perhaps most obviously, cultivating realistic optimism and a growth mind-set requires going beyond contemplating the perspectives we've advocated. To follow through, you'll need to make different decisions about how to respond to a given experience and then put it into practice. This means replacing what may have been a comfortable course of action with something that you would not otherwise opt to do. Consult our web materials at failbetterbydesign.com for more specific steps for doing so, and you will strengthen your capabilities. You can also enable others' resilience by encouraging them to reframe challenges in a learning-oriented growth mind-set instead of a limited performance mind-set.

Physical care of your body is also important. Exercise, time alone to recharge, a healthy diet, and sufficient sleep are all known to contribute to resilience. You should not shortchange yourself on these fronts.

Your behaviors as a manager can also fuel your own resilience. For example, taking decisive action, rather than ignoring stressful problems, is thought to contribute to resilience.[13] Shoring up skills in communication and problem solving could also help.

There's room for some general advice here too. Never forget that caring and supportive relationships that involve love and trust are essential for people to feel healthy and happy. They provide the bedrock for resilience. Invest in building and maintaining deep relationships. When you need it, they will help in many ways by encouraging, reassuring, and inspiring you.

Concluding Thoughts

We set out to provide you with an array of ideas to explore, each selected to spur your thoughts about your mind-set for leading, managing, and working on projects for innovation and change. Consider the ideas laid out in this chapter to be food for thought connected to starting points for implementing Fail Better. You do not need to take on every idea at once or to follow them in sequence. Select one idea to start with, reflect on it, learn more, try out a change in your approach, and see if it works. Then come back for more.

We don't want to pretend that every step will be easy. Making failure work for your team will require you to change how things are done. It will call on your management and leadership skills.

In choosing to fail better, you're embarking on a journey that will likely involve unpredictable challenges.

How you get there matters.

Regardless of how far you go in adopting elements of the Fail Better approach, we want to encourage you in this part of the work. To enable you to embed your learning from each project, chapter 6 provides guidance for assessing and updating your own practices. Draw on the same methods to reflect on and crystallize the personal principles that will support your efforts to lead innovation and change in every project.

Eventually, if your ambitions reach farther and you seek to enable your organization to embrace a Fail Better approach, people will need to know its underlying principles, to advance them consistently, and to defend them in use. To get to this point, your early actions within your team and project will be important. Leaders at all levels face special responsibilities because visible violations of the ideas they espouse can undermine everyone's commitment to the approach.

You'll also encounter tests along the way. Some can appear to be small, even mundane. More often than not, good intentions to change behaviors go awry as the result of drifting back to old habits. Team members start skipping a step, fail to hold each other accountable, or lapse into their old finger-pointing ways. Meetings intended to design the action steps so that they pressure-test your project's hypotheses may turn into more traditional divide-and-conquer work planning over time, but the drift may be slow.

Sooner or later, you could also encounter more dramatic challenges that try your ability to manage in the moment. To survive such challenges, you'll need to be able to present and preserve—possibly even to defend against attack—the principles that guide your approach, linking them to the actions that are needed.

Being personally prepared will equip you with the language, ideas, and conviction you'll need in these moments. Focusing on your own mind-set could help you be prepared. And by identifying the ideas and approaches you will infuse into your projects, you'll be attuned to signs that they are being undermined and ready to support the key ideas in practice.

The rewards will be great if you emerge the wiser for it. In fact, we think that the approaches mentioned here provide a path for your own development. If you can learn from your actions, and along the way nurture effective dialogue about failure, enable the right time frames, advance positive collaboration, and shore up resilience, you can remake your workplace. You could even make the world a better place.

CHAPTER 8

Our Design-for-Learning Foundations

Why do some failures lead to eventual success when so many others do not? We've argued that the difference lies in what's learned from each experience. Because there's power in understanding what makes for instructive mistakes, we'd like to introduce you to the foundations that underlie the Fail Better method and provide the rationale behind its steps.

Our goal is to equip you with knowledge and guidance for making the Fail Better approach work for you, your team, and your organization. Learning about the conditions that enable instructive failure can help you implement the method more effectively and avoid unproductive missteps.

There's a second benefit to understanding these design-for-learning principles. Appreciating how learning is woven into the Fail Better steps can help your team to stay the course when you encounter challenges. It can help shore up motivation—your own and your team's—to adopt and maintain the practices we've described. Knowing why you are undertaking a given activity is often essential for carrying it out, particularly when you are adopting something new.

The third benefit of learning about Fail Better's foundations is that they empower you to make the method your own. Once you're familiar with the underlying principles, you'll be equipped to improvise as you go. If you can master the core ideas behind them, you can use them to adjust and innovate new approaches in response to your team's and your project's needs.

The Only Benefit of Failing Is Your Learning

Learning from experience is not a straightforward process. In chapter 1, you learned about the impediments posed by dynamic complexity. Complexity hinders our ability to make appropriate predictions and draw the right inferences, both of which are needed for learning. Overlay the complexities of career, workplace, and team factors, and the challenges to learning multiply.

Yet we have much to draw on. Many different fields offer useful insights for understanding how people learn—or fail to learn—from experience. Research into adult education, training and development, and communities of practice sheds light on workplace learning. Techniques for innovation and improvement from the real-world domains of manufacturing, software development, product design, and other areas provide field-tested, integrated approaches to experimentation and learning from errors. Behavioral research, social psychology, and the study of cognitive functioning contribute valuable clues about handling failure, while philosophy, sociology, and organizational research provide grounding for understanding the implications of failure. We've distilled some key ideas from these domains to equip you to overhaul how you design your own work, your team's assignments, and your next project.

As we've argued, the *only* value of failure lies in its ability to generate new ideas, insights, or understanding. Why, then, do we see so much advice extolling failure's upside but so little attention to what is required in order to learn from it? A lack of attention to the learning process is part of the problem. Perhaps a lack of knowledge is to blame.

But before we look into why, let's begin with a basic definition.

Narrowing In on Learning

Learning is more than the process of acquiring knowledge or skill. For our purposes, it's also about the *modification of behavior* through practice, training, or experience. Particularly when it comes to professional performance, we're interested in how information that resides in people's heads and the skill sets they possess translate into changed behaviors that generate better results.

Unfortunately, most managers know little about how people learn. The topic is rarely taught in business school curricula, for example. Fostering learning is not part of most managers' evaluations. We've learned that managers devote surprisingly little attention to learning on the job and their role in enabling it. As a result, many miss the chance to spur their organization's innovation, adaptation, and improvement by supporting their team's (and their own) learning. No wonder learning from failure can be so elusive!

While we're all in favor of learning for its own sake, we focus here on learning most closely linked to getting work done: learning that leads to performance improvement or innovation. Thanks to their specific goals paired with time and resource limits, projects are excellent vehicles for learning.

Considering the value of projects as learning environments leads to a related point that helps us narrow our present focus. We are setting aside some forms of learning that reside in individual expertise. Think of how you build the muscle memory and technique underlying a hard-earned golf swing, for instance. This learning emerges from practice, guidance, and effective feedback. In fact, excellent feedback can offset the need for guidance, which is why you encounter self-taught experts in some areas, such as playing the piano (pianists hear their own playing and can then strive to improve it, trying out mini-tests to see if variations in technique deliver better results).

Some kinds of professional expertise are the product of a similar form of learning. Expert investors, firefighters, doctors, teachers, and all sorts of professionals at the top of their game accumulate innate, tacit expertise that enables them to make effective snap judgments and instinctual decisions, seemingly without thinking. Their initial training combined with vast accumulated experience enables them to act automatically.

Most projects involve a level of complexity that precludes these types of automatic and expert learning. Because they entail discovery, projects offer the potential for even more complex learning than those described above. It would be foolish to rely on such embedded expertise emerging on its own in project teams. Projects are simply too complex, varied, and multifaceted, and the context in which they operate too changeable, to reliably give rise to tacit, automatic team-level expertise. Many are one-off collaborations. Hence the need for a more deliberate approach to learning from failure.

This orchestrated learning is our focus. We've boiled down its requirements to three basic elements:

- People need calibrated challenges that stretch them in the right way.
- They need the right amount of freedom paired with safety to enable varied and creative action.
- They need meaningful feedback that is specific, timely, and consequential.

Calibrated Challenges

A quick look at how schools design for learning provides a familiar example to ground our discussion.

The best educational environments present children with a mix of assignments. Some routinize specific skills. Consider how children master core techniques for solving problems. They work through addition and subtraction drills before moving on to multiplication and division. The challenge in these repeated practice assignments is to improve on speed and error rates (and in so doing shore up the automatic type of learning mentioned above). This approach can help train production workers, software users, or radiologists interpreting scans. But people do not learn from training alone. Other school assignments stretch students by calling on them to create, link, or otherwise expand what they are already comfortable doing. Science projects, for example, involve novel research that is connected to content and frameworks that students have already learned via more structured methods.

The art of designing challenging assignments lies in equipping learners with *some* of the needed inputs to ensure that the more open-ended, difficult aspects of the work are lined up with its learning objectives. It's pointless to assign science projects without first equipping students with relevant ideas about the scientific method, for example. A poorly designed assignment stymies learning by forcing learners to grapple with issues unrelated to its educational goals.

This is not to say that everything should simply be handed to the student. Depending on their development and capabilities, learners can be helped to discover these needed inputs themselves. But guidance is always needed, as is a backdrop of mastery of the foundational domain and procedural knowledge that students draw on in their challenge assignments.

How does this apply to your project? It may be helpful to think of your work streams as assignments whose learning design you can shape. What aspect of the assignment is the "challenge" portion, where team members will be called on to do something new or creative (and hence may fail), and what aspect do you expect to be more routine, tapping into known skills, capabilities, and knowledge?

To learn at work, team members need to be equipped with resources, knowledge, and skills for the task. Aligning assignments with team members' capabilities requires understanding how strong their foundations are so that any failures emerge in the challenge aspect of the work at hand rather than in the more routine aspects. Technical, knowledge, and resource inputs are also obvious requirements to enable the work to be carried out and learning to take place.

For projects, team-level skills also come into play. These include the ability to surface and challenge assumptions and mental models, the capacity to connect cause and effect via systems thinking, and the practical skills of teamwork, collaboration, communication, and difficult conversations. We touched on these requirements in chapter 4, then showed them in action in chapter 5.

Doubtless, you already take into account such inputs when you line up your project teams (our launch checklists in chapter 4 are designed to assist in the process). But now, viewed through a learning lens, you may refine how you equip your team to *both* learn and perform. Design assignments and tasks so that the team is equipped to draw on some provided inputs while also being called on to discover or develop something new.

Plan how much guidance and help to offer for each task, and think through where in the assignment your team members will need to innovate. Can you reframe a project step to make it a better learning opportunity by highlighting the initial hypotheses underlying your approach?

Instead of requesting a task to be executed, consider adding a design aspect to an assignment. Rather than simply asking people to update a website with new dates, contact names, or other information, you may also ask them to consider a specific, higher-level goal for the site update, such as enabling more customer interactions via the site.

Another way to add a calibrated challenge to a work task is to go beyond the procedural. For example, instead of having your team simply borrow a plan from a previous project, consider bringing in an expert to instruct the team in its underlying approach. This new knowledge could enable your team to better use the existing plan by adapting it to the work at hand. As they do this, they will be learning.

As a manager, then, your job is to ensure team members have the information, training, and overall understanding they need in order to carry out the work of their project. This includes orienting individuals toward the approach you are using to guide the project as well as providing needed technical training and information. For instance, teaching people specific practices for quality improvement, such as kanban, *plus* the underlying philosophy of the quality approach is much more effective than focusing on the practices alone. It allows team members to connect the dots of their efforts to overall intent and to improvise within the guidance offered by the principles. This is why we suggest that in your earliest team meetings, and at touch points throughout the project, you discuss your use of the Fail Better method with team members to make the underlying rationale and approach visible to everyone.

To calibrate the learning challenge, it's also helpful to know where each team member most wants to develop, as these personal goals tie into individual motivation to learn. Research on professional and workplace education underscores the importance of enabling adult learners to see the value of what they are learning in terms of the practical implications for their work and lives. We've built this idea into our launch advice (see chapter 4).

The main insight is that the assignments that are best at generating learning stretch you a bit but not too much, enable you to find or discover what you need when you need it, and are personally meaningful.

Planning for Learning

In the rush to results, planning your project to enable learning may seem like a luxury you cannot afford. Yet it need not be a daunting task. One simple step is to set aside some early time to plan for the knowledge and informational inputs your team needs. Instead of falling prey to exigency by sanctioning the quickest of initial searches, relying too much on precedence, or borrowing what others have done, plan for some time to figure out what your team needs to know or have access to in order to come up with even better ideas for carrying out the project work. Identify where you want the team to innovate and create—this is the challenge part of the assignment—and where you want them to rely on established knowledge and practice—the foundational aspects of the assignment, in which you expect them to draw on what they have already mastered or have ready access to.

Foreknowledge of potential traps could help. Sometimes, the way in which a project is set up gets in the way of embedding calibrated challenges into the work. If teams are being asked to be creative or innovative without taking account of informational inputs, they may feel that they should just go ahead and make things up. If, on the other hand, they are under time pressure, they may simply blindly repeat past practices or use what's convenient. But we've learned that real innovation is best fueled by equipping the team with resources and knowledge that its members can use to develop their thinking in new ways. For example, to tackle the problem of avoidable in-hospital medication and treatment errors, the Institute for Healthcare Improvement (IHI) studied how Toyota engineers had improved their design and manufacturing processes over decades, learning its methods in detail. IHI and its partner hospitals took a page out of the auto manufacturer's book by setting up project management structures and discipline for every improvement effort. They also trained staff at partner hospitals to measure the incidence of adverse events, plotting results on charts to enable both prediction and goal-setting for error reduction, a practice that Toyota had used to great effect.[1] IHI's resulting campaign reduced avoidable hospital deaths dramatically, saving 100,000 lives over the course of an eighteen-month campaign that reached 3,100 US hospitals.

Recognizing that the team may lack knowledge of approaches outside the organization or industry, management often brings in consultants for such tasks. Yet too much outsourcing can mean your team does not learn as much as it could. Our advice: exploit your consultants to serve as teachers, not just deliverers of a final report. And don't overlook the expertise available within your own organization or professional communities. Not only is such input free, but it also benefits you and your team by expanding your professional network and revealing potential allies and collaborators. Many firms provide directories of employees and their specific areas of expertise to enable quick access to the abilities that reside within the company. You can also use social networks, in person or online, to track down expert input. Our launch checklists in chapter 4 direct you to scout for such opportunities, and the embed guidance in chapter 6 helps you to pay it back, contributing to others' needs by making your learning more accessible to others.

To sum up our calibrated challenge design principles: invest in designing assignments that stretch your team. Enable your team members to perform and learn by lining up the right inputs and foundations for action. Value the early-stage search and research aspects of your project. And to calibrate the challenges, find skill gaps that would impede learning, then invest the resources needed to address them. If you seek innovation, help your team to gather inspiring ideas and useful knowledge from other domains rather than simply telling them to be creative.

Freedom and Safety

We've been extolling learning from failure. To realize its benefits, you need two things. First is freedom to choose your actions, including the scope to try things that may not work out. But such freedom must be supported by safety—the sense that you will not pay too high a price if things do not work out as hoped.

Allowing Freedom

Actively learning involves designing and taking actions that put your thinking and understanding to the test in some way. Without the ability to freely decide how to solve a problem, it's difficult to learn from experience.

Freedom of this kind allows learners latitude to design their approach, choose tactics, and create content in response to a specific challenge. When people are free to decide what to try, the feedback that follows becomes more important to them. By spurring effort and engagement, freedom to choose actions enables several important ingredients for learning from failure: thinking and deliberation, active testing of understanding, and a drive to learn more.

To reap its benefits, combine freedom to experiment with the scope to try ideas in a repeated sequence. Iteration provides an engine for learning in this situation: back-to-back rounds of interaction with the domain enable people to refine ideas and skills as they learn them. Knowledge gained early in the process triggers sensemaking, and because there's another opportunity to act, the reflection process takes a practical turn as team members design their next steps. Layers of comprehension emerge with each round of acting, reflecting, and designing. Iteration also supports a key learning accelerator: multiplicity of interactions. Learners do better when they have a number of opportunities to interact with the material and domain.

Freedom to shape action steps can also increase the variety of interactions, another factor that enhances learning. When team members are encouraged to design diverse ways to explore, test, probe, and examine their ideas, they interact with multiple angles of the problem and its potential solutions. To research community needs, a team empowered to try varied approaches may use surveys, key informant interviews, historical and current documents, comparative examples, observations, and focus group discussions. The combination of methods yields a deeper understanding of the situation.

Freedom to explore new ideas does not mean freedom from rigor. We've highlighted the central role of hypothesis testing in your key action-loop steps (see chapter 5). Forming predictions before taking action, then reviewing results systematically will help your team to make the most of their freedom to act while avoiding impediments to learning—the sense that you sort of knew it all along or the tendency to ignore or downplay challenging results.

Your mind-set will come into play here. If your project incorporates learning via creative exploration, it will generate some surprise results along the way. This means that you need to be willing to tolerate some level of risk-taking and failure and to help your team handle disappointing results. You'll also need the flexibility to adapt plans to exploit fortuitous discoveries.

Enabling Safety

Your team members' basic safety is an obvious requirement for both performance and learning. Because it's difficult to try out new things when your well-being is threatened in a dangerous environment, physical safety is one of the basic requirements for learning. Psychological safety is just as important for learning, but often overlooked. Will team members feel free of the threat of abuse, job loss, extreme reputation damage, and other serious penalties if they take risks in their statements or actions? If they sense that they will be harshly penalized for missteps, employees are less able to learn because they do not take risks in what they say or do. Bullying, belittlement, abuse, and blaming are impediments to learning.

More subtly, feeling that your job or personal reputation is at risk can also create a level of uneasiness that inhibits learning. This is why it is so important to clarify expectations for performance, risk taking, and failure. Creating psychological safety through clear and supportive communication, making boundaries for action and risk explicit, and providing meaningful feedback reinforce team members' learning.

But psychological safety does not rule out accountability, nor does it preclude calling out mistakes, wrongdoing, or shoddy performance. Constructive criticism, identification of acceptable and unacceptable failure, and timely correction all help learning, not only because they eliminate bad ideas but also because they stimulate deeper thinking about cause and effect by triggering the team to acknowledge and make sense of negative results.

It's also important to understand that some stress can serve learning, particularly in forming associations about what to avoid and in building meaning and motivation for challenging tasks. In this way, raising the salience of the downsides and risks that your failures could entail could actually be helpful if it adds an adaptive level of stress. On the other hand, too much stress undermines thinking and reflection, impeding learning. Individuals' sensitivity to stress varies, so this is something to monitor as a leader of the team. Look for signals of stress, such as anxiety, and take the time to ask team members how they are coping.

It might feel strange to think about creating the right levels of stress for your team, but whenever you select the scale of your action steps and decide how visible you'll make the findings, you are shaping the potential stressfulness of a failure result. If you want to make it easier for your team to handle failure, design smaller steps that put less on the line each time. And if you want to stimulate deeper thinking and challenge conventional thinking, raise the stakes by making action steps more risky, large-scale, and visible.

Taken together, freedom and safety provide us with several practical implications for the design of your project. To enable their benefits, design linked cycles of action over which team members have influence. Then ensure your team feels sufficiently safe to undertake appropriately varied experimentation and testing. At launch, assess and communicate the size of tolerable failure, which in turn will allow results to be processed with the right level of attention, rather than triggering dysfunctionally high levels of stress and scrutiny or, on the flip side, creating too little emphasis that the results matter. If you can scale and respond to failures appropriately, avoiding blame and recrimination along the way, you can maximize learning.

Meaningful Feedback

Our third design-for-learning principle is linked to ideas we've already been exploring. We're all in favor of the creative action that freedom and safety enable, but unless you align and frame your team's efforts with respect to goals and understanding that matter to the team, and then support them in making sense of results with reference to data, your team may be missing opportunities to learn. Think of feedback as the information generated by a course of action to inform subsequent decisions. It goes beyond the colloquial sense of the term—what people tell you about your performance—to include results from tests, responses by competitors in the market, and other kinds of reactions to what you do or say. Feedback that tells what worked, and what didn't, is as essential for learning as the freedom and safety to try new things.

What kind of feedback is useful? To support learning, first and foremost feedback needs to be *directionally* useful to suggest whether the team is heading in the right direction or should change paths. It also needs to be *frequent* enough to help guide choices. There's evidence that directionally correct but incomplete feedback trumps more detailed and accurate but less frequent feedback (hence our focus on iteration). Feedback must also be *specific* enough to support reflection and examination of key considerations that gave rise to the action step. For example, data from an experiment needs to be fine-grained enough to reveal something about the particular hypotheses you were trying to test. Finally, feedback should be meaningful.

Framing Feedback for Meaning

Learning from action is hard work. What motivates this effort for an adult learner when so many other tasks and responsibilities loom? Research suggests that personal meaningfulness motivates people to invest effort in learning, in part by stimulating them to form connections to their existing understanding and experience. As a manager, you help create meaningfulness in several ways. After all, your role involves providing individuals with performance feedback that is aligned to what they consider to be important attributes of their job. You also offer feedback in more aspirational areas connected to each person's professional development goals and interests, something we highlight in chapter 4's launch advice. But don't assume that you know what everyone thinks is important for their job. Nothing beats open and regular communication with your team members to identify what makes work meaningful and relevant to them. Then, whenever possible, tap into this information as you shape the roles, responsibilities, and tasks assigned to each person.

There's also a connection to leadership. Part of the work of any leader, whether formal or informal, is to enable meaning for others. Link the work at hand to bigger goals by helping your team connect the project to their own aspirations for the team and the organization. Enable motivation and effort by reminding the team of the end users, beneficiaries, or customers you are aiming to help. Framing how the present tasks are linked to higher aims also helps the team to maintain perspective on what is most important to accomplish.

Skills for Extracting Feedback's Lessons

You are excellent at making quick judgments. You do it every day. Whether navigating a car through traffic, disciplining a child, or responding to an email, you are constantly sizing up situations and figuring out your response on the fly. Problems arise when you overlook flaws in your own judgments and ignore the effects of limitations in information and analytical capacity. Awareness of these thinking traps may help you to avoid them.

The practical implication for your project is that you need to develop personal and team disciplines to catch ill-informed snap judgments and push for rigor when needed. As we've mentioned all along, appropriate data analysis methods are essential for making sense of feedback from your team's experiments and tests. Remember that alongside such quantitative methods as statistical analyses are qualitative techniques like extracting key themes from customer interviews or systematically combining observations of consumer behavior.

Interpreting feedback will require other skills. If you're seeking feedback to tell what worked and what didn't, your team will need to make sense of all your results, whether they appear to be positive, negative, or ambiguous. To interpret your findings at any step of the process, your team will need to talk about failures, to draw appropriate inferences from both success and failure, and to adjust plans in keeping with new information. These are complex requirements that many of us are not taught, so you'll want to be on the lookout for such skills and shore them up as you can.

Capabilities in systems thinking, logic modeling, causal mapping, surfacing and probing assumptions, and group facilitation come into play here. We show how these capabilities enable Fail Better projects in part II. For example, systems and logic modeling techniques are needed for developing your project impact map (chapter 4), skills in probing assumptions are needed to target actions for iteration and then discuss the implications of interim results (chapter 5), and group facilitation skills aid in analyzing what the team has learned and should share as part of the embed phase (chapter 6).

Surfacing and examining assumptions is an antidote to the limitations in judgment that knock many a project off track. So too is the practice of collecting and looking at the data—and as much of the data as you can—with a critical eye and an open mind.

Consider All Sources of Data as Feedback Inputs

The right data is a critical input for your team's analysis. By *data*, we mean all the rich, varied forms of information that flow from action and experience. As we described in chapter 5, data includes databases of results from a formal survey, the numbers on your financial spreadsheets, and lab results from a prototype test, along with nonverbal responses you see in meetings, audience engagement in a public presentation, the speed and care with which your collaborators respond to your messages, comments from users, and your videos of product tests.

What do all these forms of data tell you about what you need to do next? All provide useful signals and shape perceptions, but the less traditional forms of data are often overlooked in the formal activity of data analysis. Within organizations, we tend to pay explicit attention to quantitative information but are often influenced by other forms of data without realizing it. To harness the power of all the data at your disposal, and thereby benefit from more meaningful feedback, cultivate the habit of drawing attention to all forms of information. For example, a simple practice involves debriefing after meetings using methods that go beyond impressions to data (e.g., tracking how long respondents discussed different issues or reviewing key quotes your team captured in a session with stakeholders).

Advice for a Data-Savvy Kickoff

When you're embarking on a new project, you'll want to talk to others whose experience may be instructive. This approach is common for new project teams. Gathering other people's feedback on your approaches, ideas, or core questions can provide information you could not get in any other way, but a word of caution—if you are simply asking someone else to tell you their opinions based on their past experience, be aware that one person's take on things is shaped by many factors besides those you are thinking of. Drawing inferences from a few historical examples is a risky endeavor at best.

One antidote to the limits of small sample size and lack of comparison cases in naturally occurring experiments is to use triangulation, by involving multiple forms of data and multiple informants. Another useful technique is to seek outliers rather than only the typical. Good research methods (such as including contemporaneously collected information rather than only retrospective accounts or employing appropriate statistical methods to mine your datasets) can also build confidence in lessons extracted from past experience. Even if your research is informal, bear in mind that you can boost the quality of your learning by talking to a few different people and trying to find any other forms of corroborating information, such as initial plans or status reports, along with materials documenting how conclusions were drawn.

Don't neglect existing bodies of knowledge. There's useful information to be gleaned from external sources, including formal and academic repositories. Think about how much practice of medicine has advanced over the decades. Two factors contributed to its improvement: the advent of scientific methods to systematically gather information about what works and what doesn't and the development of institutions to share this knowledge with practitioners.

Evidence-based management is beginning to catch up. For example, research on influence and persuasion reveals that others are more likely to do something specific—such as reusing hotel towels instead of having them changed daily—when they learn that many others are already doing it, rather than hearing a list of reasons they should do it.[2] If your project involves behavior change, looking at the evidence on persuasion and influence could be incredibly useful.

A Reminder for the Action and Embedding Steps

Considering varied data is an important requirement, but perhaps even more crucial is using your data effectively for decision-making. Make every key choice within your project reflect your team's critical assessment of the information you collectively have access to. We have seen countless professional projects undermined by poor use of data. Team members spend hours on interviews or assessments or field tests, but then when they come together to make decisions we often see very little reference to the data itself being used to back up or interrogate the team's key choices. Instead it's the other way around—people pull out the data that support what they aimed to do anyway.

Another common failure mode is when data collected by a subset of the team is not investigated by the entire team—instead the rest of the team is given just the conclusions and moves on without examining the data itself, thereby missing a chance to reap the benefit of the larger group's involvement. Since people often advance and advocate for a given course of action using less rigorous methods, such as a persuasive anecdote that has little to do with the data they have painstakingly collected, it's important to have other team members involved in both analyzing data and drawing conclusions.

From Data to Feedback

Data by itself does not really tell you what to do. For data to find use as feedback, it needs to be contrasted against goals or expectations. Without a way of judging results, outcomes of tests, experiments, or other actions are difficult to assess.

Maximize the learning potential of *every* action you target for learning by forming explicit predictions of what you expect to happen. To avoid hindsight bias and other flaws in attribution, when you review your results, juxtapose them against your prior predictions. If you don't set up a clear statement of your expectations for the result of a given test or experiment, it can be easy to reframe what you find after the action to suggest that the results were as expected or simply to make you look good in the eyes of others. But critical thought and insight are triggered by surprise, not confirmation. If the results don't jibe with predictions, you'll be prompted to figure out what it means. It is in this effort to understand surprises that you'll find the value of failures.

Concluding Thoughts

Equipped with the core concepts that underlie our approach, you can now more effectively leverage the Fail Better method to turn your projects into real learning opportunities. Understanding our design-for-learning principles will also, we hope, help you to innovate and improvise as you make the approach your own.

Could the approach transform how work is done? We think so, but to get there, we realize that many managers, leaders, change agents, and others will be needed to join our collective Fail Better efforts. To help you lead the charge within your domain, we've explained and illustrated the method, provided insight to cultivate the right mind-set, and shared the fundamental principles that drive learning at work. In chapter 9, you'll also benefit from seeing how the method as a whole plays out successfully in a complex and challenging environment.

CHAPTER 9

Practical Fail-to-Succeed Lessons from a Frugal Innovator

Bangladesh's vast deltas empty into the Bay of Bengal, its rivers fed by the Himalayas to the north. It's among the most populous countries in the world, yet its land area is smaller than Iowa. Bangladeshis are proud of their rich artistic, intellectual, and cultural traditions. The country is admired for its commitment to interweaving Hindu, Christian, and Buddhist minorities with its Muslim mainstream, and its groundbreaking advances in promoting social equity.

The country has faced its share of catastrophes: recurring floods, droughts, and famine (and now, the effects of climate change), exacerbated by its population's economic vulnerability. Thanks to recent growth, annual per capita income reached the milestone mark of $1,044 in 2013, but up to a third of Bangladesh's 160 million citizens still subsist on less than $2 per day.[1]

Bangladesh's history foreshadows the situation it faces today, marked by both triumphs and problems. After war in 1971, it won independence, but with political costs that continue to be felt. Weak economic development made the country dependent on external support. Adding to these challenges, Bangladesh endured unthinkable humanitarian burdens: fast on the heels of a 1970 cyclone—by most accounts the most lethal storm in human history—followed wartime massacres, then the displacement of tens of millions of refugees and migrants seeking to escape the violence. Observers were pessimistic about the new nation's prospects. As the *New York Times* reported in 1972, the US ambassador to Bangladesh infamously called the country "an international basket case."[2]

At this time, a young chartered accountant named Fazle Hasan Abed (later to be Sir Fazle Hasan Abed) felt he had to do something about the problems his country faced. He left his comfortable position at the Shell Oil Company with the idea of using his business skills, access to funds, and connections to acquire and distribute relief supplies to the rural poor. The organization now known as BRAC was born in 1972.

Over forty years later, BRAC is by several measures the world's largest non-governmental organization. By 2013, it employed 120,000 individuals in Bangladesh alone. Its scale is difficult to comprehend. BRAC operates over forty-four thousand schools. Its legal centers outnumber Bangladesh's police stations. It serves almost 5 million microfinance borrowers, each of whom now has a better shot at lifting her entire family out of poverty. It provides water and sanitation services to some 30 million Bangladeshis and pre- and postnatal health care to a similar number of women, along with a host of other health, legal, poverty-reduction, educational, agricultural, and community development services. In 2012, BRAC delivered direct services to 135 million people in Bangladesh and beyond.[3] Not every program that BRAC launches is successful, but what it chooses to retain and grow is both efficient and effective.

Since its first international program in 2002, BRAC has grown globally. By 2014, it was delivering programs—many at a national scale—in Uganda, Afghanistan, South Sudan, Pakistan, Haiti, Sierra Leone, and elsewhere in Africa and Asia. To fund its operations, the organization runs dozens of revenue-generating enterprises, including a chain of retail stores that feature a wide array of craft and artisan products. These and other for-profit business lines provide essential services and manufacture products that are linked to BRAC's activities while also filling gaps in the Bangladesh market. In 2013, BRAC businesses included a dairy, livestock artificial insemination services, poultry production, poultry rearing, feed mills, fisheries, industrial salt production, the manufacture and sales of sanitary napkins and maternal delivery kits, sericulture, printing, bio-gas and solar energy services, recycled handmade paper production, and plant nurseries. The organization has invested in tea production, a mobile money system, and large-scale cold storage facilities. It runs a university, a bank, and more. Overall, an astonishing 70 percent or more of BRAC's programs are self-funded by the organization's own enterprises and operations.

The story of how BRAC developed into a results-focused operational and financial powerhouse with global reach is fascinating, but the organization's evolution is not our focus. We want to tell you about how BRAC works because in collaborating with its staff, visiting its headquarters and sites, interviewing its beneficiaries, and studying its programs, organizational culture, and methods, we discovered an organization that has innovated, routinized, and embedded into practice every element underpinning the Fail Better approach.

That the method is working in some of the most challenging settings, amid pressing constraints, to make real progress against some of the world's most persistent challenges, suggests to us that it could work anywhere. To focus our discussion as much as possible, we'll look at BRAC through the lens of one of its ongoing efforts, its maternal health program. We'll start with its foundations.

Delivering Low-Cost Health Interventions to Many

In 2005, BRAC's leaders could take measure of the impressive progress their organization had made in vaccination campaigns, which were delivering the world standard of care to 80 percent of the country's children. To do so, they had built on BRAC's earliest efforts to save children's lives.

When BRAC was founded, cholera and diarrheal diseases were taking a huge toll on the population. Intravenous saline injections, the traditional medical treatment, were not feasible in the setting. In what experts called "the medical advance of the century," researchers at the International Centre for Diarrheal Disease Research, Bangladesh (then the Cholera Research Laboratory) developed a low-tech alternative: oral rehydration solution (ORS), a mix of commonly available ingredients, and established its effectiveness in children with cholera, and adults and children with non-cholera diarrheal diseases.[4] Recognizing the vast challenge of delivering the simple treatment to those who most needed it, BRAC went to work. Starting in the 1980s and through the 1990s, BRAC's field staff, managers, and health researchers refined, and then refined again, cost-effective, medically efficacious, and easy-to-spread ways to prevent children from dying of diarrhea. To scale up its response, BRAC volunteers went house to house in every part of the country, including the remotest rural settings. At each doorstep, volunteers taught mothers and caregivers how to make the right mix of salt, sugar/molasses, and water to provide the electrolytes needed for recovery.

The trick was not just to perfect the recipe with inexpensive, locally available ingredients (the BRAC team redesigned the instructions several times, returning to the drawing board every time they uncovered a new problem in the field), but also to figure out how to reliably teach it to mothers, another step that necessitated iteration and field testing. BRAC developed a cadre of community workers from each village whom they trained carefully. By 1990, BRAC had provided direct instruction to 13 million women and lifesaving benefits to their families.

Close monitoring allowed BRAC to verify via follow-up testing that recipients of its training understood how to use the solution appropriately. BRAC was always frugal. Even at the height of its campaign, the program used no more than three jeeps and twelve motorcycles to implement services.[5] By 2007, ORS was credited with saving the lives of *50 million* children, thanks in large part to BRAC's efforts.[6]

The Maternal Health Challenge

Over the years, Bangladesh had seen a decline in maternal deaths, but in 2005 the country was still far from reaching the substantial reduction in the number of women dying in childbirth specified in the United Nations Millennium Development Goals. BRAC had applied what it learned about operational excellence from its experience to increase vaccination delivery, but could the lessons help reduce maternal and newborn deaths?

Delivering healthy children and ensuring their mothers' health offer even more complex challenges than providing vaccinations or instructions for home treatment of diarrhea. To tackle maternal health goals, BRAC needed a different approach. New services had to reach women, and they would need to go beyond the organization's existing core microfinance, health, and education programs. Health interventions would succeed only if they were appropriately designed to meet women's needs and preferences. The solution would have to bridge the gaps in a health-care system that often failed to connect communities to the services and facilities they needed. The new effort would need to balance demand at the community level with the readiness of facilities to respond quickly to that demand. To be cost-effective, it would need to quickly find and manage more complex and emergent cases while serving a high volume of primary care and standard cases through frontline workers. And to empower mothers to use these services, they, their families, and their communities would need to be involved too.[7]

IMNCS—The Rural Program

In 2005 BRAC piloted a new program in rural Bangladesh in collaboration with UNICEF and the leadership of the government of Bangladesh. The program, called Improving Maternal, Neonatal and Child Survival (IMNCS), targeted the disadvantaged. It aimed to improve four key ingredients for mother and child health:

- Knowledge and practices related to aspects of maternal, neonatal, and child health.
- Household and community access to high-quality maternal, neonatal, and child health services.
- Availability of facilities providing a continuum of maternal, neonatal, and child health care and services.
- Awareness and usage of community, facility, and referral services.

To ensure that its efforts were aligned to needs, a fifth objective was added: to increase participation, accountability, and responsiveness to communities' voice in the delivery and design of these health services.

Leveraging Launch Activities

BRAC's IMNCS team invested carefully in its launch, especially when it came to gleaning lessons from the past and inventorying the assets that could aid their new effort. Its operational platform was the organization's Essential Health Care program, also known as EHC, first established in 1991. The program had been instrumental in the widespread success of the ORS program to combat diarrhea and the national vaccination effort. Now, BRAC continued its strategy of using the EHC platform to reach the most vulnerable groups, drawing on global best practices and proven interventions that the design team contextualized to the needs of Bangladesh.

Its own recent experience also informed the design. A short-term program based on the same platform, called Saving Newborn Lives, concluded in 2004. As part of its comprehensive documentation, the program's subsequent impacts were studied until mid-2005, offering critical lessons for IMNCS just as it got going. The experience of Saving Newborn Lives underscored the need for BRAC to get its maternal programs operating more quickly than it had in the past, the need to factor in community participation, and the need for more integrated care that spanned a longer time frame. It also highlighted challenges in ensuring that women received the full set of four antenatal care visits before giving birth. Its lessons were scrupulously documented in a public report, and they were available to the IMNCS team at the right moment as they launched their new effort.[8] The Saving Newborn Lives team had identified the drawbacks of more modest interventions, while showing the benefit of combining education and behavior change with the provision of more medical services. IMNCS was a more ambitious program by design.

Second, as part of the IMNCS launch effort, the team scouted for the capabilities and existing programs that BRAC already had to offer, leading its designers to think carefully about how to make the most of the core community health workers that the organization had already invested in, without overburdening them. Over the years, the Essential Health Care program had developed a large group of community-based health workers (CHWs). The IMNCS team surveyed the workers' capabilities and coverage, designing a program to draw on their strengths in reaching women at their doorsteps and in enabling behavior change via face-to-face and community meetings. Recognizing that most rural women gave birth at home, the BRAC team added skilled birth attendants who were familiar with the communities' needs and who could provide hands-on care at birth. Together, CHWs and birth attendants provided frontline family planning, pregnancy, childbirth-related, newborn, and under-five child care directly to households. Following the practice first developed for the oral rehydration program, the reporting structure was carefully designed. Field workers' supervisors oversaw the pre- and postnatal services that they delivered. They also had a new responsibility: linking patients as needed to health facilities that could serve more complicated cases. IMNCS added another staff role, referral program organizer, as well as new services (such as mobile phone communication and transportation services) to enable women and babies who needed to reach hospitals and available services promptly.

Iterating to Reach Scale and Finding the Learning

To guide the evolution of the IMNCS program, the BRAC team harnessed the power of iteration. The program was launched in the poverty-stricken districts of Nilphamari in northern Bangladesh. Over the next two years, BRAC developed and refined the program with an eye to expansion.

The three districts that were added in 2008 represented a significant growth in coverage and variation in complexity and challenges, all of which forced the team to solve new problems and to improve program design so that it could achieve a significant reduction in maternal and child mortality. At the same time, BRAC's research and evaluation team (discussed in more detail later) studied the impact of the second iteration of the program longitudinally in all four districts, along with two districts that did not get the intervention and served as controls for the study. Their research results, along with the project's own data, fueled the third iteration of the program.

By 2010, the third iteration was in full swing. Thanks to a streamlined intervention design that reduced costs and improved monitoring, it had grown from four to ten districts and was reaching close to 20 million women. The evidence was revealing its impact: the women in the first IMNCS district saw their risk of dying in childbirth fall by around half from 2001 to 2011. The improvement in their maternal mortality risk significantly outperformed gains elsewhere in the country.

Manoshi—The Urban Program

Even as the IMNCS team was iterating on its rural program, BRAC launched another effort, this time to target the urban poor. The new team had to identify what was applicable from the rural program and pinpoint where they needed to innovate. They faced a new set of challenges, thanks to differences in the settings and populations and because BRAC had less accumulated experience in delivering health services in urban slums.

A third of Bangladesh's population lives in urban areas, and this fraction is expected to grow. In some respects, health outcomes in city slums were worse than anywhere in the country. In part because their populations were more transient, they offered fewer social supports. To address the needs of families living in urban slums, BRAC created the Manoshi Maternal, Neonatal and Child Health Project in 2007. Like IMNCS, Manoshi aimed to provide integrated prenatal, childbirth, neonatal, maternal, and child health care customized to each community's needs.

To start, Manoshi faced an ambitious set of requirements. It needed to create demand for these services in the community by increasing knowledge about mother and child health needs, build the capacity of health workers and service providers, link community with facilities by enabling access to obstetric and newborn care at public and private health-care facilities, and develop effective referral processes for emergency obstetric care.

The Manoshi team quickly realized that IMNCS could not simply be copied. In-home services and referrals alone would not be sufficient to improve outcomes. A lack of privacy for childbirth, along with pervasive pollution, crowding, and unhygienic environments, complicated the challenges of poverty facing pregnant women in urban settings. The Manoshi team's innovation was to establish delivery centers to ensure clean and safe delivery that also served as mini-hubs for prompt diagnosis and referral of complications to better-equipped facilities. Each modestly provisioned Manoshi birthing center had two Urban Birth Attendants and served a small catchment area within walking distance of the women they sought to attract. Their two-room design allowed for privacy and dignity while keeping infrastructure costs low.

To ensure that women got the health care they needed, Manoshi assigned a female CHW to every two hundred houses. In monthly visits to each house, the CHW would identify when a woman became pregnant, which she would then report to her supervisor. CHWs would visit the expectant mother every month and provide antenatal care, inviting her to the birthing center for delivery. At the center, trained birth attendants delivered the baby with the support and supervision of Manoshi midwives. If there were complications, the mother was referred to a nearby clinic or hospital that offered a broader scope of care. BRAC Referral Staff were stationed in public hospitals to provide physical support to referred cases. The care did not stop at birth: CHWs continued to follow up with the family for postnatal, infant, and pediatric care until around age five.

In 2010, Manoshi reached 5.7 million individuals in slums across six city corporations. By the five-year mark, it had expanded to another two cities, closing in on its goal of providing services to 8 million women. Results from the first six cities showed that home delivery rates had fallen in these urban areas from 86 percent to 18 percent, evidence of a significant change in behavior. Both neonatal and maternal mortality declined in Manoshi program areas. The country marked a milestone in 2011 when a national study showed that Bangladesh would attain the improvements in maternal health set by the Millennium Development Goals, outperforming all expectations.[9]

Launch: How Manoshi Built on BRAC Capabilities

Manoshi followed the BRAC recipe for success. Its team drew on the lessons of the rural IMNCS project. Its designers benefited from the deep knowledge and relationship base BRAC had established in communities across Bangladesh.

The program's launch was guided by the organization's twin hallmarks, linking a "just try it" approach with a deep research infrastructure that facilitated timely and implementable feedback as the program evolved.

As BRAC launched Manoshi in early 2007, it undertook a careful investigation of its target market with a multimethod study of potential users in Dhaka slums.[10] Over the course of nine months of field study, its staff conducted observations, in-depth interviews, case studies, network analysis, surveys, and a mix of informal, structured, and focus group discussions.

The result was rich documentation of the characteristics of the community, including beliefs about practices related to maternal, neonatal, and child health, a mapping of existing facilities and service providers, and inventories of stakeholder community groups and networks.

Some specific insights emerged:

- Despite the presence of a variety of services and providers, there were open questions about their quality (thanks in part to wide reliance on cheap, unregulated care providers) and inadequate referral to clinics and hospitals when needed.
- Community members had superficial but insufficient knowledge of maternal, neonatal, and child care to ensure optimal health outcomes.
- Prevailing cultural beliefs and practices favored home delivery without skilled assistance.
- Men worried about expense, and women worried about the care experience, including delivering at hospitals.
- There was poor social support for health, even in comparison with other needs.

The findings directly influenced Manoshi's program design and provided the team with all-important context. They also enabled the team to focus on the felt needs of people they aimed to serve, putting the users and their situation in clear view.

Iterate: Using Data Throughout the Action Loop

As Manoshi rolled out, its team continued to look at all the information BRAC could glean from the field. Intertwining data collection and assessment with service delivery enabled real-time innovations. Both quantitative and qualitative data—the latter generated by frequent site visits, observations, and staff conversations—enabled the BRAC team to pay attention to specific cultural, economic, and environmental differences in the varied urban slums. This allowed results to be viewed in context and the program to be customized locally.

We'll take a look at three specific insights arising from data-driven experimentation and iteration in Manoshi: uncovering and addressing unexpected challenges with CHWs, reexamining willingness to pay for services, and trying out an innovation in real-time data tracking and program monitoring.

Discovering and Responding to an Implementation Surprise

Early in its implementation, Manoshi's management team encountered an unexpected finding that prompted reexamination of the CHW role. Despite BRAC's thirty-seven years of success with community health workers as the mainstay of health-care delivery in rural communities, the approach didn't seem to be working as well for Manoshi in urban slums. Research and discussions revealed that turnover could be high.[11] Even when CHWs stayed on in their positions, some were becoming inactive, with their health-promoting activities dwindling over time. The Manoshi team commissioned a study to explore factors affecting CHW performance, specifically in Dhaka slums. It showed that financial incentives influenced performance: CHWs who saw their families as economically dependent on their work with Manoshi were three times as likely to be active as others. Social prestige and positive family attitude toward the CHW role were also associated with better performance.

Manoshi's leaders realized that they needed to be better attuned to the market of potential employment opportunities their CHWs faced so that they could more appropriately present the role and its benefits, and that selection of workers for the position should target those who saw both economic and nonfinancial benefits to the role. But because the team was experienced, they also decided not to overreact, reasoning that this program and role were new and still developing. Indeed, by 2014 as Manoshi had matured, CHW retention and activity levels had both increased.[12]

Valuing the Service: Participants' Willingness to Pay

Some versions of Manoshi's initial design called for users to be charged a small fee. Right away, it became clear that fees would not work if the goal was to maximize access to maternal services, and the idea of nominal fees was dropped.[13] But the team did not completely give up on the idea of charging fees, because they knew that revenue would be important for the program to survive over time.

Using the Manoshi pilot structure, BRAC researched the question. A study to explore whether service recipients would be willing to pay for delivery center services found that most would be willing to pay a registration fee. The researchers suggested that users pay in installments, with an option for waivers as a safety net. Along with a high level of private demand for Manoshi's delivery centers, the study identified factors that the program could change to influence household or individual willingness to pay.

This study added more insight to the assumptions behind the Manoshi program. Even as the team worked to roll out the program as a free service, it showed an openness to testing the hypotheses underlying the overall design. By 2012, the team was considering how to introduce limited charges for a subset of services at a newly designed delivery center which offered upgraded delivery care.

There was another benefit to revisiting the question of fees. Even if it was not on the table for the first-round implementation of Manoshi, by gathering this information early on, the team could guide program choices in the free version of the program that would set the stage for moving to a fee-for-service model.

Getting Better Data Faster

Using the infrastructure and process that BRAC had built to support Manoshi, the team launched a test project equipping CHWs with mobile phone–based software. The goal was to allow CHWs to more efficiently and accurately track and report critical patient information in a simple and standardized format.[14] Software company Click Diagnostics, later rechristened mPower, partnered with BRAC for this effort. To design the new mobile tool, the collaborators drew on existing data on CHWs' needs and challenges in collecting information. The result was a simple mobile phone application that could track women's health data.

Consulting physicians could view the data on a secure site and advise on patients' care, sending recommendations directly to the CHW's mobile phone. To manage potential risks, an algorithm categorized patients by defined risk categories. The server could also alert Manoshi field staff as needed and equip CHWs to prioritize high-risk patients. Supervisors could monitor the data sent by CHWs in various ways, and the system could send supervisors text alerts if workers missed visitation targets.

Here, too, BRAC used Manoshi to run experiments that would inform its *next* steps. Based on insight from the initial mobile intervention, a new phase launched in 2014 in both rural and urban programs. Data collection software was integrated with a call center, enabling health consults to patients remotely, addressing minor ailments, and facilitating referrals.

Embedding the Learning

As it does with all programs and initiatives, BRAC launched Manoshi with an evaluation and research plan in place.

To influence policy and help replicate the model at a national level in Bangladesh, Manoshi shared findings from the project with national, government, and NGO stakeholders, funders, United Nations and other multilateral organizations, and research and advocacy organizations. BRAC also leveraged its own global network of operations and stakeholder relationships to disseminate the lessons it learned from Manoshi. To make results even more widely available, by 2014, BRAC had published dozens of papers on various aspects of the program, including many by its own Research and Evaluation Division (RED). RED analyzes and evaluates the organization's activities, enabling BRAC to use results to improve programming, share findings with others, and provide direction for the organization to expand and evolve.[15]

A focus on high-quality research exemplified by RED can come with some downsides. While its website lists some two thousand research papers, including hundreds of peer-reviewed publications, it's difficult to find written records of decision-making processes, management approach and design, and its iterative learning methods. There's a dearth of contemporaneous documentation, so we rarely get a blow-by-blow feel for the dilemmas, options, and surprises that BRAC's managers and leaders encounter in the course of their project work. Most of BRAC's documentation is through the lens of retrospect and rather formal in nature. As a result, it's difficult to appreciate the people who are involved in the efforts we read about. It's heartening that BRAC documents its programmatic failures, but few appear to be examined with an eye to their implications for how management could be improved.

But perhaps this critique is not fair. BRAC is excellent at documenting its results and accounting for them rigorously, which by itself provides an enormous contribution to the world. And if its staff were to spend more time writing, perhaps they would have less time to do great things!

More materials are being produced all the time. Blog posts and opinion pieces are joining the compelling books that tell the story of BRAC's experience with its landmark innovations in oral rehydration and tuberculosis treatment, along with others that explain how the organization grew to be so cost-effective and operationally efficient.[16] And management researchers are studying the organization to learn its secret of frugal innovation.

BRAC values evaluative processes and has built a culture that embraces them. Manoshi received support from the Bill & Melinda

Gates Foundation that enabled expanded documentation by the International Centre for Diarrhoeal Disease Research, Bangladesh, the outside research organization that had pioneered ORS. Its study resulted in an extensive collection of eighteen in-depth working papers between 2009 and 2012.[17]

These external papers, together with the trove of materials produced by RED and other BRAC personnel, tracked outcomes, explored potential challenges and innovations, and documented program elements during Manoshi's launch, iteration, and scale-up. They set the stage for the next set of projects by testing ideas that Manoshi was not yet able to implement but that held promise for increasing quality, reducing cost, or increasing revenue in the future. As we found in the course of preparing this chapter, all these resources also help others to identify and spread the lessons offered from the program's experience.

Concluding Thoughts: What BRAC Reveals about Failing Better

BRAC's operational and programmatic strengths are evident from its results. As we've seen, its low-cost programs, ability to develop and spread innovations, and design for scale would not be possible without its managers and leaders being able to track data quickly and effectively enough to uncover and respond to surprises. This capability yields an impressive success rate: BRAC insiders say that only about 20 percent of BRAC pilots are discontinued, and the proportion is less than 10 percent for those that are scaled at least once.

What could your organization borrow from BRAC to make better use of data to test ideas and pivot your plans as needed?

To launch projects, BRAC teams often start quickly, trying out new ideas that are informed by past experiences—including limitations revealed by earlier projects. And from the outset, at a point when others would be looking only at implementation, the organization begins to assess each new effort's early results, providing the fodder for the next iteration. The organization has built a discipline that allows it to go from a large pilot to an even larger second iteration, often by design in less favorable settings. A new round of assessment sets the stage for scaling up, often at breakneck speed. It's a learning-by-doing approach that brings rigor and planning for scale to the fore.

Could your efforts draw on similar approaches to combine the benefits of testing ideas early and often with the benefits of planning to reach many?

BRAC has mastered the action loop at the heart of the Fail Better approach. Our examples of data-driven iteration illustrate why BRAC is one of the most impressive learning organizations in the world. And unlike corporations striving to maintain competitive advantage by keeping their processes and program under wraps, BRAC, in partnership with its funders, has a strong, mission-driven incentive to widely share its findings in ways that can help scale solutions.

To support this learning, its members draw on three rich streams of information that have developed over the years and that embed the learning from every experience. First, every project develops its own programmatic data used for ongoing planning, management, and program refinement, and all layers of BRAC management are skilled in using these field data, reports, and databases. Second, insights and evidence-based findings are produced by RED, BRAC's internal research arm, which has built a formidable capability and massive set of materials over the organization's existence. The third data set is more informal, the result of the organization's vast experience base and low turnover. Innovators can draw on their peers' shared stories and BRAC's many in-house experts. There's much to learn from looking for analogies across programs, time periods, and settings.

BRAC is among the best in the world at what it
organization cannot match these capabilities, don't fea
BRAC was once just a handful of people who had to
out as they went. Because they invested in a systemat
their projects, they built an engine for learning and
If they could do this without the wealth of informati
inspiration that today's technology provides, imagine
accomplish with access to a greater number of resourc

The lessons we can learn from BRAC drive ho
happen when Fail Better capabilities are integrated a
at an institutional level. You may not be in a work c
there yet. But that's the beauty of the Fail Better appro
many layers of benefits when it comes to your own p
team, and your project; there's much that you can cont

CHAPTER 10

Fail Better Can Change the World

Before moving on to our big ideas for changing the world, we thought we'd reflect briefly on how we got here.

Our Own Journey

Having invested in our own planning, project mapping, and predictions, tried many experiments, and explored how to embed what we've learned, we followed our own advice to reach this point.

We began working together when we realized that our professional experience had shown each of us many project failures—and that our grounding in research provided promising ideas for how to address them. We experimented with various iterations of our methods in many different organizations over the course of close to ten years, documenting our efforts at each step. Along the way, we encountered our share of instructive failures (we will spare you the details here!).

As we refined our ideas, we studied productive managers to uncover how their work habits enabled successful projects. Sifting through research articles, books, news stories, blog posts, and presentations, we tested our ideas against the evidence and grounded our efforts in existing knowledge. In fact, you've seen some of this research playing out in our advice on tackling dynamic complexity, managing time frames, cultivating helpfulness, and building resilience.

Throughout this effort, we kept the focus on understanding how to improve and harness the everyday work of projects so that they deliver on the promise of changing work life, organizations, markets, and society for the better.

Along with overall support for our method and real-world illustrations of its use, our explorations provided us with new insights into current management thinking. In published research, the press, blog posts, and elsewhere, we noticed, much attention is devoted to large advanced-economy companies, often consumer-focused or high-tech firms. Yet in our professional experience, we've seen potentially useful ideas being tried out in different and inspiring ways across other settings, too: in small businesses, nonprofits, governmental organizations, services, lower-tech industries, and emerging markets. We think more could be learned about effective action by examining a greater variety of settings and juxtaposing examples. We suspect there are useful ideas to glean from all quarters.

In this chapter we take a wider perspective. Maximizing the full potential of Fail Better calls for going beyond one project or even one organization to systematically connect different efforts.

We'll explore this bold idea in two ways. Our explorations, we hope, will inspire you to aim high and take bold action. Looking to the future, we'll consider ReThink Health, an ambitious effort now underway to change health and health care in America. To review our method, we'll look back in time, examining how the US Civil Rights Movement exemplified many of the ideas we've been developing. We send you off on your way with a final word or two of advice.

ReThink Health: Stewardship, Organizing, and System Dynamics

There's a health-care crisis facing the United States today. Costs are growing. Rates of obesity, cardiovascular disease, and diabetes keep rising. Emergency room visits are too often the inadequate stand-in for proper primary care. If diet, physical activity, and preventive care continue to follow trends, by 2030 half of all Americans will be not just overweight but obese.[1] There's widespread agreement that the US health-care system as a whole is failing to deliver the outcomes everyone wants. Throw political complexity into the mix, with the unfolding effects of the Affordable Care Act playing out over years, and it's no surprise that many agree that no single action will change all the interacting elements in the system for the better. How will progress emerge?

In 2007, the New Jersey–based Fannie E. Rippel Foundation embarked on a new effort that sought to "enable a genuine metamorphosis within the health system."[2] The initial idea emerged when thought leaders in health, business, economics, energy, and academia met to explore the potential for fundamental changes in health care. Action soon followed. The effort, called ReThink Health, has grown to include varied implementation and funding partners. Its threefold goals are ambitious: better health, better care, and lower costs.

ReThink Health's leaders believe the origins of health and health care are local. Even if the United States needs radical changes in health care at the national level, they argue, it cannot happen without change within communities. So the program is building community collaborations designed to nurture effective innovation that could transform health.

What could enable such transformation? As described by the organization's staff, the approach connects innovations in three linked domains:

- **Active stewardship** focuses on the conditions for diverse stakeholders to work across boundaries to shift cultures, influence change, and sustainably steer health systems toward common aspirations.

- **Effective strategy** equips leaders with data and dynamic models to see the system in which they work, play out plausible scenarios, spot opportunities, and set priorities for action.
- **Sustainable finance** questions what it takes to gather and direct resources to sustain system-wide impacts.[3]

To combine these three spheres into practical systematic actions, ReThink Health designed a program in consultation with the experts who sparked the effort. The goal was to create a disciplined way for each community to explore how they could improve everyone's health by involving local stakeholders—including business, government, and social sector leaders who rarely collaborate systematically to plan a joint future. Each effort would be driven by a community that invited in the program team. Together, they would take on pressing questions about needs, opportunities, and desires driven by the stakeholders themselves.

Participants would start by examining the current health system within the region to identify existing or potential failure modes, in essence creating a list of things they did not want to occur. Working within a carefully designed process, they then come up with new ideas for collaborations, policy changes, and shared priorities. Everyone is encouraged to think boldly and to look to the future without discounting the transitions needed to get there. To develop a deeper collective understanding of how different factors influence health outcomes, to test suggestions rigorously, and to enable ideas and plans to be shared, ReThink Health put computer-based systems modeling at the center of every project.

The effort is still new, but it offers an up-to-the-minute example of the promise of Fail Better to enable innovation. Careful planning and design make the theory of change explicit. ReThink Health's premise is that bringing stakeholders together using structured systems and thinking tools can help them find their own unexpected solutions to meet shared goals. The program is designed not just to show that improvement is possible but to help make it happen in order to transform health care.

One way that ReThink Health aims to do this is by ensuring that a varied set of stakeholders is in the room from the start. A second ingredient is a structured method for tapping into their perspectives and ideas. Stakeholders' interaction is supported by a process and tools designed to help them think together in new ways and build commitment to action. To this end, the team starts by gathering information, mapping cause-and-effect relationships related to the community's health and other important outcomes, then generating and testing different hypotheses about changes that the community proposes.

Computer Simulation as a Test Bed for Innovation

A simulation model brings rigor to these tests, revealing unexpected interactions and exposing relationships among different factors and objectives. In exploring the simulation results, the stakeholders reach a new level of systems thinking about trade-offs and dynamics that reveals additional options and builds understanding about why some approaches may lead to subpar results and others can put the community on a path to ongoing improvement.

ReThink's experts explain why systems thinking supports are important: "Carefully crafted tools, like simulation modeling, bring greater foresight, evidence, and creativity to the process of multistakeholder planning and action."[4] Computer models designed to realistically represent known factors and processes give stakeholders a tangible way to wrestle with their ideas—and to incorporate many different kinds of empirical data that boost validity. Models can show the implications of policy decisions and incorporate the effects of shifts and trends by representing population health, health-care delivery, health equity, workforce productivity, and health-care costs. In ReThink's case the simulations are not used to form specific projections of the future, because no model of something so complex can predict fine-grained details without an extensive investment in calibrating and testing hundreds of varied effects and factors. But the models have been validated for their high-level fidelity to the systems they represent by a team of domain experts. Using them enforces a level of discipline in thinking, enables conversations and interactions about complex issues, and supports what-if analysis. Once the community team comes to an agreement on plans, they specify detailed studies required to make specific investment and policy decisions.

ReThink Health uses modeling within its projects as the test bed for iterating on ideas generated by the community team. The formal systems approach benefits ReThink Health's aims in three ways. It's a vehicle for learning before doing, because it can enable virtual experiments to be run at practically no cost. And the models are also themselves objects in a learning interaction among the stakeholders participating in the process. If the goal is to reach a common solution, sometimes it's easier to disagree about a model than to disagree with each other directly, because the model can be changed to represent the different views. The result of talking about and interacting with each other around the simulation model yields better mental models that are shared among the participants. This opens the door to bold initiatives.

The models also perform a third function: because they are updated over time in response to stakeholder interactions, they provide a vehicle for the ReThink core team to learn from its own and others' experience. Each project session reveals new insights and ideas that inform the simulation model itself. So the learning loop also operates at the collective level.

Although it's still in the early days for ReThink Health, the results are encouraging. In Pueblo County, Colorado, a vigorous collaboration emerged from the process. The Pueblo Triple Aim Coalition grew to forty-five senior leaders from across health-care, education, and economic development sectors. Working with ReThink Health, together they ran extensive experiments with the simulation model to develop and test ideas for improving their communities' health. The result was agreement on a set of high-leverage policies, together with a durable financing strategy and a plan for sequencing their efforts.[5] Visit the website to learn about this and other ReThink Health efforts and to explore their interactive modeling process in Georgia, California, and elsewhere.[6]

ReThink Health is an innovative effort that aspires to help communities with an approach that takes into account real-world complexity. It aims to combine learning and action within and across communities while further developing its own and its partners' capabilities—and at the same time ensuring a level of rigor in thought and approach. If it delivers on its goals, it could help reshape communities and improve health for many.

Is progress of such magnitude even within the realm of possibility? History suggests that it may be. Let's look at the efforts involved in the US Civil Rights Movement. How did the strategies, resources, and actions of a few people help orchestrate massive change?

The US Civil Rights Movement: Iterative Action, Scaled Failures, Reflective Practice

"You must do more than pray and read the Bible," Martin Luther King Jr. urged a meeting of church leaders in Birmingham, Alabama.[7] It was early 1955, and King aimed to initiate a new phase in the movement for civil rights that would change the course of history.

Seven years earlier, America's vanguard civil rights organization, the NAACP, had developed a concerted strategy to push for changes to reduce the pervasive inequalities that African Americans faced in daily life. To enact the strategy, case after case had been filed in the courts. In 1950, the effort met with success when the University of Texas was told to desegregate its graduate education programs. In the following years, a collection of lawsuits seeking equal access to public schools known as *Brown v. Board of Education* reached the Supreme Court, which found that racial segregation in schools violated the US Constitution. In 1955, the Court ordered desegregation to take place "with all deliberate speed." The movement had given years to litigation and lobbying.

The surprising turn was that just as the movement appeared to be finally reaching success, new leaders pushed for a radical change in its strategy. They advocated a new focus on nonviolent civil disobedience that emphasized direct action coupled with political participation. King found inspiration in the techniques used by Mahatma Gandhi and the Quit India movement to advance the end of British rule. By eschewing violence, the new US civil rights movement could take the moral high ground, train frontline people relatively simply (thereby scaling up quickly), and attract media attention. If many participated, the collective spirit and impact of the movement could expand rapidly. Momentum could be built. And new supporters could be won over to the cause by bringing the struggle right into the communities in which the organizers sought change instead of playing out in courtrooms far removed from the front lines of daily life.

To strengthen the movement's appeal to others, participants in planned actions were to wear their Sunday best and behave politely, no matter what. Targeted collective economic action, grassroots organizing, and voter registration would give the movement power and visibility. In going beyond schools, it would reach a wide range of institutions and settings. By taking action instead of waiting, it would demonstrate its commitment to the idea that justice delayed was justice denied.

The movement would also step up and take on conflict when it was needed. "We *wanted* confrontation, nonviolent confrontation, to see if it would work," explained Birmingham leader Fred Shuttlesworth. "We were trying to launch a systematic, wholehearted battle against segregation which would set the pace for the nation."[8] The overall approach first took form in the early 1950s when King and fellow clergyman Ralph Abernathy agreed to collaborate on systematic, nonviolent efforts that could be embraced by both whites and blacks.[9]

In the years that followed, acts of civil disobedience played out in buses, housing estates, swimming pools, luncheonettes, churches, parks, and schools. Along with other leaders and many supporters, King was arrested and jailed. Their tactics included boycotts, demonstrations, and marches. Even young children were involved. Many endured taunting, incarceration, and even violence.

Although the work needed to make an equal and just society continues today, the results from this period were dramatic. Between the *Brown v. Board of Education* Supreme Court ruling and the Civil Rights and Voting Rights Acts, the legal and social landscape of America was transformed. In less than a decade, public attitudes had shifted and support for segregation dwindled.[10]

Launching a New Movement

What lessons can we draw? Let's go back to the beginnings of this phase of the civil rights movement. In the mid-1950s, just as the prevailing movement was reaching the legal outcomes it had diligently worked toward for the better part of a decade, King and his colleagues chose to introduce a different approach to the struggle for civil rights. Looking at it today, we appreciate their boldness in embarking on their new project even while the jury was still out (the Supreme Court finding that school segregation violated the Fourteenth Amendment's Equal Protection clause was issued in 1954, before King's January 1955 exhortation to action, but the Court's remedy ruling ordering speedy desegregation followed it). On that January day, we can imagine a plausible speech in its place advocating even more legal action on the heels of the growing success of the civil rights efforts in the courts.

In launching their new effort, the new civil rights leaders were rejecting the prevailing notion that had guided their movement since 1948: that their battle should be fought, patiently, within the legal and judicial systems, school by school. By 1955, they were aware that progress since the war's end had been slow, and in some settings mandated changes were being avoided altogether. Efforts to dismantle "separate but equal" structures, even when ordered by the highest court, were being met with massive resistance by whites in the South. The movement's leaders realized that legal victories alone would not deliver social transformation in the schools. In addition, unequal access to voting persisted. Other institutions saw continued discrimination that could not be remedied with lawsuits.

We imagine that it took courage in 1955 to say that the diligent efforts of the movement's mainstay were insufficient. The new effort was risky, to say the least.

But the leaders did their homework. As we explained above, this new civil rights effort was built on an explicit theory that accounted for how the specific confrontational actions would create the change that the movement sought, which in turn revealed a sophisticated systems view of the challenges and opportunities. A realistic assessment of the current situation, rather than wishful thinking, was also a foundation. So was learning from others, including the lessons offered by experience in the battle for independence in India. Building the Southern Christian Leadership Conference and other linked organizations enabled the team to coordinate resources, share information, and provide assets and capabilities to its members. At the same time, the new movement capitalized on established capabilities and legitimacy by allying with the existing movement's leading organization, the NAACP. The stage was well set.

Clearly, the civil rights movement was made up of more than one project and led by more than one man: it involved many linked efforts, some of which worked well and some of which did not. It also engaged multiple organizations and approaches. The NAACP tackled legal and judicial issues, including helping to release imprisoned movement leaders. It organized the 1963 March on Washington for Jobs and Freedom. Yet NAACP leaders chose not to fully commit their organization to the new movement's all-out strategy of direct action.[11]

Not everyone involved in the effort did the same thing. Styles and tactics varied greatly. But learning was shared. When we examined the sequence of the movement's experiences in the 1950s and 1960s, we found many examples of small failures leading to bigger successes. We found evidence that harnessing these failures helped to make change possible.

The Civil Rights Movement as a Fail Better Effort

Applying the Fail Better lens to this complex effort reveals that many of the ideas we've been exploring throughout the book formed the basis for effective action across settings, teams, and domains. We'll consider the evidence that our method could aid in a bigger movement—in efforts that go beyond single projects. We hope to show you the promise that Fail Better could indeed help to change the world.

We've already discussed the launch efforts built into the mid-1950s beginnings of the civil rights effort led by King and his colleagues. In the next phase of the movement, its leaders and members gleaned insights by trying out many experiments: quiet sit-ins at lunch counters and kneel-ins at churches, the orchestrated disobedience of Rosa Parks, registration drives, and mass marches.

Iterating on the Front Lines

Amid all their activity, the movements' members examined their experience to continually learn from every failure and success. For example, in late 1961, King and his colleagues embarked on a nine-month effort to tackle discrimination in Albany, Georgia. Despite their concerted efforts, the Albany campaign fell short of success. But it yielded important lessons that, according to King, immediately shifted the movement's approach:

> The mistake I made there was to protest against segregation generally rather than against a single and distinct facet of it. Our protest was so vague that we got nothing, and the people were left very depressed and in despair. It would have been much better to have concentrated upon integrating the buses or the lunch counters. One victory of this kind would have been symbolic, would have galvanized support and boosted morale . . . [W]hat we learned from our mistakes in Albany helped our later campaigns in other cities to be more effective. We never since scattered our efforts in a general attack on segregation, but focused upon specific, symbolic objectives.[12]

So King derived tactical lessons from the experience. Historian Howard Zinn, who also participated in the Albany campaign, offers a different take:

> Social movements may have many "defeats"—failing to achieve objectives in the short run—but in the course of the struggle the strength of the old order begins to erode, the

> minds of people begin to change . . . Albany was changed forever by the tumultuous events of 1961 and 1962, however much things looked the same . . . [13]

Zinn drew his lessons from considering the time horizon: movements need to act in the short run, but their effects may be manifested, he argued, only later on.

The movement's activities in one project cycle built capabilities that were harnessed for others. Experienced organizers traveled to communities to assist with public civil disobedience and share their learning. As the movement refined its field-tested advice, it developed training manuals. People representing the public face of the movement—most visibly Martin Luther King—seized one opportunity after another to give speeches and tell their story, gaining skills and learning to frame issues in compelling ways what would appeal to many.

And the lessons continued to accrue. At the end of 1962, after the failure in Albany, the movement took on challenges in deeply divided Birmingham, Alabama. But learning from one mistake and avoiding its traps did not guarantee success in the next attempt. Despite carefully targeting their campaign in the city, early efforts failed to build the momentum King and his colleagues sought: boycotts did not shift business behavior; pressure for the city to change its hiring had little impact; and the events they orchestrated failed to catch on with both citizens and outsiders.[14]

In part because attendance at its mass events in Birmingham had been sparse, in 1963 the movement's leaders hit on an approach that came to be called the "Children's Crusade." After much debate, they agreed to allow schoolchildren to participate in demonstrations and events. The sheer number of protesters drew harsh responses from local authorities. The result was powerful: the sight of hundreds of children being set upon by police dogs, cattle prods, and water cannons attracted widespread attention and forced the crisis that

King predicted would catalyze change. Soon afterward, civil unrest escalated into riots, and civic leaders agreed to changes that would desegregate Birmingham. King and his colleagues celebrated their victory, even if it turned out to be only one step in a longer journey for Birmingham. In the years that followed the city's citizens and government took on the work of turning the ideals of the movement into change within the city.

The year 1963 was a momentous one for the civil rights movement. The march on Washington took place that summer. The work continued in the ensuing years, even as focus and methods shifted in the aftermath of the tumultuous events of the 1960s.

Embedding the Learning

How did the movement identify, embed, and disseminate what its leaders and members learned from their action in those early years?

The civil rights movement generated a wealth of specific insights to share. Some were personal. In the early 1960s, D'Army Bailey's anti-segregation activism got him expelled from college. Years later, he articulated what the experience taught him: "As a black, I was in a weak position when it came to living in a white world. I realized I must … not feel bad for myself, but rather I should allow it to reinforce my determination to carry my protest as far as I can carry it."[15]

Other insights informed the movement. In the 1970s, movement leader James Bevel explained a lesson on the importance of drama he drew from his experience: "Every nonviolent movement is a dialogue between two forces . . . and you have to develop a drama, to dramatize the dialogue, to reveal the contradictions in the guys you're dialoguing with."[16]

More broadly, our study reveals that personal and interpersonal aspects of learning were key in the civil rights movement.

For example, reflection was always part of the approach, even in the thick of campaigns. The movement's leaders reflected on their own, often in writing, and via discussions that played out over days, weeks, or even longer. They spent time with each other, cultivating perspectives that influenced the careers of movement members such as Andrew Young, who had been involved early on. The discussions, debates, and sensemaking sessions in which Young participated contributed to his strategy and negotiation skills, shaping his subsequent work as ambassador to the United Nations, mayor of Atlanta, and congressional representative and his development as a thought leader for the country.

Perhaps the most obvious way the civil rights movement embedded its learning into the system was by the passage of civil rights legislation that now serves as a cornerstone of American life and shapes our national values of rights and equality.

The movement's ideas have infused our culture in other ways. Thanks to their practice of documenting their thoughts and experiences, its leaders helped to embed their learning more broadly, via accounts in books, letters, essays, and notes (after his assassination, King's voluminous notes and other materials allowed scholar Clayborne Carson to construct a first-person account of King's life).[17] Movement members were generous in talking with the press, permitting photographs and other recordings, giving speeches, and otherwise sharing the story. Enabling others—historians, film documentarians, even artists—to draw on their work, experience, and ideas brings the movement's ideals and learning to our national consciousness in rich and varied ways.

Sociologists, historians, and today's movement leaders link what was learned from the civil rights movement to subsequent efforts to address gay rights, gender equity, immigrants' issues, animal rights, environmental issues, and labor rights. Nelson Mandela and Aung San Suu Kyi invoked King's example as they led nonviolent movements for freedom in their countries.

Build on the Lessons, Use the Method, and Initiate Larger-Scale Change

The changes unleashed during the brief period from 1954 to 1968 did not instantly reform American society: the work of ending racism and ensuring equal rights for all continues today. Nor did it all start in 1954. In America, a century earlier, the forces that gave rise to the Civil War shaped events and themes that eventually led to the movement. In the first half of the twentieth century, the NAACP took on the horrific scourge of lynchings and created changes that laid the foundation for the later movement. Ordinary citizens' contributions to World War II efforts made real the values that the movement drew on, and the postwar movement for universal human rights emerged. At the same time, lessons came in from India and elsewhere. And as the movement gained momentum, thousands upon thousands of unsung Americans contributed significantly to its efforts.

Connecting to the past and to others along with a dedication to learning from experience were crucial ingredients for the movement to gain momentum. Martin Luther King and his colleagues provide a vivid illustration of the core idea behind Fail Better: *to advance your efforts in a complex world, develop an ongoing practice of reflecting on your experiences, and build shared capabilities to both explicate the thinking behind your plans and analyze the lessons of your experiences so you can shed light on the quality of your ideas.* Learning from experience is the only way to make progress when you face complex challenges that cannot be solved analytically.

We gleaned other insights from studying the civil rights leaders. Among these: develop direct and meaningful ways to tell the story so that others can learn from your tactics *and* the thinking behind them. It may be difficult to present honest first-person accounts of your experiences, particularly if they involve failure, but we can think of no better way to build an authentic voice. It is also inspiring to hear of others' struggles along with their victories. When presenting new and possibly difficult-to-accept ideas, help others to connect the past to aspirations for the future, and call on texts, stories, and themes that resonate, as King did in his speeches connecting to Biblical passages.

The movement's history drives home the power of working together. Distribute the work by enabling multiple efforts instead of centralizing and controlling. At the same time, harness the power of learning by iterating sequentially when you can. Try to identify one lesson from each failure experience that you can act on in your next iteration. Collaborate not just to share the work but to learn and coordinate. Talk to other people so that you can link your efforts with theirs.

And for large-scale change, enable system leadership. Cultivate the skills of looking at the big picture. Be willing to take action even when it would be plausible to stay the old course instead of risking something new.

The US Civil Rights Movement shows that astounding change can happen in a relatively short period of time. Remember its history when you feel disheartened by your work experiences. Just one decade separated the *Brown* ruling and the landmark 1964 Civil Rights Act. American public opinion had changed radically by the end of the 1960s. If such change is possible across an entire nation, surely you should not give up on the prospects for change within your organization!

START TODAY

We started with a mission statement of sorts:

> The right kind of failure instructs, refines, and improves ideas, work products, skills, capacities, and teamwork. We aim to support your efforts to generate small, smart mistakes that enable your team to meet its work requirements (a first-order performance goal) while building capacity, habits, and insight (the second-order, deeper change). In other words, we want to help you harness the right kind of failure to get your day-to-day work done while you learn.

Throughout the book, we've provided advice on how to do this. To bring our learning journey to a close, we offer some parting suggestions for putting the method into practice.

Advancing the Fail Better Approach

We see vast potential for the Fail Better method to help all kinds of projects across varied settings. Think of the organizations we've drawn on in this book, from high-tech lean start-ups to established social-sector organizations. Each offers insight and ideas that could help others.

What would it take for people in all kinds of organizations to embed learning into their own work by designing projects to get off to an effective start, iterate via action, and then retain and share what works best?

We would like both research and practice to more directly address the work of managers in the middle. We'd like to see a growing bank of evidence that connects professional habits and techniques used within projects to organizational outcomes so that we can better understand the potential for alignment between performance and learning.

We'd also like to advance our collective understanding of projects as the method for professionals to make change happen. And we seek to bring learning into the workplace by embedding it into every project.

To enable Fail Better to spread, not only do we need research to continue but we also need to shift public professional dialogues and norms to recognize the value of learning. Training programs, executive education, business schools, and other professional schools could incorporate ideas about learning into their teaching. MBAs could learn how to ground their management techniques in a solid understanding of how adults learn. Other professional schools could do the same. Managers could be evaluated for how well they enable others to learn—individuals, teams, and even within their organizations and industry.

Realism for Your Own Journey

We opened this book by discussing why it's so difficult to design and take action that creates positive and enduring change. Inescapable delays, surprising nonlinearities, and evolving interactions conspire together to make the dynamics that play out in organizations, markets, societies, and ecosystems difficult to understand and even harder to predict. Cognitive challenges in understanding cause-and-effect relationships mean that sometimes connections go unnoticed, and other times attributions are made with too much confidence—or are just wrong. Social-psychological factors loom over people's ability to make sense of failure and handle its repercussions effectively.

These unavoidable consequences of dynamic complexity stymie our learning from direct experience. They provide the rationale for Fail Better, of course, since our method is designed to reduce their negative effects. But considering these factors also injects a dose of realism into our advice for your journey. It turns out that no team operating in a real-world project can know with full certainty why things turn out the way they do. So the age-old problem of knowledge and action persists: *learning from experience requires you to take action and assess the results, but the basis for action will always be incomplete knowledge, and the data and methods you use to assess results will inevitably be flawed.* You need to take action while recognizing that the underlying thinking is provisional; and you need to identify lessons learned while bearing in mind that your understanding is limited. Doing well in the world rests, at least in part, on your ability to maintain both perspectives and recognize that you could be wrong about pretty much anything even as you move ahead decisively.

A second challenge, perhaps less existential in origin, is almost as ubiquitous: to get the payoffs in the long run, you may need to pay up in the short run. Putting Fail Better methods into practice will require investment in your skills and practices as well as those of your team in order to squeeze learning out of every action. We believe that by aligning the work at hand with individual and team capability development, Fail Better offers the dual value of getting things done within the constraints of a project while getting better. But it's important not to overstate the case for the approaches we advocate. Along with the benefits come some very real costs. For the Fail Better method as a whole to work, you need to take on each step of your project with diligence. Setting the groundwork, iterating, and embedding the learning might call for an extra level of commitment and discipline. Maintaining an open mind and defending the process against the tendency to slide back to old ways both require effort.

Our tools will, we hope, soon save you money and time and help you to succeed sooner, because they allow you to pull the plug earlier on ideas that do not work. But the effort saved and mistakes avoided will accrue value only over time and are unlikely to immediately offset the investment needed to get going. To implement Fail Better you may need to invest *more* time at the beginning for developing, examining, and documenting your maps, plans, data, analysis, learning, and results.

And to build the full complement of skills for all phases of the Fail Better approach, you may need to learn new tools and build your abilities. On your to-do list:

- Develop the discipline to launch your project and plan your action steps so that you prioritize activities that will advance your understanding and test your ideas.
- Learn how to map out your assumptions to highlight the connections between your work steps and the change you seek to create in the world.
- Develop habits that remind to you link your project activities and their results to your overall aims.
- Find a documentation method that works for you, and use it consistently to capture your steps and results sufficiently to thoroughly draw lessons from your experiences.
- Shore up your ability to gather and analyze data and information effectively, from qualitative methods to statistics, so that you draw the right lessons from apparent successes and failures in your tests.
- Develop the skills for negotiation, persuasion, facilitation, systems thinking, inquiry, and the ability to have difficult conversations.

- Hone your ability to call it when you encounter—or even create—preventable, wasteful, and uninstructive failures.
- Build the capabilities to tell your story compellingly.
- Check on your project's eventual impact, even after the deliverables are in.
- Extract a handful of lessons from every project.

You also need to be ready to fail.

So as you form your plans for leading your team to ever-more-effective failures, also plan for the extra effort you'll need to invest to do so. And remember to nurture your resilience!

How You Can Change the World

If Fail Better methods can help with distributed change efforts that span multiple projects, they may provide a way to take on the world's most pressing problems. Research on complex systems—not to mention human experience across a vast reach of time and space—teaches us that big problems are never solved by a single stroke of genius. Could our approach help society tackle messy, complex challenges?

Climate change, shortcomings in education, declining communities, the need for nation-building in fragile states, failures in health care—none of these can be "solved" with a single solution created by a group of people in a room somewhere, no matter how brilliant. Nor can markets always fix them. Instead, people will have to keep working at them, bit by bit, in one community and one effort at a time. Learning will be essential.

Humankind has already encountered failures in taking on grand challenges, and there are sure to be more. We've been arguing for more projects to use the Fail Better approach so that every individual effort is more effective. But maybe we could go a step further and connect efforts with each other. If our method helps to build deeper understanding and improve how we account for results, then we have a better chance of learning from each other. The promise that we can build better ways to connect disparate efforts and enable each to build on its predecessors—using the Fail Better approach *across* communities—makes us hopeful that human ingenuity can be harnessed in new ways to make progress on even the biggest challenges. The promise is that we can iterate across projects and settings, not just within each project. Imagine how much we could learn if we had better ways of sharing lessons learned from the varied and distributed efforts to tackle major challenges.

To deliver on this promise, we'd like to build a movement that supports your efforts to do things better and make things better. We'd like to connect you to others and inspire you to learn from new examples. To join us, go to failbetterbydesign.com.

And Now . . .

We have high hopes for what you will accomplish in your work with the ideas we have shared with you. Taken together, the Fail Better steps could help to remake work experiences, one project at a time. If they deliver on the promise we foresee, you will be able to advance your professional practice: to go from execution-focused projects that, if you are lucky, generate the specified deliverables, to Fail Better projects that build insight, capabilities, innovation, and learning. Your projects could surpass the original plans for deliverables and simultaneously make work more meaningful for everyone on your team. You could even help change the world.

Start today.

NOTES

CHAPTER 1

1. Mark O'Connell, "The Stunning Success of 'Fail Better': How Samuel Beckett Became Silicon Valley's Life Coach," *Slate.com*, January 29, 2014, http://www.slate.com/articles/arts/culturebox/2014/01/samuel_beckett_s_quote_fail_better_becomes_the_mantra_of_silicon_valley.html.

2. Project Management Institute, "The High Cost of Low Performance," March 2013, http://www.pmi.org/~/media/PDF/Business-Solutions/PMI-Pulse%20Report-2013Mar4.ashx.

3. Michael Bloch, Sven Blumberg, and Jürgen Laartz, "Delivering Large-Scale IT Projects on Time, on Budget, and on Value," October 2012, http://www.mckinsey.com/insights/business_technology/delivering_large-scale_it_projects_on_time_on_budget_and_on_value.

4. Scott Keller, Mary Meaney, and Caroline Pung, "What Successful Transformations Share: McKinsey Global Survey Results March 2010," March 2010, http://www.mckinsey.com/insights/organization/what_successful_transformations_share_mckinsey_global_survey_results.

5. George Castellion and Stephen K. Markham, "Perspective: New Product Failure Rates: Influence of *Argumentum ad Populum* and Self-Interest," *Journal of Product Innovation Management* 30, no. 5 (2013): 976–979.

6. Sheena Iyengar, *The Art of Choosing* (New York: Hachette: Twelve, 2011).

For more: Barry Schwartz, "Is the Famous 'Paradox of Choice' a Myth?" PBS Newshour, January 29, 2014, http://www.pbs.org/newshour/making-sense/is-the-famous-paradox-of-choic/.

7. Matthew A. Cronin, Cleotilde Gonzalez, and John D. Sterman, "Why Don't Well-Educated Adults Understand Accumulation? A Challenge to Researchers, Educators, and Citizens," *Organizational Behavior and Human Decision Processes* 108 (2009): 116–130.

For more: John D. Sterman, "Misperceptions of Feedback in Dynamic Decision Making," *Organizational Behavior and Human Decision Processes* 43 (1989): 301–335; Mark Paich and John D. Sterman, "Boom, Bust, and Failures to Learn in Experimental Markets," *Management Science* 39, no. 12 (1993): 1439–1458; Ernst Diehl and John D. Sterman, "Effects of Feedback Complexity on Dynamic Decision Making," *Organizational Behavior and Human Decision Processes* 62 (1995): 198–215; Michael Shane Gary, Giovanni Dosi, and Daniel Lovallo, "Boom and Bust Behavior: On the Persistence of Strategic Decision Biases," in *The Oxford Handbook of Organizational Decision Making*, ed. Gerard P. Hodgkinson and William H. Starbuck (Oxford: Oxford University Press, 2008), 33–55; and Stefan N. Groesser and Martin Schaffernicht, "Mental Models of Dynamic Systems: Taking Stock and Looking Ahead," *System Dynamics Review* 28, no. 1 (2012): 46–68.

8. M. Anjali Sastry, "Problems and Paradoxes in a Model of Punctuated Organizational Change," *Administrative Science Quarterly* 42 (1997): 237–275.

9. Peter M. Senge, *The Fifth Discipline: The Art and Practice of the Learning Organization* (New York: Doubleday Currency, 1990).

For more: John D. Sterman, "Learning in and about Complex Systems," *System Dynamics Review* 10 (1994): 291–330; John Sterman, *Business Dynamics: Systems Thinking and Modeling for a Complex World* (Boston: Irwin/McGraw-Hill, 2000); Charles Perrow, *Normal Accidents: Living with High-Risk Technologies* (New York: Basic Books, 1984); Jay W. Forrester, "Counterintuitive Behavior of Social Systems," *Technology Review* 73, no. 3 (1971): 73; Dietrich Dörner, *The Logic of Failure: Recognizing and Avoiding Error in Complex Situations* (New York: Basic Books, 1997); Karl E. Weick, *The Social Psychology of Organizing* (New York: Random House, 1979); and Michael Shane Gary and Robert E. Wood, "Mental Models, Decision Rules, and Performance Heterogeneity," *Strategic Management Journal* 3, no. 2 (2011): 569–594.

10. Forrester, "Counterintuitive Behavior of Social Systems."

For more: Sterman, *Business Dynamics*; and Sterman, "Learning in and about Complex Systems."

11. Amy C. Edmondson, "Strategies for Learning from Failure," *Harvard Business Review*, April 2011, 48–55.

12. Ibid.

13. Issie Lapowsky, "Why Every Company Is Now an Incubator," *Inc.com*, December 21, 2012, http://www.inc.com/issie-lapowsky/why-everyone-is-an-incubator-now.html.

14. Project Management Institute, "Société Générale Receives Project Management Institute's 2012 Distinguished Project Award," June 13, 2012, http://www.pmi.org/en/About-Us/Press-Releases/Societe-Generale-Receives-Project-Management-Institutes-2012-Distinguished-Project-Award.aspx.

CHAPTER 2

1. All quotes taken directly from Ryan Tseng's writings as an MIT student in 2007 and 2008. This section and the close of this chapter also draw on Ryan Tseng, interview by Anjali Sastry, April 2014, and class discussions in 2007.

2. "Innovations: Zap Your Gadgets a New Way, with Ryan Tseng, WiPower, Inc., President and CNBC's Bill Griffeth," *CNBC*, November 27, 2007, http://video.cnbc.com/gallery/?video=600257970.

For more: Scott Kirsner, "Charging Pads Inching from R&D to Reality," *Boston Globe*, September 30, (2007), K.1; Donald Melanson, "WiPower Touts Breakthrough in Wireless Power," *Engadget*, September 24, 2007, http://www.engadget.com/2007/09/24/wipower-touts-breakthrough-in-wireless-power/; Sean Snyder, "WiPower Provides Wireless Transfer of Electrical Energy," *Design News*, October 22, 2007, http://www.designnews.com/document.asp?doc_id=213622.

3. Kent A. Greenes, "Peer Assist: Learning Before Doing," *NASA ASK Magazine* 42, (2010): 43–45, http://appel.nasa.gov/2010/10/17/peer-assist-learning-before-doing/.

4. Dantar P. Oosterwal, *The Lean Machine: How Harley-Davidson Drove Top-Line Growth and Profitability with Revolutionary Lean Product Development* (New York: American Management Association, 2010).

5. Takashi Tanaka, Sharon Tanner, and Craig Flynn, "The Basics of Oobeya," *Toyota Engineering Co. QV System, Inc.* (2011), http://www.leanuk.org/downloads/LS_2011/mc_oobeya_basics.pdf.

For more: Takashi Tanaka and Sharon Tanner, "The Visualization of Purpose: Quickening the Pace of Executive Achievement through the Visualization of Purpose," paper presented at the Lean Executive Masterclass, near Birmingham, UK, June 27, 2011, http://www.leanuk.org/downloads/masterclass/paper_visualization_of_purpose.pdf; and "Managing Visually—A Word from Daniel T. Jones," *Lean Execution-Intelligent Metrics*, April 23, 2011, http://leanexecution.wordpress.com/2011/04/23/managing-visually-a-word-from-daniel-t-jones/.

6. Oosterwal, *The Lean Machine*.

7. Sarika Bansal, "The Power of Failure," *New York Times*, November 28, 2012, http://opinionator.blogs.nytimes.com/2012/11/28/the-power-of-failure-2/.

For more: Engineers Without Borders, "2010 Failure Report," 2010, http://issuu.com/ewb-isf/docs/failurereport2011 or http://www.ewb.ca/ideas/admitting-failure-0.

8. Ashley Good, "Fail Forward," Management Innovation Exchange, December 21, 2012, http://www.managementexchange.com/story/fail-forward.

9. Engineers Without Borders, "2010 Failure Report."

10. Good, "Fail Forward."

11. Jon Fingas, "Samsung, Qualcomm Start up Alliance for Wireless Power to take on Qi," *Engadget*, May 8, 2012, http://www.engadget.com/2012/05/08/samsung-qualcomm-start-alliance-for-wireless-power/.

12. Geoff Gordon, "Wireless Charging Gains Flexibility with Qualcomm WiPower Technology," *Qualcomm OnQ* blog, February 19, 2014, http://www.qualcomm.com/media/blog/2014/02/19/mwc-wireless-charging-gains-flexibility-qualcomm-wipower-technology.

For more: "Current Members," Rezence Alliance for Wireless Power, http://www.rezence.com/alliance/current-members; and "Qualcomm Toq," Qualcomm, https://toq.qualcomm.com/.

13. Fingas, "Samsung, Qualcomm Start up Alliance for Wireless Power to take on Qi."

CHAPTER 4

1. Edgar Schein, *Helping: How to Offer, Give, and Receive Help* (San Francisco: Berrett-Koehler Publishers, 2009).

2. "2011 C77DA Interiors/Exhibition Designer: Herman Miller Healthcare and Continuum Design Team Question and Answer," Core77 Design Awards, http://www.core77designawards.com/2011/recipients/herman-miller-compass-system/.

For more: "Herman Miller Healthcare: COMPASS," Core77 Design Awards, http://www.core77designawards.com/wp-content/uploads/2011/07/Interiors-Pro-e200-a.pdf; and "Continuum Designs New Category of Healthcare Furnishings for Herman Miller; Wins a Gold Best of NeoCon Award at the Neo Con World's Fair," *Bio Med Reports*, June 23, 2010, http://www.biomedreports.com/2010062345235/continuum-designs-new-category-of-healthcare-furnishings-for-herman-miller-wins-a-gold-best-of-neocon-award-at-the-neocon-world-s-trade-fair.html.

3. "Patient Rooms: A Changing Scene of Healing," Herman Miller Healthcare, 2014, http://www.hermanmiller.com/content/hermanmiller/northamerica/en_us/home/research/research-summaries/patient-rooms-a-changing-scene-of-healing.html.

4. Janet Wiens, "A New Direction," *Interiors & Sources*, March 7, 2011, http://www.interiorsandsources.com/article-details/articleid/11516/title/a-new-direction.aspx.

5. http://www.core77.com/blog/core77_design_awards/core77_design_award_2011_herman_miller_compass_system_notable_for_interiors_exhibitions_20526.asp.

6. Interview with Gianfranco Zaccai, http://www.hermanmiller.com/support-pages/video-modal/product/compass-system-making-of-compass.html.

CHAPTER 5

1. Behance Team, "Paul English: Getting Human," *99U.com*, http://99u.com/articles/5524/paul-english-getting-human.

2. David A. Garvin, *Learning in Action: A Guide to Putting the Learning Organization to Work* (Boston: Harvard Business School Press, 2003), 106.

3. Ibid.

4. David Christensen, "The Wildland Fire Lessons Learned Center 2002 to 2010, 2010, http://www.wildfirelessons.net/documents/Comp_Christenson_LLC_Since_2002.pdf.

For more: Michael T. DeGrosky and Charles S. Parry. "Beyond the AAR: The Action Review Cycle (ARC)," Proceedings of 11th International Wildland Fire Safety Summit, April 4–8, 2011, Missoula, MT, http://www.fireleadership.gov/toolbox/after_action_review/index.html; "After Action Reviews," Wildland Fire Leadership, http://www.fireleadership.gov/toolbox/after_action_review/index.html.

5. Leigh Buchanan, "Leadership: Armed with Data: How the Military Can Help You Learn from Your Mistakes," *Inc.com*, March 1, 2009, http://www.inc.com/magazine/20090301/leadership-armed-with-data.html; Marilyn Darling, Charles Parry, and Joseph Moore, "Learning in the Thick of It," *Harvard Business Review*, July–August, 2005, 84–92; and for some practical guidance, see "Get Better Faster: Ultimate Guide to Practicing Retrospectives," Open View Partners eBook, May 2011, http://labs.openviewpartners.com/ebook/retrospective-meetings/.

6. Darling et al., "Learning in the Thick of It," 92.

For more: Garvin, *Learning In Action*; the US Center for Army Lessons Learned, http://usacac.army.mil/CAC2/call/8; and for an interesting introduction, consult *This American Life*, episode 333, "The Center for Lessons Learned," May 25, 2007, http://www.thisamericanlife.org/radio-archives/episode/333/the-center-for-lessons-learned, for an audio podcast and transcript.

7. Marion Buchenau and Jane Fulton Suri, "Experience Prototyping," in *Proceedings of the 3rd Conference on Designing Interactive Systems: Processes, Practices, Methods, and Techniques*, ed. Daniel Boyarski and Wendy A. Kellogg (New York: Association for Computing Machinery, 2000), 424–433, http://dl.acm.org/citation.cfm?id=347802.

For more: Alan South, "Abstract Truth," *Aircraft Interiors International*, March 2004, 116–122.

8. Mark D. Cannon and Amy C. Edmondson, "Failing to Learn and Learning to Fail (Intelligently): How Great Organizations Put Failure to Work to Innovate and Improve," *Long Range Planning* 38 (2005): 299–319.

9. Thomas M. Burton, "Flop Factor: By Learning from Failures, Lilly Keeps Drug Pipeline Full—Dr. Nyikiza Uses Math Skills to Save Cancer

CHAPTER 8

1. Donald Berwick, Andrea Kabcenell, and Thomas Nolan, "No Toyota Yet, but a Start: A Cadre of Providers Seeks to Transform an Inefficient Industry—Before It's Too Late," *Modern Healthcare* 35, no. 5 (2005): 18–19.

2. Noah Goldstein, "Changing Minds and Changing Towels," *Psychology Today*, August 23, 2008, http://www.psychologytoday.com/blog/yes/200808/changing-minds-and-changing-towels.

For more: For the research behind it, see Noah J. Goldstein, Robert B. Cialdini, and Vladas Griskevicius, "A Room with a Viewpoint: Using Social Norms to Motivate Environmental Conservation in Hotels," *Journal of Consumer Research* 35, no. 3 (2008): 472–482; and for a broader introduction to the ideas, see Robert B. Cialdini, *Influence: Science and Practice*, 5th ed. (Boston: Allyn & Bacon, 2009).

CHAPTER 9

1. "Bangladesh," in Central Intelligence Agency, *The World Factbook*, https://www.cia.gov/library/publications/the-world-factbook/geos/bg.html.

For more: "Per Capita Annual Income Crosses $1000," *BDNews24.com*, September 4, 2013, http://bdnews24.com/bangladesh/2013/09/04/per-capita-annual-income-crosses-1000.

2. Rounaq Jahan, "Bangladesh in 1972: Nation Building in a New State," *Asian Survey* 13, no. 2 (1973): 199–210.

3. From BRAC USA, "FY2013 Annual Report: Creating Opportunity for the World's Poor," and "BRAC at a Glance," http://www.brac.net/, and from personal interviews by Anjali Sastry with BRAC leadership, Dhaka, Bangladesh, January–Febuary, 2012.

4. "Water with Sugar and Salt," *The Lancet* 312, no. 8084 (1978): 300–301.

5. A. Mushtaque, R. Chowdhury and Richard A. Cash, *A Simple Solution: Teaching Millions to Treat Diarrhoea at Home* (Dhaka: University Press Ltd., 1996).

6. Olivier Fontaine, Paul Garner, and M. K. Bhan, "Oral Rehydration Therapy: The Simple Solution for Saving Lives," *British Medical Journal*, January 2007, http://www.bmj.com/content/334/suppl_1/s14?view.

7. Sources for information on Saving Lives at Birth, IMNCS, Manoshi, and BRAC in general include BRAC's websites, published papers, and the RED and icddr, b repositories, along with approximately twenty days of personal site visits in January–February 2012 and March–April 2013. Also, Anjali Sastry conducted personal interviews with BRAC leadership, staff, and board members in Dhaka, January–February 2012 and March–April 2013; in Delhi, June 2012 and January 2014; and via phone and in Boston, October and December 2013 and April 2014, as well as all materials mentioned in the notes for this chapter. In the remainder of this chapter, specific references are cited where a report or resource is mentioned.

8. Abdullahel Hadi and Munir Ahmed, "Saving Newborn Lives in Rural Communities: Learning from the BRAC Experience," December 2005 Research and Evaluation Division, BRAC, http://research.brac.net/reports/Lessons_learned_from_SNL_project.pdf.

9. icddr, b, "Maternal Mortality and Health Care Survey 2010," *Health and Science Bulletin* 9, no. 2 (2011), http://www.icddrb.org/what-we-do/publications/cat_view/52-publications/10042-icddrb-periodicals/10048-health-and-science-bulletin-bangla-and-english/11089-vol-9-no-2-english-2011-/11093-maternal-mortality-and-health-care-survey-2010.

For more: National Institute of Population Research and Training (NIPORT), MEASURE Evaluation, and icddr, b, "Bangladesh Maternal Mortality and Health Care Survey 2010."

10. Syed Masud Ahmed, Awlad Hossain, Marufa Aziz Khan, Malay Kanti Mridha, Ashraful Alam, Nuzhat Choudhury, Tamanna Sharmin, Kaosar Afsana, and Abbas Bhuiya, "Using Formative Research to Develop MNCH Programme in Urban Slums in Bangladesh: Experiences from MANOSHI, BRAC," *BMC Public Health* 10 (2010): 663, http://www.biomedcentral.com/1471–2458/10/663.

For more: Khurshid Alam, Elizabeth Oliveras, and Sakiba Tasneem, "Retention of Female Volunteer Community Health Workers—A Case-Control Study in the Urban Slums of Dhaka," Manoshi-WP08, November 2009, http://www.icddrb.org/what-we-do/publications/cat_view/52-publications/10043-icddrb-documents/10058-icddrb-reports-and-working-papers/10069-manoshi-working-papers/10226-manoshi-working-paper-no-08–2009; Khurshid Alam, Sakiba Tasneem, and Elizabeth Oliveras, "Performance of Female Volunteer Community Health Workers in Dhaka's Urban Slums—A Case-Control Study," Manoshi-WP12, February 2011, http://www.icddrb.org/what-we-do/publications/cat_view/52-publications/10043-icddrb-documents/10058-icddrb-reports-and-working-papers/10069-manoshi-working-papers/10144-manoshi-working-paper-no-12–2011; Khurshid Alam, Jahangir A. M. Khan, and Damian G. Walker, "Impact of Dropout of Female Volunteer Community Health Workers: An Exploration in Dhaka Urban Slums," *BMC Health Services Research* 12 (2012), http://www.biomedcentral.com/content/pdf/1472-6963-12 260.pdf; and KhurshidAlam, Sakiba Tasneem, and Elizabeth Oliveras, "Retention of Female Volunteer Community Health Workers in Dhaka Urban Slums: A Case-Control Study," *Health Policy and Planning* 27, no. 6 (2012): 477–486, http://heapol.oxfordjournals.org/content/27/6/477.

11. Afsana Kaosar, telephone interview with Anjali Sastry, January 2014.

12. Ziaul Islam, Elizabeth Oliveras, Nirod C. Saha, Meghla Islam, Damian G. Walker, and Marge Koblinsky, "Urban Slum Dwellers' 'Willingness to Pay'—A Study of the MANOSHI Delivery Centres in Dhaka," Manoshi-WP4, 2009, http://www.icddrb.org/what-we-do/publications/doc_download/

267-urban-slum-dwellers-qwillingness-to-payq-a-study-of-the-manoshi-delivery-centres-in-dhaka-manoshi-wp04-2009.

13. "BRAC Manoshi," Center for Health Market Innovations, http://healthmarketinnovations.org/program/brac-manoshi.

14. Mafruha Alam, Tahmina Khanam, Rubayat Khan, Ananya Raihan, Mridul Chowdhury, "Assessing the Scope for Use of Mobile-Based Solution to Improve Maternal and Child Health in Bangladesh: A Case Study on Efficiency of Community Health Workers, Automated Risk Assessment of Patients and Web-Based Data Collection," working paper for ICTD 2010 London Conference, http://clickmedix.com/wp-content/uploads/2010/08/ictd-working-paper-feedback.pdf10.

15. BRAC Research and Evaluation Division, http://research.brac.net/.

16. Richard A. Cash, A. Mushtaque, R. Chowdhury, George B. Smith, and Faruque Ahmed, eds. *From One to Many: Scaling Up Health Programs in Low Income Countries* (Dhaka: The University Press Ltd., 2010).

17. BRAC Health Program, *Making Tuberculosis History: Community-Based Solutions for Millions* (Dhaka: The University Press Ltd., 2011).

18. A. Mushtaque, R. Chowdhury and Richard A. Cash, *A Simple Solution*.

19. Ian Smillie, *Freedom from Want: The Remarkable Success Story of BRAC, the Global Grassroots Organization That's Winning the Fight against Poverty* (West Hartford, CT: Kumarian Press, 2010).

20. "Manoshi Working Papers," icddrb, http://www.icddrb.org/what-we-do/publications/cat_view/52-publications/10043-icddrb-documents/10058-icddrb-reports-and-working-papers/10069-manoshi-working-papers.

CHAPTER 10

1. "A Healthier America 2013: Strategies to Move from Sick Care to Health Care in the Next Four Years," RWJF/Trust for America's Health, 2013.

2. See http://rethinkhealth.org/.

3. See http://rethinkhealth.org/wp-content/uploads/2014/02/RTH-Dynamics-Model-Summary.pdf.

4. Bobby Milstein, Gary Hirsch, and Karen Minyard, "County Officials Embark on New, Collective Endeavors to ReThink Their Local Health Systems," *Journal of County Administration*, March–April 2013, 1, 5–10, http://icma.org/Documents/Document/Document/304830.

5. Bobby Milstein, Jack Homer, Peter Briss, Deron Burton, and Terry Pechacek, "Why Behavioral and Environmental Interventions Are Needed to Improve Health at Lower Cost," *Health Affairs* 30, no. 5 (2011): 823–832.

6. See http://county.pueblo.org/sites/default/files/documents/CHIP%20FINAL%20w.o.%20signatures.pdf.

7. See http://mlk-kpp01.stanford.edu/index.php/encyclopedia/chronologyentry/1955_01_23/.

8. Jon Nordheimer, "Rev. Fred L. Shuttlesworth, an Elder Statesman for Civil Rights, Dies at 89," *New York Times*, October 5, 2011, http://www.nytimes.com/2011/10/06/us/rev-fred-l-shuttlesworth-civil-rights-leader-dies-at-89.html?pagewanted=all&_r=0.

9. Richard Severo, "Ralph David Abernathy, Rights Pioneer, Is Dead at 64," *New York Times*, April 18, 1990, http://www.nytimes.com/learning/general/onthisday/bday/0311.html.

10. "An Interactive Civil Rights Chronology," Yale University, http://www.yale.edu/lawweb/jbalkin/brown/1963.html.

11. "NAACP: 100 Years of History," National Association for the Advancement of Colored People, http://www.naacp.org/pages/naacp-history.

12. "Chapter 16: The Albany Movement," The Martin Luther King, Jr. Research and Education Institute Stanford University, http://mlk-kpp01.stanford.edu/index.php/kingpapers/article/chapter_16_the_albany_movement/.

13. Howard Zinn, *You Can't Be Neutral on a Moving Train: A Personal History of Our Times* (Boston: Beacon Press, 2002), 54.

14. Jeffrey C. Alexander, *Performance and Counter-Power: The Civil Rights Movement and the Civil Sphere*, http://ccs.research.yale.edu/documents/public/alex_civRightsPerf.pdf.

15. Terre Gorham, "D'Army Bailey: Civil Rights Activist, Attorney, and Public Servant," *Memphis Downtowner*, [n.d.], http://www.memphisdowntowner.com/my2cents/D%27Army_Bailey.html.

16. Quoted in Alexander, *Performance and Counter-Power*, 17.

17. "What Is the Kings Papers Project," The Martin Luther King, Jr. Research and Education Institute Stanford University, http://mlk-kpp01.stanford.edu/index.php/kingpapers/article/what_is_the_king_papers_project/.

INDEX

Note: Page numbers followed by *f* indicate figures.

ACKNOWLEDGMENTS

Countless leaders, managers, frontline workers, students, academics, and experts of all sorts—including many whose learning came from the school of hard knocks—shared their insights with us over the years. Thank you for every phone call, site visit, meeting, email exchange, conversation, and working session. You helped us to better understand your experiences, test our ideas against your wisdom, and refine our approach in response to your thoughtful critiques.

Our book would work only if it were tied directly to practice. Thank you to everyone who shared a personal habit, told a story, sent along an article or blog post, or pointed us to a new example. We are deeply grateful to Kaosar Afsana, Eric Hjerpe, Ryan Tseng, and Elizabeth Yin for their generosity in sharing their own stories in this book.

We are humbled to work with amazing organizations that take on some of the world's most complex problems amid pressing constraints. Every day, these organizations are helping to shift communities and businesses toward more sustainable and equitable futures, delivering essential services with limited resources, and putting the people they serve first. We are more inspired than we can express.

To our editorial team, Tim Sullivan, Allison Peter, and their equally talented colleagues at Harvard Business Review Press, thank you for believing in the power of our ideas, developing a vision for the book, and seeing it through to the printed page.

And to the family, friends, and colleagues who read our drafts, offered us feedback or a testing ground for ideas, helped us juggle our many commitments, and encouraged us through our own Fail Better process to this final version, we are indebted: Dave Dagg, Harley Davis, George Deriso, Duncan Forbes, Adit Ginde, Sarah Jean-Louis, Simon Johnson, Julie Markham, Denise McMahan, Francy Milner, Bobby Milstein, Mark O'Brien, Frank Penn, Krista Penn, Roxanne Penn, Kelley Ritz, Kris Rutledge, Jeff Shames, Megan Smith, Allen Weintraub, and Kelleen Zubick. Thank you!

ABOUT THE AUTHORS

Anjali Sastry is senior lecturer at the MIT Sloan School of Management and a lecturer in the Department of Global Health and Social Medicine at Harvard Medical School. Her PhD in management science and her undergraduate physics and Russian degrees are from MIT. She has worked as assistant professor of organizational behavior at the University of Michigan, assistant professor of management science at MIT, a management consultant at Bain & Company, and a research scholar at Rocky Mountain Institute.

Anjali has two decades of experience teaching and researching organizational change, system dynamics, and action learning. She added global health delivery to her portfolio in 2007 to further develop her groundbreaking approach to learning by doing. Her perennially oversubscribed MIT lab courses pair field projects with classroom instruction and faculty mentoring, and she has been conducting research to investigate the impact of her efforts in the field.

Anjali presents her work to many audiences, through executive education, academic conferences and publications, blog posts, and press articles (find links at failbetterbydesign.com), and guest lectures in the United States, Africa, and elsewhere. She serves on the board of directors of the global nongovernmental organization Management Sciences for Health and collaborates with MIT's Tata Center for Technology and Design, the University of Cape Town's Bertha Centre for Social Innovation, WonderWork, the Lemelson-MIT

Program, the MIT IDEAS Competition, among other programs and organizations. Her book, *Parenting Your Child with Autism: Practical Solutions, Strategies, and Advice for Helping Your Family*, coauthored with Blaise Aguirre in 2012, draws on personal experience as well as research evidence.

Kara Penn is cofounder and principal consultant at Mission Spark, a management consulting firm dedicated to organizational change and improvement in complex and often resource-constrained settings. In guiding her clients' thinking, planning, and action, Kara focuses on best practice and implementation, an approach that puts her at the front lines of practical management in varied domains.

Kara has fifteen years of experience in senior leadership positions with organizations throughout the United States, including as founder, director, chair, and board member. She has led award-winning community collaboratives; designed, managed, and evaluated multiyear social change initiatives; and provided in-depth consulting services to more than sixty NGOs, social enterprises, corporations, and philanthropic foundations. Kara authored *Start Up for Success: Planning, Founding and Initiating a New 501(c)3*, a comprehensive and practical workbook for nonprofit start-up and early implementation published by the Community Resource Center in 2010.

Kara graduated from Colorado College, where she was a Boettcher Scholar. She completed her MPP as a Harris Fellow at the University of Chicago's Harris School of Public Policy and her MBA at the MIT Sloan School of Management. MIT Sloan recognized Kara with the Seley Award, the highest honor given to a graduating student. Kara has also been awarded several national fellowships, including the Thomas J. Watson Fellowship, which supports independent, purposeful travel to foster fellows' effective participation in the world community; the Coro Fellowship in Public Affairs to develop principled public leaders; and the Forté Fellowship to promote women leaders in business.